DEVELOPMENT IN THE WORKPLACE

DEVELOPMENT IN THE WORKPLACE

Edited by

Jack Demick
Patrice M. Miller
Suffolk University

LEA LAWRENCE ERLBAUM ASSOCIATES, PUBLISHERS
1993   Hillsdale, New Jersey   Hove and London

Lawrence Erlbaum Associates, Inc., Publishers
365 Broadway
Hillsdale, New Jersey 07642

Library of Congress Cataloging-in-Publication Data

Development in the workplace / edited by Jack Demick, Patrice M.
    Miller.
        p.   cm.
    Includes bibliographical references and indexes.
    ISBN 0-8058-1191-5
    1. Work—Psychological aspects.   2. Adulthood—Psychological
aspects.   3. Developmental psychology.   I. Demick, Jack.
                                                    BF481.D47   1993
                                                    158.7—dc20   92-8457
                                                                          CIP

Printed in the United States of America
10   9   8   7   6   5   4   3   2   1

To our colleagues in the Psychology Department of Suffolk University (Bob, Carrie, Debra H., Debra K., Debra R., Ed, Elliot, Harvey, Kris, Maria, Michael, Paul, Rose, Silvia, and Wilma) who help foster our own development in the workplace on a daily basis.

Contents

Preface

The chapters in this volume were solicited from among papers presented at the Sixth Adult Development Symposium, which was jointly sponsored by the Department of Psychology at Suffolk University, Boston, Massachusetts and by the Society for Research in Adult Development. The symposium was held on July 12–14, 1991 at Suffolk University. The chapters have been extensively edited to reflect both discussion and comments at the symposium as well as the editors' comments.

The current volume brings together theorizing from the fields of developmental psychology and organizational psychology. It seems useful to place the volume in perspective compared to other recent volumes in the field of adult development. First, there has been, more recently, a strong emphasis on positive adult development rather than the earlier focus on decline and degeneration. Second, there has also been considerable discussion and theorizing about stages of development that have been postulated to be both more complex than and qualitatively distinct from Piaget's descriptions of formal operations. Third, there has been an increasing amount of work that attempts to go beyond studies of pure cognition or reasoning and, by so doing, to make significantly more use of interdisciplinary approaches. To some extent, the current volume reflects all of these trends.

ACKNOWLEDGMENTS

There are many people whom we wish to thank for their assistance in completing this project. Members of the Department of Psychology at Suffolk University, most notably Krisanne Bursik, Rosemarie DiBiase, Harvey Katz, and Robert Webb, were invaluable in planning and carrying out the symposium itself. Suffolk University also provided outstanding physical facilities and support in terms of audiovisual needs (Masahiro Hasegawa), food services (Ellen Schwarz), and publicity (Louis Connelly). Carrie Andreoletti, one of the most able assistants with whom we have ever worked, spent many long hours retyping and formatting manuscripts. Our families also helped by being tolerant of extended hours and harried interludes. Most important perhaps, we wish to thank the participants of this and the other Adult Development symposia for their always enthusiastic interest in thinking, talking, and writing about adults and their development.

Jack Demick
Patrice M. Miller

Introduction

Jack Demick
Patrice M. Miller
Suffolk University

The chapters in this volume, although exploratory in nature, seek to un-cover some possible relationships between the fields of organizational and developmental psychology with particular emphasis on the grand developmental theories of Lawrence Kohlberg (1969), Jean Piaget (1967), Lev Vygotsky (1978), Heinz Werner (1957), and their descendants. These relationships are subsumed under the more general rubric of develop-ment in the workplace. All of these chapters, with the exception of the final integrative piece by Demick and Miller (chapter 13), were present-ed at the conference on which this and related volumes are based. To orient the reader, our general organizational framework followed by a brief synopsis of each chapter is presented.

On the most general level, the chapters on development in the work-place are organized on the basis of the authors' chosen unit of analysis. That is, the chapters in Part I (chapters 1–8) address the development of the *individual* in the workplace. Part II (chapters 9 and 10) treats a larger unit of analysis, namely, the development of the *dyad* and *group* in the workplace. In Part III, the authors (chapters 11 and 12) consider an even broader unit (viz., the development of *organizational culture* in the workplace). Finally, Part IV (chapter 13) is directed toward un-covering both similarities and differences among the authors' theoreti-cal positions with an eye toward delineating some possible directions for future research in the general area of development in the workplace.

Part I begins with Melvin Miller and Alan West's (chapter 1) presentation of data concerning the influence of individuals' underlying world views (or generalized beliefs about how the world works) on personality, epistemology (as reflected in cognitive style), and choice of profession. Based on data from five occupational groups (clergy, lawyers, military personnel, physical scientists, social scientists), they suggest that "one's world view may be at the root of . . . personality and cognitive characteristics and perhaps the basis of career selection for many" (p. 18).

Cheryl Armon (chapter 2) presents select findings from a 12-year study of a small, highly educated sample of adults. By extending Piaget's (1967) and Kohlberg's (1969) groundbreaking work on cognitive and moral development respectively, she demonstrates that a structural–developmental approach is equally applicable to understanding developmental differences in reasoning about *good work*. In addition to showing that reasoning about good work is related to variables such as age, education, and socioeconomic status and that certain stages of this reasoning are unique to adulthood, she draws out many significant, practical implications for the construction of adult education, training and re-training, career education, and psychological intervention programs and methods.

Dorothy Rulon (chapter 3) discusses the interrelationship between workers' moral reasoning and the sociomoral complexity of their jobs as well as the influence of this relationship on workers' ability to resolve workplace dilemmas. Employing Kohlberg's (1969) theory of moral development as a theoretical framework, she illustrates the ways in which some intriguing interventions (e.g., the just community model) have indicated the potential to advance the moral development of select occupational groups such as teachers and health-care workers.

Doreen Cleave-Hogg and Linda Muzzin (chapter 4) present the findings of their comparative assessment of the developmental levels of beginning pharmacy and medical students, using Perry's (1970) constructivist–development framework of intellectual and ethical development. After delineating the differences, these authors employ their findings to speculate about some possible changes in standard admission procedures as well as curriculum designs for these types of students.

Rita Weathersby (chapter 5) provides another demonstration of the powerful heuristic potential of constructivist–developmental theory coupled with the usefulness of cross-cultural research. Specifically, she addresses the issue of Sri Lankan managers' conceptions of leadership as a function of their level of ego development (Loevinger & Wessler, 1970). Through a comparison of her data with those obtained from American managers, she illustrates how cross-cultural differences may affect the transferability of leadership models. She concludes with a discussion of leadership as a dynamic interaction between the developmental level of the leader and the cultural expectations of the society.

Carl Goldberg (chapter 6) addresses issues of maturation in the seasoned psychotherapist. After acknowledging that the vast amount of material examining clinical practice and the lifestyle of the practitioner has focused almost exclusively on understanding the neophyte psychotherapist, he then presents some preliminary results of his empirical research on developmental issues in mature (middle-aged and aging) psychotherapists. Based on these preliminary data, he goes on to paint the broad brush strokes of his own dialectical theory of adult development that has largely been influenced by the important work of Jung (1989), Kelly (1963), and Levinson (1978).

Lorraine Mangione (chapter 7) aptly demonstrates the usefulness of phenomenological analysis in her portrait of a single artist. Employing the concept of life themes (Spotts & Shontz, 1980), she illustrates the ways in which this construct represents "a somewhat different view of development (and in this case, female development) than has recently been promulgated by the emphasis in women's development on relatedness and the relational context (e.g., Chodorow, 1978; Gilligan, 1982; Surrey, 1984)" (p. 124).

Peter Bachiochi (chapter 8), through the use of the quasi-experimental method, presents the results of an empirical study on the relationship between career maturity and the salience of one's roles as worker and leisurite. On the most general level, he reports that the career planning in which individuals take part is significantly related to the salience of their leisure roles; and that career planning as well as career exploration are significantly related to the salience of individuals' work roles. Based on these findings, he then discusses the implications of this work for the specific area of career development.

Using a method similar to Bachiochi but focusing on a larger unit of analysis (workplace dyads), Janet Barnes-Farrell (chapter 9) provides empirical evidence to support the generalization that contextual variables may affect individuals' career development. Specifically, in a field study of 87 supervisor–subordinate dyads, nondirectional measures of perceived and actual age disparity were found to account for significant variance in ratings of promotability. She then discusses both the theoretical and practical implications of her findings for minimizing potential age bias in the workplace.

Jan Sinnott (chapter 10) begins by acknowledging the Vygotskian (1978) position that "thinking and complex problem solving occur taking into account products of several minds, not of one mind alone" (p. 155). She then argues that participation in a thinking group inevitably leads to intragroup conflict. Drawing on theories from biology, cognitive science, developmental psychology, mathematics, and physics, she presents her own integrative theory of intragroup conflict. Using case history and phenomenological data, she illustrates how we (as individuals or groups) can make conscious use of our conflict experiences to foster adult development. While her grand theory is applicable to groups in any context, she provides numerous examples from the workplace to support her theory.

Linda Morris (chapter 11) provides information on current theory, research, and practice surrounding the concept of the "learning organization" (one that facilitates, while constantly transforming itself, the learning and personal development of all its employees). By providing numerous examples of this concept in action, she delineates the implications of this model both for theory and practice in (adult) developmental and organizational psychology.

Michael Commons, Sharon Krause, Gregory Fayer, and Maryellen Meaney (chapter 12) investigate the relationship between individual moral development and the developmental stage of a workplace environment. Specifically, they hypothesize that the interaction of individuals and organizational atmosphere reinforces behaviors at specific stages, thereby fostering or constraining individual development. Using their General Stage Model of adult development, they attempt to demonstrate their ability to characterize this interaction with a high degree of precision. They believe that such characterization is necessary because contemporary challenges in the workplace increasingly call for postconventional responses from both individuals and organizations.

Finally, toward integrating the chapters and suggesting directions for future research, Jack Demick and Patrice Miller (chapter 13) conclude the volume by uncovering similarities and differences among the authors' theoretical approaches and their own. From a recent extension (Wapner & Demick, 1990) of Werner's (1957) organismic–developmental theory, they focus their suggestions for future research on such issues as unit of analysis; the holistic and systemic nature of human behavior and experience; broader conceptualizations of the person, of the environment, and of development; the need for methodological eclecticism; and the complementarity of basic and applied research. Through this lens, they shed light on reasons underlying why the majority of authors have focused on the individual worker as unit of analysis and then propose that future researchers more broadly define the basic concept of development in the workplace.

REFERENCES

Chodorow, N. (1978). *The reproduction of mothering*. Berkeley, CA: University of California Press.
Gilligan, C. (1982). *In a different voice: Psychological theory and women's development*. Cambridge, MA: Harvard University Press.

Jung, C. G. (1989). *Memories, dreams and reflections*. New York: Random House.

Kelly, G. (1963). *A theory of personality*. New York: Norton.

Kohlberg, L. (1969). Stage and sequence: The cognitive-developmental approach to socialization. In D. A. Goslin (Ed.), *Handbook of socialization theory and research* (pp. 347–480). Chicago: Rand McNally.

Levinson, D. J. (1978). *The seasons of a man's life*. New York: Ballentine.

Loevinger, J., & Wessler, R. (1970). *Measuring ego development* (Vol. 1). San Francisco: Jossey-Bass.

Perry, W. G. (1970). *Forms of intellectual and ethical development in the college years*. New York: Holt, Rinehart & Winston.

Piaget, J. (1967). *Six psychological studies*. New York: Random House.

Spotts, J. V., & Shontz, F. C. (1980). *Cocaine users: A representative case approach*. New York: The Free Press.

Surrey, J. L. (1984). Self-in relation: A theory of women's development. *Works in progress*. Wellesley, MA: Stone Center.

Vygotsky, L. S. (1978). *Mind in society: The development of higher psychological processes*. Cambridge, MA: Harvard University Press.

Wapner, S., & Demick, J. (1990). Development of experience and action: Levels of integration in human functioning. In G. Greenberg & E. Tobach (Ed.), *Theories of the evolution of knowing: The T. C. Schneirla conference series* (pp. 47–68). Hillsdale, NJ: Lawrence Erlbaum Associates.

Werner, H. (1957). *Comparative psychology of mental development*. New York: International Universities Press.

PART ONE

DEVELOPMENT OF THE INDIVIDUAL IN THE WORKPLACE

CHAPTER ONE

Influences of World View on Personality, Epistemology, and Choice of Profession

Melvin E. Miller
Norwich University

Alan N. West
Veterans Administration Hospital and Dartmouth Medical School

What leads an individual to pursue a particular profession? Aside from its potential rewards, both extrinsic and intrinsic, as well as various seren-dipitous factors, one's choice of career must, to some extent, reflect one's philosophical orientation and one's fundamental assumptions regarding the sources of basic truths and the proper goals of life. Do certain profes-sions attract members who hold similar world views? Alternatively, does each discipline's unique training include some form of indoctrination into the world view of the profession? Are some professions more homogene-ous than others with respect to prevailing philosophies?

To address such questions, we categorized the world views and used hypothetically related measures of personality and cognitive style ob-tained from members of five distinctive professional groups. World view classifications were derived from an extensive interview-based procedure with good interrater agreement. Group differences in predominant world views supported the construct validity of a world view classification system.

WORLD VIEW DEFINITIONS

A world view can be thought of as a particular set of mental constructs that make one's world meaningful. A world view acts as a "filter" through which phenomena are perceived and comprehended. As the set of con-

3

ceptual rules representing one's core beliefs, it guides one's significant actions.

This definition extends the Piagetian notions of cognitive structure and development; it is more in line with the postformal theories proposed by Richards and Commons (1990), Basseches (1984), and Kegan (1982). Our conceptualization of cognitive structure holds open the possibility of cognitive development after the formal operations stage has been reached. Such postformal thinking involves metasystematic and dialectical thought. Some individuals transcend "mere" formal operations and develop more complex structures through which they process information about themselves and the world.

Koplowitz (1990) engaged in some exploratory research that has investigated the possibility of encouraging postformal developments in thought in the context of the workplace. Further, Torbert (1991) discussed cultivating postformal development in business management training programs. These exceptions notwithstanding, very little has been written in the psychological literature about world views and cognitive/personality development within a postformal context.

A study of professional world views, or frames of reference, was attempted in the field of sociology. Holzner, Mitroff, and Fisher (1980) conducted an exploratory study on philosophical frames of reference using a case study approach with six distinguished professionals in the fields of psychology, psychiatry, sociology, and the law. Interviews with these individuals focused on how their philosophical frames of reference related to their professional thinking and behavior. All six individuals had world views that could be articulated with varying degrees of specificity and clarity. Moreover, some of them reflected more consciously upon the specifics of their world views (and how they impacted their professional lives) than did others. Further, to explore how an individual's "core beliefs" are formed, Shapiro (1989) studied a sample of professionals in the "consciousness disciplines" (e.g., therapists, teachers of meditation and/ or martial arts). He asked questions such as: "Are there catalytic events that cause one to change one's view of ultimate reality?" and "Do we voluntarily and consciously choose this belief or does it seem as if we 'receive' it, almost as if it 'comes to us' and is beyond our control?" (p. 18). Shapiro's subjects claimed that their belief systems were developed in both ways; some were even able to explain the process in detail. Absent from this study, however, was any assessment of personality or cognitive variables and/or comparisons of belief systems across disciplines.

To compare world views among different professional groups, we decided to construct a classification system that would permit the clarification of world view differences in a systematic fashion. Before developing the classification system, an interview that explored world view questions had to be constructed.

CONSTRUCTION OF THE WORLD VIEW INTERVIEW

The World View Interview (Miller, 1982) was developed to meet the need for a reliable technique in this largely unstudied area. An extensive review of the literature in a variety of disciplines yielded a list of the most likely dimensions comprising a comprehensive world view. Significant variables and constructs were found in Pepper's (1970) book on *World Hypotheses*, in the anthropological–sociological research of Kluckhohn (1967), and in Churchman's (1971) text, *The Design of Inquiring Systems*.

From these studies, Miller (1982) constructed a list of variables or dimensions that hypothetically belonged in a comprehensive world view. The list included items relating to the subject's degree of reflectivity (with respect to one's world view); degree and kinds of commitments made; degree of cognitive rigidity versus cognitive flexibility; a locus of control estimate; an ego level score; a Perry (1970) epistemological position estimate; an estimate of the subject's ability to articulate a world view; and, finally, an estimate of the degree of the comprehensiveness of the subject's world view.

The World View Interview was written in a semi-structured format to incorporate these variables and to provide subjects the opportunity to talk about their world views in an open-ended manner. Questions similar to the following were used: Do you think that you have a world view? When did you first develop one? How often do you think of it? Under what circumstances do you think of it? How do changes in your world view transpire? Do you actively work to change or modify it?[1] Additional questions were added to the interview to probe for other variables that seemed to merit investigation (e.g., questions that addressed the interplay between personality dynamics and the choice of/development of one's world view).

WORLD VIEW CLASSIFICATION SYSTEM

Many extant theoretical notions (Churchman, 1971; Pepper, 1970) that were drawn upon in the process of developing the World View Interview were also used in the construction of the World View Classification system. From their descriptions of world views, along with estimates of the personality and epistemological characteristics of likely adherents to such world views, Miller (1982) developed the World View Classification Grid (see Table 1.1).

---

[1]Sample questions presented in the text are modified and condensed versions of ones used in the World View Interview. Due to space limitations, the complete interview could not be included in this chapter. The actual World View Interview is available upon request from the first author (Melvin E. Miller, Psychology Department, Norwich University, North field, VT 05663).

TABLE 1.1
World View Classification Grid

	The Teleological-Metaphysical Dimension (One's Relationship to Meanings, Goals, Nature, and God)		
Epistemological Dimension (One's Source of Truth)	Anti-Teleological (Against Telos)	A-Teleological (Without Telos)	Teleological (For Telos)
General Descriptors	WV#1	WV#2	WV#3
1-Reflectivity: (Low to Mod.)	Atomism	Stoicism	Traditional Theism
2-Commitment to: (Mod. to High) Law & Order	(Mechanistic-Reductionistic)	(The Do-er & Experiencer)	(Law & Order Position)
Objective — Church &/or Dogma			
(Outside) — Scientific Paradigm			
"You; It" — Experience Itself			
"I-It" 3-Rigidity (Mod. to High)			
4-Locus of Control (External)			
5-Ego Level: Mod.			
6-Perry Pos. 1-4	—Transition—	—Transition—	—Transition—
1-Reflectivity (Mod. to High)	WV#4	WV#5	WV#6

6

	Nihilism	Skepticism-Agnosticism	Traditional Humanism
	(Nothing is Knowable)	(The Doubter & Questioner)	("Man is the Measure . . .")
Subjective (Within) "Self; I'"			
2-Commitment to: (Low to Mod.) Self & Self-Preoccupation			
3-Rigidity (Low to Mod.)			
4-Locus of Control (Internal)			
5-Ego Level (Mod. to High)			
6-Perry Pos. 4-6	—Transition—	—Transition—	—Transition—

	WV#7	WV#8	WV#9
	Pantheistic Monism	Integrated-Committed Existentialism	Integrated-Committed Theism & Humanism
	(Eastern Mysticism)	(A "Maker of Meaning")	(True Commitment Beyond Self)
Dialogical (In relationship) "I-Thou" "I-Other" "Man-God"			
1-Reflectivity (Mod. to High)			
2-Commitment to: (High w/ "Care") Something Beyond Self; e.g., Social Projects & One's Own Life Project			
3-Rigidity: Mod. (Dialogical)			
4-Locus of Control (Dialogical)			
5-Ego Level (Mod. to High)			
6-Perry Pos. 7-9	—Transition—	—Transition—	—Transition—

The World View Classification Grid is a two-dimensional grid comprised of three rows and three columns. The horizontal rows comprise the Epistemological Dimension and the columns make up the Teleological–Metaphysical Dimension. There are three world views in each row, creating a total of nine world views.

Along the Epistemological Dimension, there are qualitative differences found among the world views of the different tiers or rows. An important question relating to one's placement in a particular row is: Where is the individual's locus or source of truth? It is assumed to be "outside of self"—in events, objects, or authorities—for those in the first tier or Objective row. It is assumed to be "within self" for those in the Subjective row and it is expected to be dialogical or dialectical for those in the Dialogical row. Specifically, those in the Dialogical row would find truth and meaning in relationship with events and nature as well as in dialogue (give-and-take relationships) with significant others.

The columns of the World View Classification Grid also depict substantive differences in the world views of the subjects. The columns help to differentiate among world views that are: *Teleological* (belief in "ends," "ultimate designs," and "purposes"); *Anti-Teleological* (consciously opposed to a belief in ultimate designs and purposes); and *A-Teleological* (suspended or withheld belief about ultimate designs and purposes). Also addressed in this dimension are issues relating to the subject's perception of being and reality (ultimate reality). Thus, this dimension is most appropriately called the Teleological–Metaphysical Dimension.

The interplay of the underlying epistemological and teleological variables forms the foundation for the nine different world views. General descriptions of the world views (Table 1.2) were developed with these underlying factors in mind.

Some of the theoretical assumptions behind the development of the World View Classification Grid are as follows:

1. All nine of the world views are most likely manifestations of formal operational thinking.
2. Nevertheless, a general developmental sequence is implied. Those subjects with more cognitive and emotional maturity more likely will be found in the Subjective and Dialogical rows. These same subjects will also be more likely to demonstrate postformal thinking. Although a general developmental sequence is implied in the layout of the Grid, an invariant hierarchical sequence is not.
3. Those with world views on the first tier, or Objective row, seem to want or need a frame of reference that is fairly tight and struc-

TABLE 1.2

World View 1—Atomism

It makes the most sense to me to think of all reality as being comprised of small particles called atoms. And, I believe that to make sense of things, we only need to break them down into their atomic parts and study the relationships that exist among them. Most often, these relationships are precise enough to formulate them with mathematical precision. Phenomena as diverse as human relationships and events in the physical world all can be treated with equal precision. We need no gods nor a deity to give meaning to existence. Science can give us all the answers we need.

World View 2—Stoicism

I would say that there really is no rhyme or reason to events that occur, and that there are no fixed orders, purposes, or meanings in life. Given this state of affairs, it seems that the best thing for people to do is to keep busy and take care of their own little corners of the world. I like to keep busy. I may not be able to control things on a larger perspective, but I can control my attitude toward what happens and what I do with my life.

World View 3—Traditional Theism

It seems to me that there is a universal purpose and meaning to life. These purposes and meanings are most likely predetermined, and are likely determined by a deity or God or some "higher" form of intelligence. Our purpose in life is to understand these meanings and to live in accordance with them. The unhappiness that exists in the world is a result of people and nations not living in accordance with these realizations.

World View 4—Nihilism

I do not think that anything can be claimed to be true with any sense of certainty. There is no such thing as reliable knowledge, and no God or gods or moral order in the universe. Given these facts, people can do with their lives whatever they wish. Everything is entirely up to the individual, for in the long run, nothing really matters anyhow.

World View 5—Skepticism–Agnosticism

I do not know what—if anything—human beings can know for sure. I tend to doubt anybody or any system that says that they have the ultimate truth about anything, and I am especially suspicious of any claims to "official" truths whether they come in the form of religion or science. At best, everything is relative. Despite this doubting position, I believe that I keep an open mind that receives new input and information.

World View 6—Traditional Humanism

I would say that we cannot be certain of any fixed purposes or predetermined meanings or "ends" toward which the universe and/or individual lives are moving. Despite this absence of certainty, things do matter and there is a general direction in which the world and human lives move. We are in charge of our own lives, and the community of the world is in charge of "Spaceship Earth." Both individuals and groups must endeavor to establish appropriate and positive meanings and goals. The ecology movement, the human potential movement and the peace movement are considered important causes.

(Continued)

TABLE 1.2
(Continued)

World View 7—Pantheistic Monism

Personal and/or spiritual awareness are the most important things to be worked at during this life, so that I can more greatly appreciate the specialness and uniqueness of each moment. Activities and aesthetic pursuits are valuable in and of themselves. I am not working toward ultimate goals that are predetermined, nor do I believe in a personal god who oversees everything. But, I do commit myself to understanding myself and the world more completely, and to appreciate all of life.

World View 8—Integrated–Committed Existentialism

Nothing is intrinsically or ultimately meaningful. What is "right"—and the particular goals that are important to work toward—can best be arrived at through conversation and dialogue with concerned others. I am committed to care for people and the world despite the lack of a master plan or blueprint, and despite the apparent relativistic nature of things. I see my life as being comprised of a series of ongoing commitments to self-exploration and the world's needs.

World View 9—Integrated–Committed Theism & Humanism

I believe in a god or gods—or something greater than myself, but I do not see things as being predetermined or part of a preordained divine scheme. I think that one should remain in dialogue with that which is perceived as being divine or greater than the self. Through self-introspection, an exploration of values and this dialogical relationship, one can orient oneself and commit oneself to worthwhile goals and projects. It seems that there is a general "direction" in which lives and worlds should move, but things are not fixed or etched in stone. Lives and events can change and improve through individual and collective human effort. Human relationships, social causes, ecology, and world peace are the kinds of commitments in which I might invest time and energy.

Note: This table includes only abbreviated descriptions of the nine world views included in the World View Classification Grid. See Miller (1982) for more detailed descriptions.

tured, regardless of whether their particular world view is a scientific one or a traditional theistic one. The degree of reflectivity or consciousness brought to the choice of world view by these individuals will tend to be low. Moderate to high degrees of cognitive rigidity are expected from this group along with moderate levels of ego development and an external locus of control.

4. Those with world views on the second tier, or the Subjective row, are expected to be in the somewhat relativistic and "internal"—and perhaps even self-conscious—position. The degree of reflectivity and consciousness brought to this position is expected to be moderate or high and these subjects are expected to be the most "open-minded" or cognitively flexible of those in the study. Lo-

cus of control is expected to be internal and the ego levels are anticipated to range from moderate to high. At times, these individuals have difficulty making commitments to causes, people, and events beyond themselves.

5. Those with world views on the third tier, or on the Dialogical row, are assumed to think in a more dialectical or dialogical manner. They arrive at "truth" in relationship with the other. They actively think about reality and events in a more dialectical and conscious manner. Levels of reflectivity are assumed to be moderate to high and the subjects are predicted to be fairly open-minded. The ego levels of these individuals will be found in the moderate to high range and their locus of control is considered to be "dialogical." These subjects are committed to projects and events "beyond self" such as social projects and environmental concerns. Their "projects" appear to be consistent with and consciously evolve from their world views.

METHOD

Subjects

The subjects were 40 adult males between the ages of 28 and 57. The average age of the subjects was 37 years. Subjects were drawn from this age range because: (a) it was assumed that about 30 years of experience are needed for an individual to arrive at a fairly crystallized and expressible world view; and (b) follow-up interviews are planned to span a 20- to 30-year interval. Subjects were recruited from five professions (i.e., social scientists, "hard" or physical scientists, lawyers, military personnel—both officers and noncommissioned officers—and ministers/priests). There were eight subjects in each of the five professional groups.

Most subjects had advanced degrees, either academic or professional (average formal education = 19.2 years). There were 6 PhDs, 2 ABDs ("all but dissertation"), 7 JDs (Juris Doctorate), 2 MBAs, 6 with either the MA or MS degree, and 6 with the Bachelor's degree. All the remaining subjects had some kind of post-high school formal education. At least 10 subjects had more than one advanced degree. Collectively, the research sample was certainly of above average intelligence and was comprised of highly motivated and professionally oriented individuals. Subjects were volunteers and were contacted through friends, colleagues, and officers at various institutions (e.g., university and government offices).

Procedure

Each subject was administered the World View Interview by the first author. Beforehand, the subjects completed both the Dogmatism Scale (Rokeach, 1960) and the Washington University Sentence Completion Test (Loevinger & Wessler, 1970)—two standardized instruments offering data relevant to personality and cognitive variables. The interviews generally required 3 to 5 hours to complete.

Subsequently, the interview protocols were scored according to a specific set of guidelines (Miller, 1982); each subject was then assigned to one of the nine World View (WV) categories depicted on the World View Classification Grid. To assess interrater reliability, a second rater was trained in the scoring and world view placement procedure. The second rater agreed substantially on category assignments (Kappa = .70).

The Washington University Sentence Completion Test (WUSCT) was scored according to the Loevinger and Wessler (1970) guidelines. Responses to the 36 sentence stems were scored individually. Then the cumulative frequency distribution of each subject's scores was compared to Loevinger's "automatic ogive" table to derive an overall test score. This ogive score was standardized to a 10-point scale.

The Dogmatism Scale (Rokeach, 1960), a self-report scale of "open- or closed-mindedness" (cognitive flexibility vs. cognitive rigidity) also was administered. It includes 40 statements to which a subject expresses agreement or disagreement at various levels (e.g., + 3: "I disagree very much" to − 3: "I agree very much"). The "0" point is excluded to force responses toward agreement or disagreement. For scoring purposes, responses were converted to a 1 to 7 scale by adding a constant of 4 to each item score. An individual's total score is the sum of scores obtained on all 40 items on the test (Rokeach, 1960).

Subjects also were assigned to one of the Perry positions of "intellectual and ethical development" (Perry, 1970). These assignments were based on their responses to specific World View Interview questions as well as from an overall impressionistic rating of their responses throughout the interview. The Perry scheme was used to facilitate the process of making a "scaled judgment" concerning the subject's level and quality of commitments. The issue of commitment is especially critical in determining the assignment of a subject to the Dialogical row group in the Epistemological Dimension of the World View Classification Grid.

RESULTS

Regardless of professional orientation, all of the subjects had world views (WVs) that could be categorized according to the World View Classification Grid. The distribution of subjects among the different world views is displayed in Table 1.3.

Inspection of Table 1.3 reveals that subjects were distributed fairly evenly across the Epistemological Dimension (rows). On the Teleological-Metaphysical Dimension, however, the distribution was skewed. A majority held Teleological world views, whereas 11 subjects were A-Teleological and only 4 were Anti-Teleological. For purposes of analysis, these latter two positions were collapsed into a "Non-Teleological" category.

Some striking general observations were noted when the grid was collapsed from 3 × 3 to 2 × 3 (see Table 1.4). The military personnel were distributed fairly evenly throughout the top two rows of the grid. No military personnel were found in the Dialogical row. All but two of the lawyers were assigned to the Teleological column.

All clergy were in the Teleological column as well—in World Views 3 or 9. All physical scientists except one, on the other hand, were placed in the Non-Teleological column, and all except one were in either the Objective or Dialogical rows. The social scientists were all assigned to either the Subjective or Dialogical rows. Two social scientists were Non-Teleological, whereas 6 were Teleological in their orientations. Across the entire sample, the correlation between ego level and dogmatism (or cognitive rigidity) was negative ($r = -.48, p < .01$). Hence, subjects with higher levels of ego development tended to be less dogmatic. Correla-

TABLE 1.3
World View Placements by Professional Affiliations

Epistemological Dimension	The Teleological-Metaphysical Dimension		
	Anti-Teleological	A-Teleological	Teleological
Objective	WV 1	WV 2	WV 3
	2 Scientists	2 Military	5 Clergy
	1 Lawyer	1 Scientist	4 Lawyers
$n = 17$			2 Military
	$n = 3$	$n = 3$	$n = 11$
Subjective	WV 4	WV 5	WV 6
		2 Military	3 Soc. Sci.
		2 Soc. Sci.	2 Military
$n = 12$		1 Lawyer	1 Scientist
		1 Scientist	
	$n = 0$	$n = 6$	$n = 6$
Dialogical	WV 7	WV 8	WV 9
	1 Scientist	2 Scientists	3 Clergy
			3 Soc. Sci.
$n = 11$			2 Lawyers
	$n = 1$	$n = 2$	$n = 8$
	col. $n = 4$	col. $n = 11$	col. $n = 25$

TABLE 1.4
Collapsed World View Placements by Professional Affiliations

Epistemological Dimension	The Teleological-Metaphysical Dimension	
	Non-Teleological	Teleological
Objective	WV 1 & WV 2	WV 3
	3 Scientists	5 Clergy
	2 Military	4 Lawyers
n = 17	1 Lawyer	2 Military
	n = 6	n = 11
Subjective	WV 4 & WV 5	WV 6
	2 Military	3 Soc. Sci.
	2 Soc. Sci.	2 Military
n = 12	1 Lawyer	1 Scientist
	1 Scientist	
	n = 6	n = 6
Dialogical	WV 7 & WV 8	WV 9
	3 Scientists	3 Clergy
		3 Soc. Sci.
n = 11		2 Lawyers
	n = 3	n = 8
	col. n = 15	col. n = 25

tions between ego level and dogmatism were also computed for each of the five professional groups separately. Strong negative correlations emerged for physical scientists (r = $-.81, p < .02$), and for the military professionals (r = $-.76, p < .03$). For the other three groups, however, ego development and dogmatism were not significantly related.

The WUSCT ego level scores, Dogmatism scores, and Perry Position scores were submitted to separate 2 (Teleological) × 3 (Epistemological) analyses of variance. Subjects at different epistemological levels differed significantly with regard to ego development scores, $F(2,34) = 5.12, p < .05$. Specifically, those in the Subjective and Dialogical rows had higher levels of ego development than those in the Objective row. Epistemological rows also differed significantly with regard to dogmatism, $F(2,34) = 4.74, p < .05$. Objective row subjects were more dogmatic or cognitively inflexible than the others, whereas Subjective row subjects were the most open-minded or cognitively flexible of the three groups of subjects. Epistemological rows differed with respect to the Perry Positions of ethical and intellectual development, $F(2,34) = 3.40, p < .05$. Dialogical row subjects showed higher levels of development than the other groups.

For all measures, there were no significant main effects for Teleology nor for its interaction with Epistemology. These measures (WUSCT, Dogmatism, and Perry Position) were also submitted to separate one-factor (i.e., professional group) ANOVAs. Significance emerged only from the analysis of Perry Positions, $F(4,35) = 5.69$, $p < .01$. Compared to the other groups, Military personnel had significantly lower Perry scores. No other group differences emerged.

DISCUSSION

These results, although admittedly from a small sample, attest to the usefulness and construct validity of the World View Interview and its associated classification grid in several ways. First, we demonstrated good interrater agreement in the assignment of subjects to positions on the World View Classification Grid. Hence, the information generated through the interview and the categorization criteria are sufficiently comprehensive and comprehendible for raters to assess world views reliably.

Second, world view dimensions were related to professional identity and to measures of personality and cognitive style, yet these personality and cognitive measures were largely unrelated to professional group per se. This finding suggests that world view somehow mediates between the traits we studied and one's choice of profession. Because we assume that one's world view represents a sort of filter mechanism through which life events are interpreted and rendered meaningful, we suggest that it may be at the root of other personality and cognitive characteristics as well as the basis for career selection.

Third, and most compellingly, our world view categorizations were quite compatible with subjects' career choices. For example, all of the clergy had world views in the Teleological column of the World View Grid (WVs 6 or 9). Clergy members seemed to see their world in terms of "ends," "designs," and "purposes"; most seemed to believe that it is up to individuals (and organized religion) to discover what these "ends" are and to live in accordance with them. Those in World View 3 (Traditional Theism) appeared to look for their answers in more conventional ways and in conventional religious beliefs consistent with those espoused by the mainstream Judeo-Christian perspective.

In contrast, those in World View 9 (Integrated Committed Theism and Humanism) seemed to believe in more individually realized or discovered beliefs that may or may not be sanctioned by mainstream religion. Some of the subjects in World View 9 were still part of mainstream religious groups, and three were ministers or priests. Nonetheless, the nature of their religious orientation was more unique and personal. None of the clergy were found in the Subjective Epistemological row. Hence, it appears that none of them saw the source of "truth" as within themselves only.

Physical scientists, on the other hand, held world views almost exclusively (7 of 8) in the Non-Teleological column. Three of these scientists were in the Objective row and three were in the Dialogical row. Hence, physical scientists, by and large, believe in truths that are "out there," but that are not teleologically oriented nor based on traditional religious beliefs. The atomistic and reductionistic approach of traditional science is as much about the belief in a method of investigation as in anything else. Such scientists were perhaps more likely than the other professionals to be logical positivists and so believe in the orderliness of reality—without ascribing a teleological direction or orientation to this orderliness.

Although six of the eight lawyers were found in the Teleological column (they had a distribution similar to that of the clergy), beyond that there was no strong pattern to the results. Four were assigned to WV 3 (Traditional Theism), something that, at first glance, appears to be difficult to explain. However, if we note the subtitle to WV 3, that is, Law and Order Position, their placements were more understandable. Those in the WV 3 in the Objective row were wedded firmly to the structure of law and order in a manner not unlike the theists in this group who were wedded to strict religious beliefs. Two lawyers were found in WV 9 (Integrated-Committed Theism and Humanism). This may be best understood from within the context of Kohlberg's (1981) Stage 5 representatives who espouse the importance of the social contract. These individuals understand the relative and contractual nature of laws and are committed to using the legal system for the collective good. The remaining two lawyers were found in World Views 1 and 5.

The military personnel were equally distributed among the top four cells of the 2 × 3 grid. There were two with Teleological orientations and two with Non-Teleological views; there were two in the Objective–Epistemological row and two in the Subjective row. This finding seems to suggest that with the military personnel—as with the lawyers—no generally accepted professional philosophy or set of values obtained. One's personal orientation prevailed over those that may be suggested by the profession itself, although it could be argued that the military personnel take either one of two positions (viz., either "I take orders from you" or "You take orders from me"). In any case, "There is no room for negotiations" and "Our relationship is not reciprocal." None of the military personnel were in the Dialogical–Epistemological row. Finally, five social scientists held world views in the Subjective row (more than any other professional group) and three in the Dialogical row. None of the social scientists took the Objective Epistemological stance. Their source of truth or knowledge came either from within themselves or was arrived at through dialogue or interpersonal exchange. They seemed to rely on an inner yardstick with which to measure what was "right." It often was as if some new bit of information or idea had to "feel right" in order to be accepted. As a group, they seemed to be both self-aware and aware of the "other."

An initially puzzling finding with respect to the social scientists is that six of the eight were placed in the Teleological column. They expressed an expectation of design and order to the universe and human lives in a manner similar to many of the clergy, but their teleological orientation was not traditionally theistic. It could be said that they subscribed to a somewhat secular teleology. One might wonder if the general sense of order, direction, and purpose that many social scientists experience in their personal lives carries over into their professional lives. It also could be argued that the "direction" implicit in developmental sequences—in the growth and development tenets in psychology texts—have become almost "normal science" in the field of psychology and the social sciences. If this is the case, then we might argue that the accepted tenets of the discipline essentially shape the thinking and world views of individual social scientists.

Beyond professional group differences, other findings also support the World View Classification Grid and system. For example, an analysis of ego development (WUSCT scores) showed that subjects with Objective world views had lower scores than those with Subjective or Dialogical world views. Objective subjects apparently are less likely to trust their own impressions and look beyond themselves for "the truth." Consistent with this finding is the significantly higher dogmatism of these subjects. (For the entire sample, dogmatism and ego development were negatively skewed.) These high Dogmatism/Objective row subjects appeared to have very firm ideas of what was right or wrong in a number of realms (e.g., theological, political, and interpersonal). They seemed to make decisions firmly and were not open to alternative points of view.

Subjects in the Subjective row had the lowest dogmatism scores. They tended to be quite open-minded and receptive to any number of new or different ideas. The position that it is "all relative anyhow" was espoused by a few subjects in this group. In one or two specific cases, it appeared as if the subjects were almost drowning in a sea of relativism and could not find a direction in their lives. On the other hand, the subjects in the Dialogical row were found to be slightly less cognitively flexible than those in the Subjective row. They had more specific likes and dislikes and appeared to be committed to certain ideas and a life course. Nonetheless, they were not dogmatic or rigid about these choices or positions—especially in comparison to those in the Objective row. In general, they engaged in meta-systematic thinking and were able to process multiple positions or frames of reference at the same time.

The ANOVA on Perry Position scores revealed that Dialogical subjects had significantly higher levels of development than either Subjective or Objective subjects. Dialogical subjects had either made the initial commitments that Perry (1970) described; most (6 of 11 subjects) had begun to explore the "subjective and stylistic issues of responsibility" (Perry, 1970) connected to such commitments. One Dialogical row subject (the only one in the entire sample) obtained the highest possible Perry Position score of 9. This subject was most comfortable with the commitments that he had made and was able to articulate the necessity of constantly modifying these commitments in a manner consistent with his evolving lifestyle and professional interests.

Finally, we should note that, in terms of the placement of the subjects among the nine different worlds views in the World View Classification Grid, we found the distribution to be varied and uneven (see Table 1.3). Some world views had large numbers of subjects in them, and one world view (4 Nihilism) had no subjects placed in it. Perhaps this world view does not belong in the classification system or perhaps this result is a reflection of the culturally restrictive nature of our research sample. World View 7 (Pantheistic Monism) had only one subject, and World View 8 (Integrated-Committed Existentialism) had only two. The relatively small sample size, the nature of the personal and professional orientations of the subjects, and the aforementioned cultural restrictedness of the sample are presented as explanations of this outcome. However, the paucity of subjects in these three world views is not, at this point, taken as an indication that the World View Classification System needs to be modified.

SUMMARY

This chapter explored world views, cognitive style, and personality variables as they relate to professional choices. The results revealed significant world view differences across professions, thus attesting to the usefulness and construct validity of the World View Interview and the World View Classification Grid. World view dimensions were related to professional identity and to measures of personality and cognitive style. It appears that world view somehow mediates among the traits studied and one's choice of profession. Furthermore, we suggest that one's world view may be at the root of other personality and cognitive characteristics and perhaps the basis of career selection for many.

REFERENCES

Basseches, M. A. (1984). Dialectical thinking as metasystematic forms of cognitive organization. In M. L. Commons, F. A. Richards, & C. Armon (Eds.), *Beyond formal operations: Late adolescent and adult cognitive development* (pp. 216–238). New York: Praeger.

Churchman, C. W. (1971). *The design of inquiring systems: Basic concepts of systems and organization*. New York: Basic Books.

Holzner, B., Mitroff, I., & Fisher, E. (1980). *An empirical investigation of frames of reference: Case studies in the sociology of inquiry*. Unpublished manuscript, University of Pittsburgh, Pittsburgh, PA.

Kegan, R. (1982). *The evolving self: Problems and process in human development*. Cambridge, MA: Harvard University Press.

Kluckhohn, C. (1967). The study of values. In D. Barrett (Ed.), *Values in America*. Notre Dame, IN: University of Notre Dame Press.

Kohlberg, L. (1981). *The philosophy of moral development: Moral stages and the idea of justice*. New York: Harper & Row.

Koplowitz, H. (1990, June). *Control of mind and development of mind in the workplace*. Paper presented at fifth annual Adult Development Symposium, Boston, MA.

Loevinger, J., & Wessler, R. (1970). *Measuring ego development, Vol. 1: Construction and use of a sentence completion test*. San Francisco: Jossey-Bass.

Miller, M. E. (1982). World views and ego development in adulthood. *Dissertation Abstracts International, 42,* 3459–3460.

Pepper, S. (1970). *World hypotheses*. Berkeley: University of California Press. (Original work published 1942)

Perry, W. G. (1970). *Forms of intellectual and ethical development in the college years*. New York: Holt, Rinehart & Winston.

Richards, F., & Commons, M. L. (1990). Postformal cognitive-developmental theory and research: A review of its current status. In C. Alexander & E. Langer (Eds.), *Higher stages of human development* (pp. 139–161). New York: Oxford University Press.

Rokeach, M. (1960). *The open and closed mind*. New York: Basic Books.

Shapiro, D. (1989). Exploring our most deeply held belief about ultimate reality. *ReVision, 12*(1), 15–28.

Torbert, W. R. (1991). *Cultivating post-formal adult development: Theory and practice*. Manuscript submitted for publication.

CHAPTER TWO

Developmental Conceptions of Good Work: A Longitudinal Study

Cheryl Armon
Antioch University Los Angeles

Since Piaget's groundbreaking work in cognitive development, substantive research using the structural–developmental approach has appeared in a variety of conceptual domains. This approach claims that particular aspects of human reasoning develop through an invariant sequence of stages. The existence of such stages must be demonstrated using rigorous criteria; the sequence must also be demonstrated longitudinally. If the criteria are met, the stages should be sufficiently generalizable not only to predict reasoning across structured tasks within a domain, but also to explain some of the variation in everyday behavior within that domain.

In the social domain, Kohlberg's work on reasoning about justice has been particularly robust, supporting the validity of a sequential stage model in the development of certain aspects of moral judgment (Colby & Kohlberg, 1987; Kohlberg, 1981, 1984). In addition to numerous studies replicating and modifying Kohlberg's studies of justice reasoning, variations of the approach have been used in different domains such as parent–child relations (Selman, 1981), ego development (Loevinger, 1976), faith development (Fowler, 1981), and self-understanding (Damon & Hart, 1988). This chapter reports the results of a 12-year study of a small, select sample of adults. The study applies the structural–developmental approach to the examination of reasoning about good work.

WORK VALUES

There has been no other research that explicitly investigates adults' ideals of work. Most closely related, however, may be the research on "work values," which has been carried out primarily with nondevelopmental survey approaches. The most common of these are cross-sectional studies that have relied on point assignment and forced-choice, self-administered questionnaires. The majority of these studies have had as their goal the identification and measurement of specific values that individuals hold concerning their work as well as the examination of relations between the fulfillment of such values and job outcome measures (e.g., job satisfaction). Typical inventories have included a wide range of values such as responsibility, job security, influence in the organization, co-workers, convenience of hours, contribution to society, and the like (e.g., see Cherrington, 1980; Elizur, 1984; Ravlin & Meglino, 1987).

Authors reviewing the literature on work values often comment that, in view of the large numbers of studies, it is surprising to find so little attention devoted to understanding the basic unit of study. For example, Billings and Cornelius (1980) emphasized the necessity for basic research on the nature of work values, focusing on the need for a better understanding of the dimensions of the domain.

Although a review of these studies has indicated a fairly consistent inventory of work values, there remains little knowledge about the source, meaning, or impact of such values to different individuals. In contrast, a structural–developmental perspective would: (a) explain differences in salience of particular values to particular persons and between persons, (b) use appropriate research methods to track the development of such values, and (c) incorporate the philosophical perspective required of any study of values. A philosophical perspective is required because the study of the nature of values goes beyond empirical psychology and into the realm of ethics or moral philosophy (Kohlberg, 1981).

LIFE-SPAN, NONSTRUCTURAL
DEVELOPMENTAL APPROACHES

In the area of career development and career choice, researchers have attempted "developmental" approaches. These approaches have typically investigated the likelihood of a sequential order in the development of one's career. Typically, these studies referred to "stages" in such development as well as attaching specific age periods to each stage. "Personal values," interests, and lifestyle preferences have been described as central considerations at each of the stages. A typical model is that of Greenhaus (1988), who described the major tasks involved in five stages of the development of a career from "preparation for work" (0–25 years) through "late career" (55 years–retirement).

Although researchers have discussed the importance of personal values in choosing and maintaining a satisfactory career, these values are characterized as idiosyncratic, a result of the individual's childhood experiences (Stevens-Long & Commons, 1991). No model has, as of yet, provided for how such values might "develop," if they do. Most importantly, there has been little specificity as to the nature of "personal values." Similar to the work described on "work values," few distinctions have been made between values (e.g., moral vs. nonmoral values). From this perspective, all values are apparently "personal."

Other criticisms of this approach lead one to question its "developmental" nature. There has been no longitudinal evidence that many individuals actually procede through these stages, or that they do so in the order proscribed, or that they do so at the ages suggested (Stevens-Long & Commons, 1991). Moreover, there has been some question as to whether these types of models are applicable to women at all (Ornstein & Isabella, 1990). Finally, it has also been reported that many adults change their careers two or three times during their productive years. Thus, it is unlikely that such models are actually developmental in any real sense; the "stages" described are probably better thought of as "types" or "positions" in a career development model. Indeed, such models can be seen to be *anti*developmental in that although "reappraisal" is mentioned at times, a set of value choices made early in adulthood is basically "played out" during the balance of the individual's work life.

ADULT STRUCTURAL DEVELOPMENT

In addition to the goal of more clearly understanding the nature of value in adult ideals of work, an important aspect of this study is the investigation of *structural development* in adulthood. Since the 1980s, different approaches have been utilized to study the possibilities of extending Piaget's model of cognitive development beyond the formal operational stage as well as beyond adolescence and adulthood (e.g., see Alexander & Langer, 1990; Commons, Richards, & Armon, 1984). The study described here attempts to demonstrate not only the presence of structural stage development in adulthood, but also the existence of exclusively adult stages.

Kohlberg (1969, 1984) and others have posulated several prerequisites for continued structural development in the area of justice reasoning. An important prerequisite has been sociomoral experience, particularly that which includes conflict and role-taking opportunities. Empirical research on adult justice reasoning development, however, has been scarce. Kohlberg's longitudinal study, which followed individuals into their late 30s, provided only a glimpse of how adult moral development occurs. For example, Colby, Kohlberg, Gibbs, and Lieberman (1983) reported that advanced stage attainment in adolescence did not predict advanced development in adulthood. They also demonstrated that adult levels of education were a strong predictor of higher stage development, a finding corroborated by others (e.g., Walker, 1986).

Several studies have examined adult justice reasoning stages and their relation to specific life roles and activities. Relevant to the present study is Candee, Graham, and Kohlberg's (1978) examination of adults' work roles. These authors argued convincingly that individuals who reasoned at higher stages tended to be in positions that included greater responsibility for others. Although these findings have been useful in examining behavioral corrolaries of structural–developmental stages, they revealed little about the prevalence of, or causal factors in, actual development in adulthood.

A few studies of reasoning in other areas have proposed structural development in adulthood. For instance, Fowler (1981) described development in the area of faith and the interpretation of life's meaning with older adults. Armon (1984b) also found significant development over a 4-year period in the area of ideals incomplete. In summary, we still know very little about adult structural development.

THE GOOD LIFE STUDY

The study of adult conceptions of good work is part of a larger study of conceptions of the good life (Armon, 1984a, 1984b, 1988). In the study of developing conceptions of the good life, moral philosophy has informed empirical observation in an attempt to identify ultimate or essential values that individuals refer to in their evaluation of the good life. These ultimate values are sought in individuals' reasoning about the good life and then examined over time in an effort to identify a consistent pattern of change. The analyses of this longitudinal study focus on this evaluative reasoning in a variety of domains.

This chapter describes only the aspects of the study related to the development of evaluative reasoning in the domain of work, and only in adulthood. It is argued that the structural–developmental approach is effective for investigating these phenomena. It is demonstrated that sequential stage development in this domain does occur in adulthood and is significantly related to age as well as to other variables. In addition, the importance of focusing on actual work experience in studying adult development is discussed.

METHOD

Subjects

At the first interview occasion (1977), 50 predominantly Caucasian, middle-class individuals, ranging in age from 5 to 72 years, were chosen from a larger pool elicited through advertisements in the city of Los Angeles. The adult group (n = 33), ranging in age from 23 to 72 years, has an approximately equal distribution of males and females. Levels of education ranged from high school completion to doctoral degrees. Male and female adults were roughly matched on educational attainment. Due to their higher levels of education, most middle-age and older adults occupied white-collar, professional work roles. Thus, these adults represent a group whose education is higher than average.

Procedure

The structural–developmental research approach (Colby & Kohlberg, 1987; Piaget, 1932/1965, 1972) was used to collect and analyze interview data four times at 4-year intervals from 1977 to 1990. The Good Life Interview (Armon, 1984b), administered on each test occasion, consists of open-ended questions in each domain (e.g., "What is good work?") combined with multiple probe questions to elicit subjects' underlying reasoning (e.g., "Why is that good?"). Subjects were also asked to describe "real-life" decisions and actions that occurred when their values were in conflict. Finally, demographic and personal life history information was collected.

CONSTRUCTION OF THE SCORING SCHEME

Content/Structure Analysis

Working from cross-sectional data in 1977, five preliminary stages of evaluative reasoning were identified (Erdynast, Armon, & Nelson, 1978). After the second wave of data collection, the hypothesis of *structural* stages of evaluative reasoning was tested. The goal of a structural analysis of this sort is the identification of consistent, logically organized patterns of reasoning that appear to be part of a self-regulated system. These patterns are thought to contain the fundamental organizing principles of thought at each stage. In this sense, structures use values to make appraisals of self, other people, objects, and experiences.

A significant problem in the identification of structural stages is the tendency to confound *content* and *structure*. For this analysis, much of the content of reasoning was coded using categories of value adopted from traditional ethics (discussed later). By classifying the value content of responses, structures of thought are more readily identified. Twelve construction cases (each with two interviews administered 4 years apart) were used for this analysis. Only four domains (good life, good work, good friend, good person) were used. The 24 sets of responses in the four domains were then analyzed independently.

By holding content constant, five general evaluative reasoning stage definitions were constructed that described the identified thought organizations, which appeared to be qualitatively distinct. These five stages were ordered hierarchically in terms of their increasing cognitive complexity (primarily inclusiveness) and increasing social perspective-taking ability.

Five stages were then identified in each of the four domains and a scoring manual was constructed, which was then used to score the remaining cases. The reliability of the evaluative reasoning scoring scheme is robust, including interrater as well as long- and short-term test–retest reliability. (See Armon, 1984b, for a complete discussion of the analytic procedures and the reliability results.)

Good Life Stages.   Good life stages represent the most general model of evaluative reasoning, of which good work is a part. The five-stage sequence begins in early childhood with an egocentric conception of the good, derived primarily from pleasure-seeking fantasy (e.g., "The good life is having my birthday party every day") and culminating in a complex conception of the good that encompasses complex criteria, including a preeminent societal dimension (e.g., "The good life is the worthy life. It is the integrated life—bringing the various facets of experience into balance with my interests and talents. It is also constructed in social context. To be good, it must move the society forward in some way").

The Values Dimension.   As stated earlier, there are two major dimensions to the analyses of evaluative reasoning—the value dimension (content) and the structural dimension. In actual reasoning, these two dimensions are integrated. Because the value dimension of reasoning about good work is as important as the structural dimension, it is described here in some detail. In order to maintain accuracy in the identification and delineation of the value dimension, categories of value were adopted from traditional moral philosophy. These categories allow for the distinction between values (e.g., moral and nonmoral values) as well as for more control over the value dimension while attempting to examine structural change over time. Table 2.1 presents the value categories from traditional ethics.

These philosophical categories allow for distinctions in meaning across different sorts of values. Because they may be unfamiliar to many readers, they are explained fully here. The first category, justice, contains moral values related to justice and fairness as well as the rights and obligations of individuals related to justice and fairness. In philosophy, these are called *deontic* values; and in a democratic society, all persons and organizations are expected to uphold these values. The second category, welfare, contains moral values related to beneficence, that is, values that relate to human concerns about the positive welfare of another. In philosophy, these are referred to as *teleological* values. Obligation in this category is more ambiguous than in that of justice since it requires a definition of positive welfare upon which individuals can agree. The third category contains values of character, referred to in philosophy as *aretaic* values. Such values concern ethical and moral traits of character that, as a culture, we define as good. Generosity and selflessness are examples. It can be argued that these virtues or traits have a very different quality than the moral values of justice, for example. Individuals cannot, in any practical sense, be obligated to act on such virtues or to have such traits because the development of these forms of moral character occurs over a lifetime. The fourth category, intrinsic nonmoral good, includes values of a nonmoral nature that are espoused to hold intrinsic values, that is, value in and of itself. Knowledge, beauty, and pleasure are examples of such values. The last category contains values of a nonmoral, extrinsic nature. These are values that are not considered good in themselves

TABLE 2.1
Value Categories from Traditional Ethics

Moral Right	Moral Good	Moral Worth (aretaic)	Nonmoral Good (intrinsic)	Nonmoral Good (extrinsic)
justice, fairness, rights, obligations, duties	care & responsiveness, welfare, consequences to others	motives, character (e.g., conscientious, generosity, self-sacrifice)	ends (e.g., autonomy, knowledge, self-realization, intelligence, nature, freedom, consciousness)	means (e.g., paintings, cars, travel, education)

but, rather, good for the consequences they bring. An obvious example of an American value in this category is money. (See Frankena, 1973, for a further discussion of these categories.)

These categories allow for the multifaceted nature of values. They provide ways to examine the moral and nonmoral qualities of values and, therefore, to discuss more clearly the prescriptive nature of certain values over others. In general, they provide information for a greater understanding of values and philosophical justification for the prioritizing of values.

RESULTS

Stages of Good Work

The five-stage definitions of good work are presented in Table 2.2. Stages 3, 4, and 5 are found in adulthood and are described here. At Stages 1 and 2, ideals of good work focus on fantasy and concrete need fulfillment. There is rarely the mention of other persons, and the rewards of good work are sensory and material. At Stage 3, however, reasoning about the meaning of good work is constructed within an abstract system of value. Relations between the self and other, and the self and object, are conceived of within that system. This system includes the self and the groups with which the individual has face-to-face relations (e.g., family, office colleagues, students, etc.). These groups are seen to have single sets of norms and values. The needs, interests, and goals of the self and others provide the necessary value elements of the system. Good work is evaluated primarily through an appraisal of the positive and negative affective experiences between persons that occur while engaged in the work. Thus, for work to be good, it must provide direct and visible impact on the immediate social environment in terms of positive feelings.

The importance of having impact on those in the immediate environment, the criterion of positive affect, and the absence of referents outside of that environment are illustrated in the following interview excerpt:

> WHAT IS GOOD WORK? Working with people is good work. Trying to help others. WHY IS THAT GOOD? Like in teaching, I feel a certain satisfaction in having the opportunity to touch a few lives. I enjoy working with children for this reason . . . I am getting back from it all the time. WHY IS IT IMPORTANT TO BE WITH OTHER PEOPLE AS PART OF GOOD WORK? Because I feel happiest when I am reacting to people.

In this example, there is consistent reference to others. These references,

TABLE 2.2
Stages of Good Work

Stage 1: Egoistic Hedonism

Good work consists of physical or sensory activities, fantasized or experienced, that are pleasurable and desired by the self. There is an absence of a conception of the instrumental value of work to provide for the self's material needs.

Stage 2: Instrumental Hedonism

The recognition of the reciprocal relation between work and its consequences of serving the self's needs is clear. There is the presence of a self, separated from the work concept, that can evaluate work activities and consequences. Work roles are conceived in terms of their stereotypical, surface features, such as concrete, visible activities and results. Doing good work is seen not only as a source of material reward but also as a source of personal gratification as it can provide both praise and personal freedom. Good work is rarely distinguished from hard work.

Stage 3: Interpersonalism

Good work is identified with work roles that provide interactive mutuality between the self and other in the immediate work environment. Good work results in the positive, affective experiences of personal enhancement. The means to these ends is through interpersonal interaction, particularly helping and being helped by others.

Stage 4: Individualism

Good work is a self-chosen activity that meets standards of personal choice, worth, and meaningfulness. Multiple criteria for good work are ordered hierarchically in terms of ascending value to the individual. Although ultimate value is individually and culturally relative, good work is of some benefit to others in addition to the self.

Stage 5: Autonomy

Good work is evaluated through and must be consistent with the individual's self-consciously constructed ethical philosophy. The values of good work are generalizable to others and focus on the greater understanding and the improvement of the self, society, and nature. Personal satisfaction of work must be balanced with social utility.

---

however, are framed within a single system of face-to-face relations. Such reasoning within a single system of direct interaction is further illustrated by another subject:

WHAT IS GOOD WORK? Helping people . . . feeling like I'm able to do things for them or help them to feel good. WHY IS THAT IMPORTANT? I think it is important to get positive feedback and to feel some progress with the people that I am working with.

Thus at Stage 3, the central component of good work is to have positive relations with the people with whom one works. Concerns about the effect of one's work on larger social systems are not salient.

At Stage 4, the evaluative system of good work is expanded to include an abstract conception of the impact of one's work on the greater society. With this conception comes the recognition that the self's good may not be consistent with the society's good. This conflict is resolved with a certain relativism concerning societal value. Personal, individualistic criteria are emphasized such that the work role and its consequences must be worthy and meaningful in terms of the self's particular interests and values. These elements can be seen in the following examples of Stage 4 responses:

> WHAT IS GOOD WORK? Any work is good work as long as it's productive of something useful . . . something you love doing . . . something you can construe as useful to society by almost any terminology you can imagine. WHAT IS MOST IMPORTANT IN GOOD WORK? You have to enjoy what you are doing, that you are good at it, and it has meaning for you.

> WHAT IS GOOD WORK? In the first place, it should be something useful. In the second place it should be something you enjoy doing. It should be of some value to yourself and the society at large or to an ideal you are committed to. Virtually anything can be of value.

The reasoning apparent in these two examples differs from Stage 3 reasoning not only in its recognition of the effect of one's work on society, but also by its focus on the self's need to pursue its particular goals, independent of the norms of the immediate social milieu.

At the fifth stage, the good for the self and the good for society become integrated, making complementary what was potentially opposed. The criteria used in the evaluation of good work go beyond the self's particular (usually relativistic) values and result from a self-consciously constructed, consistent ethical philosophy. In the following example, the subject stresses the possibility for the self and the society to advance one another's mutual interests.

> WHAT IS GOOD WORK? First, I think the work must include upward mobility . . . it must continue to be challenging and stimulating to contribute to the development of the worker. But, at the same time, the work includes a trade-off between self-satisfaction and service. I think, ultimately, good work is when you get satisfaction out of human service.

There are many explicit suggestions of a broader, more exhaustive system of value at Stage 5. This is well illustrated in the following example.

> WHAT IS GOOD WORK? I think good work allows a person to participate in something greater than the person. You have to be willing to take on the conflicts and hardships in the name of something larger than yourself. And you have to be able to see that the products are indeed useful by standards beyond your own.

Finally, in one last example, we find a most explicit system of value that contains the connections of the self to nature and culture.

WHAT IS GOOD WORK? Good work has to take place in a context; so if we're talking about the ideal work, the context would be humanity or, rather, the entire environment. Within that context, good work would be realizing your potential, which is not an egotistical activity. Since you are a part of the whole, to actualize yourself is to actualize the world—for better or worse. If each person were to realize their potential, she would be realizing a better world. The specific work activities would obviously vary. The constant would be that whatever the work was it would be consonant with the true nature of the self as it relates to the whole.

Invariant Sequence

Evaluative reasoning was hypothesized not only to represent structural stages, but also to change via an ordered developmental sequence. To meet the criteria for invariant sequence, it must be demonstrated that, beyond measurement error, no subject's stage score at T + 1 is less than their score at T (regression) and that no subject skipped a stage while developing progressively through the sequence. These criteria were partially supported with the follow-up data in 1980 (Armon, 1984b) and more strongly supported with the long-term longitudinal data (Armon, in preparation). Although significant stage change did not occur in all subjects on each test occasion, for those whose reasoning did change, it changed toward the next successive stage.

Relations With Other Variables

Good work-stage scores were found to be significantly related to other variables. Regression analyses were used to assess the relationship between variables such as age, education, and social class and subjects' good work-stage classifications. These regression analyses were conducted at each of the four assessment occasions. Because results were similar and significant at each of the assessment occasions, only representative findings are presented. For example, stages of good work were positively and significantly related to age. Figure 2.1 presents the data points and the curvilinear relationship between age and good work stage in 1985, R^2 = .19, $F(1,28)$ = 6.6, $p < .05$.

There were no significant positive relationships between stages of good work and income. Indeed, at some interview periods, the relationship was negative. In contrast, stages of good work were significantly positively related to educational attainment (e.g., from the 1985 assessment period, R^2 = .47, $F(1,28)$ = 25.16, $p < .001$). Stages of good work were also significantly correlated with Hollingshead and Redlich's (1958)

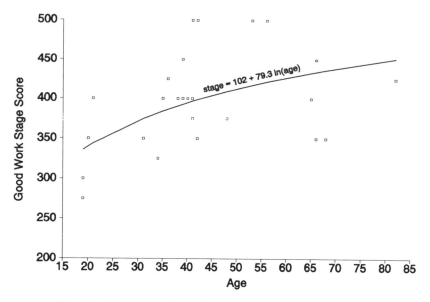

FIG. 2.1. Regression of good work stage scores and age in 1985.

Occupational Scale scores at each of the four interview periods (e.g., from 1985, R^2 = .46, $F(1,27)$ = 22.82, p < .001).

Adult Development

Although it has been shown that good work stage and age are correlated, this finding does not demonstrate actual development in adulthood nor does it demonstrate that particular stages are reserved for adulthood. These preliminary analyses address these two distinct questions. First, does development in this area occur in adulthood?

An average of 10% of the subjects developed one-quarter stage, 20% developed one-half stage, 3% developed three-quarter stage, and 10% developed a full stage or more during any one of the 4-year periods. During the entire 12-year period, 5% of the subjects developed one-quarter stage, 33% developed a one-half or three-quarter stage, and 27% developed one full stage or more. Thus, during the entire study period, well over half of the adult subjects demonstrated significant stage change.

The second question was whether there are stages of good work that should be considered exclusively as adulthood stages. One subject attained a Stage 4 score at age 19, the next youngest was 23 years, and the next 31 years. No subject attained a Stage 4/5 score prior to age 31 (then 34 and 45) and no subject attained a Stage 5 score prior to age 41. These findings indicate the existence of exclusively adult stages.

Yet, because such development does not occur with age alone, it appears that specific life events can be said to be related to structural change in adulthood when it does occur. So far, only education has been carefully examined in this way and has proved to be significant. Simply put, adults who continued in school or returned to school during the study period were more likely to show an increase in their good work reasoning stage scores than those who terminated their education or did not return to school in later life. Even this was no guarantee, however.

Gender Differences

No significant gender differences in reasoning about good work were found in this study. This is consistent with Walker's (1984) re-analysis of a large number of studies using Colby and Kohlberg's (1987) moral judgment measure that showed that, when educational attainment were controlled, gender differences previously identified were not significant. In this study, the male and female subjects were approximately equal in their educational attainment and socioeconomic status (SES). Although there were no significant gender differences overall, older women tended to score lower than younger women. The older women in this sample maintained more traditional female roles in their families and pursued less challenging professions than the younger women, which may help to explain this difference.

Good Work Stages and Actual Work Experience

Stages of good work were compared to the actual work roles of the adult subjects. Table 2.3 presents these data. As can be seen from Table 2.3, the general complexity of actual work roles, in terms of both things and people, increases with good work stage. This would be expected given the high correlation with the Hollingshead scale. Work roles in the Stage 4 and above category tend to have greater responsibility and to produce more generally distributed outcomes. Although there are exceptions, they do not in most cases contradict this trend. For example, the "handyman," one of the highest stage reasoners in the study, is severely limited in the work he can do due to health problems; he is, however, committed to complex roles in the community. In another case, a higher stage elementary teacher is the master teacher of the district. Thus, work role labels are limited and should be used only for examination of general trends.

TABLE 2.3
Good Work Stages and Actual Work Roles

Stage 3		Stage 4+	
Work Roles	*n*	*Work Roles*	*n*
Elementary/Middle School Teacher	8	Psychologist/College Professor	6
Retail/Wholesale Sales	6	High School Teacher/Adult Ed.	3
Adult Ed./Social Work	2	Medical Doctor/Dentist	2
Assistant Principal	1	Magazine Editor/Writer	2
Secretary	1	Wholesale Drug Dealer	1
Nurse's Assistant	1	School Principal	1
Actor	1	International Manager	1
Customs Officer	1	Systems Engineer	1
Electrician	1	Actor	1
Film Editor	1	Handyman	1
Hair Dresser	1		

Real-Life Events

As explained earlier, adults were asked to describe life experiences from the last 4 years in which a conflict of their moral values and also of their good life (or personal) values occurred. Because it is claimed theoretically that conflict and challenge in a domain may be a prerequisite of development in that domain, such conflicts in the work area are of special interest.

Preliminary analyses revealed that out of the 51 events reported in 1989, which included 22 different types, 20 were work-related events. These events can be placed in one of two categories. The first category contains moral events. These events involve subjects' difficulties with what they perceive to be unethical activities in the workplace. They are, at best, required to ignore and, at worst, required to perform these activities in order to maintain their positions. The second category contains issues of identity or self-realization. Here, the issues involve subjects' concerns that their work does not provide satisfaction because of its non-challenging qualities or because it provides a poor fit with their interests and talents.

These findings demonstrate the salience not only of work in adult lives, but also of morality and value in adult work. Further content analyses need to be performed to examine work experience more deeply. In particular, it would be useful to examine whether certain sorts of work experiences were consistently related to individual development in this or other domains.

DISCUSSION

This brief report has outlined some of the preliminary findings from a 12-year longitudinal study investigating how individuals reason about good work. The construct of evaluative reasoning of good work was identified and traced through a developmental sequence of five stages. Subjects' evaluative reasoning was shown to be related, in a reasonable fashion, to variables such as age, education, and SES. Over half of the subjects demonstrated development across the stages during adulthood, and some stages were found to exist exclusively in the adults in the sample. Finally, it was also shown that the stages of reasoning have possible relationships to what adults actually do in their work.

Due to the size and nature of the sample, results should be interpreted cautiously. In particular, the subjects in this study represent a somewhat elite group. Their qualifications, primarily higher educational attainment, may limit generalizability. The results indicate, however, the possibility that aspects of individual reasoning about what is of value in work is neither merely subjective nor individualistic. If these findings are replicated with larger, more representative samples (the instrument and scoring model are currently being used in a variety of other studies), this could have major implications in numerous areas. For example, it would be important to include a developmental conception of adult work values in studies of motivation. People are not only more likely to be motivated by what they value, but the variability in salience of particular values that can be predicted by developmental stage needs to be taken into account.

An important finding is the prevalence of *moral* values in the subjects' appraisals of good work. As can be seen in the stage definitions and the case material presented, moral values are particularly salient in conceptions of good work and increase in importance with development. Similarly, nonmoral *intrinsic* values increasingly replace nonmoral *extrinsic* values with development.

This places an emphasis on the notion of work values that differs significantly from traditional models. These traditional models tend to view such values as subjective vehicles by which individuals satisfy personal, hedonistic needs. The ability to distinguish between subjective, relativistic values and deontic moral values would provide the justification for the hierarchical ordering of work values that has been absent in the past.

In addition, these findings should encourage researchers to take structural development in adulthood more seriously. Additional research explicitly designed to study adult structural development needs to be conducted. If the findings in this study are replicated with different populations, there are important practical applications. For example, we would need to include structural–developmental information in the construction of adult education, training and retraining programs, career education, and psychological intervention methods. Another finding to be considered in this regard was that individuals' stages of reasoning are related to the work roles they actually acquire. Yet, the process by which this occurs is still unclear. A much more specific approach to the nature of values combined with a structural–developmental understanding could inform not only career education curricula, but also individual decision making and career goal definition in ways that current work in the area is not.

The finding that many of the subjects in this study actually changed their core ideas about the nature of good work implies that any singular notion of "career" is misguided. A developmental model of how adults value work adds an important piece to the complicated puzzle of career change. When taken together with other social and economic forces, it not only provides possible explanations for why an individual might lose interest in his or her current work and wish to "move on," but it can also help to predict the direction of that move.

Finally, adults spend more of their time and energy engaged in work than in any other wakeful activity. We are, therefore, directed to examine more closely the dimensions of that context: the environment, the roles and responsibilities, the conflicts and challenges. It is here that we may find causal relations not only with worker satisfaction, but also with adult development. It appears that development *is possible* at any time in the life span, although its probability decreases with age. It is unclear, however, to what extent developmental "plateau" is a result of the paucity of developmentally challenging experiences in adulthood, particularly in the work environment.

REFERENCES

Alexander, C., & Langer, E. J. (Eds.). (1990). *Higher stages of human development*. New York: Oxford University Press.

Armon, C. (1984a). Ideals of the good life and moral judgment: Ethical reasoning across the lifespan. In M. L. Commons, F. Richards, & C. Armon (Eds.), *Beyond formal operations: Late adolescent and adult cognitive development* (pp. 357–381). New York: Praeger.

Armon, C. (1984b). *Reasoning about the good life: Evaluative reasoning in children and adults*. Unpublished doctoral dissertation, Harvard University, Cambridge, MA.

Armon, C. (1988). The place of the good in a justice reasoning approach to moral education. *Journal of Moral Education, 17*(3), 220–229.

Armon, C. (in preparation). *A twelve-year study of reasoning about the good life*. Los Angeles: Antioch University.

Billings, R. S., & Cornelius, E. T. (1980). Dimensions of work outcomes: A multi-dimensional scaling approach. *Personnel Psychology, 33,* 151–162.

Candee, D., Graham, R., & Kohlberg, L. (1978). *Moral development and life outcomes.* Report submitted to National Institute of Education, NIE Grant #NIE-6-74-0096.

Cherrington, D. (1980). *The work ethic: Working values and values that work.* New York: AMACOM.

Colby, A., & Kohlberg, L. (1987). *The measurement of moral judgment.* Cambridge: Cambridge University Press.

Colby, A., Kohlberg, L., Gibbs, J., & Lieberman, M. (1983). Report on a 20-year longitudinal study of moral development. *Monograph of the Society for Research in Child Development, 48*(1–2), 1–124.

Commons, M. L., Richards, F., & Armon, C. (Eds.). (1984). *Beyond formal operations: Late adolescent and adult cognitive development.* New York: Praeger.

Damon, W., & Hart, D. (1988). *Self-understanding in childhood and adolescence.* New York: Cambridge University Press.

Elizur, D. (1984). Facets of work values: A structural analysis of work outcomes. *Journal of Applied Psychology, 69*(3), 379–389.

Erdynast, A., Armon, C., & Nelson, J. (1978). Cognitive developmental conceptions of the true, the good, and the beautiful. *The eighth annual proceedings of Piaget and the helping professions.* Los Angeles: University of Southern California Press.

Fowler, J. (1981). *Stages of faith: The psychology of human development and the quest for meaning.* New York: Harper & Row.

Frankena, W. (1973). *Ethics.* Englewood Cliffs, NJ: Prentice-Hall.

Greenhaus, J. (1988). *Career management.* Hinsdale, IL: The Dryden Press.

Hollingshead, A. B., & Redlich, F. C. (1958). *Social class and mental illness: A community study.* New York: Wiley.

Kohlberg, L. (1969). Stage and sequence: The cognitive–developmental approach to socialization. In D. Goslin (Ed.) *Handbook of socialization theory and research* (pp. 347–480). Chicago: Rand McNally.

Kohlberg, L. (1981). *The philosophy of moral development.* New York: Harper & Row.

Kohlberg, L. (1984). *The psychology of moral development.* New York: Harper & Row.

Loevinger, J. (1976). *Ego development: Conceptions and theories.* San Francisco: Jossey-Bass.

Ornstein, S., & Isabella, L. (1990). Age vs. stage models of career attitudes of women: A partial replication and extension. *Journal of Vocational Behavior, 36,* 1–9.

Piaget, J. (1965). *Biology and knowledge.* Chicago: University of Chicago Press. (Original work published 1932)

Piaget, J. (1972). Intellectual evolution from adolescence to adulthood. *Human Development, 15,* 1–12.

Ravlin, E., & Meglino, B. (1987). Effect of values on perception and decision making: A study of alternative work values measures. *Journal of Applied Psychology, 72*(4), 666–673.

Selman, R. (1981). *The growth of interpersonal understanding.* New York: Academic Press.

Stevens-Long, J., & Commons, M. L. (1991). *Adult life: Developmental processes.* Mountain View, CA: Mayfield Publishing.

Walker, L. J. (1984). Sex differences in the development of moral reasoning: A critical review. *Child Development, 55*(3), 677–691.

Walker, L. J. (1986). Experiential and cognitive sources of moral development in adulthood. *Human Development, 28,* 113–124.

CHAPTER THREE

Significance of Job Complexity in Workers' Moral Development

Dorothy Rulon
Harvard University

If surveyed, most workers would advocate for honesty, justice, and morality in their workplace environments. Reports from recent journalistic studies of the workplace, however, have suggested that employees do not generally feel as though they are treated with honesty and justice (Levering, 1988). Specifically, employees, when interviewed, describe situations of power and manipulation; a "we–they" relationship where management takes advantage of the workers: "How do we (the managers) get them (the employees) to do something we want them to do" (p. x).

Employees learn how to work through bureaucratic and political systems employing power and manipulation. For example, Kanter (1977) suggested that employees use both the traditional organizational structure and a concealed political road map to negotiate workplace politics: "Sometimes, people could only do their work effectively and exercise whatever competence gave them personal satisfaction if they knew how to make their way through the more cumbersome and plodding official structure via the shadow political structure underneath" (p. 94). Levering suggested that, if the levels of power, politics, and honesty in the work environment allow the employee to act, a worker may be able to resolve these dilemmas. It is argued here that situations of power, politics, and honesty in the workplace are often translated into personal moral conflicts.

Recent research on workplace organizations using Kohlberg's (1976) theory of moral development has suggested that a complex relationship between moral reasoning, moral atmosphere, and moral action may exist in many different settings (Candee, 1985; Higgins, 1982, 1983, 1988; Higgins & Gordon, 1985; Howard, 1984; Kohlberg, 1984, 1985; Mackin, 1984; Power, 1984; Power, Higgins, & Kohlberg, 1990). The interrelation between the moral atmosphere, the individual's moral reasoning, and the sociomoral complexity of a job may influence a worker's ability to resolve conflicts between competing agendas.

To date, research on adult development has suggested that growth in moral reasoning can be stimulated by moral education (Arbuthnot, 1984; Candee, 1985; Higgins & Gordon, 1985; Kuhmerker, Mentkowski, & Erickson, 1980; McPhail, 1985; Oja & Sprinthall, 1978). Two major intervention strategies have been found to be effective: dilemma discussion alone or dilemma discussion in combination with a democratic atmosphere.

The bulk of the research in adult development interventions has been conducted either in academic settings (Candee, 1985; Oja & Sprinthall, 1978) or prison classrooms (Arbuthnot, 1984; McPhail, 1985). Reports from recent research on the atmosphere of groups has had a focus on collective norms and values and has suggested that differences in normative perceptions are related to actual differences in behavior (Higgins & Gordon, 1985).

The semi-laboratory setting of an academic environment has a different atmosphere and allows for the development of a different set of behavioral norms than the workplace. In an academic or semi-laboratory setting, the collective norms support open communication and the subjects' "student-like" behavior. The enhanced moral reasoning that may be developed in such a setting may be more difficult to engender in an employment setting. In the workplace, individuals function in a bureaucratic atmosphere that often generates norms of mistrust and censure. The current study took place in work settings and used on-site, real-life dilemmas as the focus for the intervention.

SOCIOMORAL COMPLEXITY ANALYSIS OF PROFESSIONS

Research in moral education has attempted a qualitative analysis of the extent to which a job allows, encourages, or necessitates taking the perspectives of others and participating in decision making and responsibility for the decisions and consequences that affect others (Higgins, 1982, 1983, 1988; Howard, 1984). This sociomoral complexity analysis of professions and organizations has suggested that work has a structure of differential moral complexity that places pressures on the worker, ranging in characteristics from somewhat simple to more complex. Lower levels of complexity allow the person doing the work to consider him or herself in relation to another or to a small group of others. Higher levels of work complexity demand that the worker take both the perspectives of the system as a whole and the individuals within the system. These higher levels pose dilemmas concerning the demands of the system that are often in conflict with the rights of the individual.

In this chapter, I discuss workers' moral conflicts, how workers are enabled to resolve them through participation in a moral education intervention, and the interrelation between workers' moral reasoning and their work settings. Specifically, the study examines the effect of an intervention on the moral reasoning (Kohlberg, 1984) of two different sets of workers, and the effect that the nature of their jobs, in terms of sociomoral complexity, has on their moral reasoning. Specifically, the study used a pretest/moral education treatment/posttest design.

METHOD

Subjects

This study was conducted with five study groups in two schools and one health-care facility. One group of health-care workers (n = 10), two groups of teachers (n = 5 in each group), and two comparison groups of teachers (n = 3 in each group) participated in the research project. There was no comparison group of health-care workers. The study of the teachers took place in two large urban high schools over the duration of 2 years. In the schools, the treatment groups consisted of teachers in a moral education program. The comparison groups consisted of teachers involved in regular high school teaching programs. Research on the health-care professionals took place in a long-term care facility over 1½ years. This group, which was comprised of department heads, attended business operations meetings every other week; on the alternate weeks, they participated in a quasi-democratic dilemma discussion intervention.

Measures

All subjects were administered Kohlberg's moral judgment interview (Colby & Kohlberg, 1987), a real-life dilemma questionnaire (Ries, 1981), and the sociomoral complexity of jobs questionnaire (Higgins, 1983, 1988), pretest and posttest. On the pretest real-life questionnaire, participants were asked to describe their workplace dilemmas and underlying reasoning for how they envisioned resolution of the conflicts. Additionally, they were asked, should the situation reoccur, whether the resolution would change.

General Settings

Of the two general types of sites employed, one type consisted of two urban high schools; the other type was a health-care facility. Because the moral education program differed in these two types of sites, each is described in some detail here, first in the general case and then in the specific.

In each school, the intervention was an integral part of a "Just Community" program comprised of 100 students and 5 teachers. The teacher intervention reported in this chapter consisted of real-life dilemmas concerning curriculum issues and staff decision making for program operations. At the onset of the program, teachers' behavior was parallel to that of the traditional school, responding to a hierarchical structure with top–down communication. Through the dilemma discussions, norms of open communication, trust, and care emerged.

In the health-care site, the intervention began with hypothetical dilemmas and changed to real-life dilemmas associated with the facility. The participants initiated their discussions with the issue of whether a method of open communication and "equal-say" could be used in the hypothetical dilemma discussion. After the norm of equity in the discussion process was developed, the discussions moved to real-life issues of health-care policy.

Schools

Governance.   Generally speaking, traditional teacher-training programs aim to enhance teachers' level of subject content. Conventional teacher education is generally perceived of as the transmission of knowledge: The majority of this training consists of taking notes, memorizing, writing papers, and taking exams. An initial separation is created between teachers and students through the lack of teacher education in interpersonal relationships and then enhanced in the school through traditional classroom management techniques. Traditional classrooms are managed through the model of teacher as authority reinforced by a dean of safety and/or a security force. Teachers in a traditional high school work in a hierarchical system that promotes top–down communication with little or no collaboration in decision making. A principal makes decisions about the operations of the school and provides directions to the teaching staff.

In contrast, the Just Community intervention model (Power, 1984; Power et al., 1990) establishes interpersonal relationships based on fairness and justice between teachers and students. Community teachers, rather than teaching in a traditional program, teach in a democratic program. In Just Community classes and meetings, teachers and students come to agreements concerning their self-governance, which includes a system for those who break the rules. These rules, rather than enforced by teacher authority or the dean of safety, are handled by the student/teacher discipline committee. Armed with one vote each, the teachers arc an integral part of the discussions concerning the violation and enforcement of rules. In addition to their responsibility in Just Community classes, the teachers have an additional role, that of English and social studies instructor. The teachers, as a team, make collaborative decisions about the operations of the program and curricular practices. These faculty members have the responsibility to teach subject classes, attend, become involved with, and advocate for issues of fairness and justice in the Just Community classes and meetings, and to participate in twice-weekly staff meetings.

Curriculum. Development of interdisciplinary English and social studies curricula and lesson plans take place in one of these two meetings. Dilemmas relating to the curriculum "Man's Inhumanity to Man" are prepared for presentation to and exploration by the subject classes. The entire teacher team collectively makes decisions in these staff meetings and all share in the implementation of the daily tasks.

Norms. A new curriculum had to be written for the coming academic year. All teachers were not equally skilled in curriculum development. Through discussion, the teacher team agreed to have everyone share in the work. Curriculum experts would work on building the scope and sequence of the curriculum; others would share in the workload by ordering books and materials and by taking care of all daily operational tasks of the program. Sharing the responsibilities symbolized trusting the other team members to accomplish the tasks. Not shirking the agreed to commitments represented caring for the other team members. The norm of caring for and trusting each other evolved through the curriculum writing. Contrary to program design and curriculum development practices in the rest of the school (where curriculum is written by the assistant principal and given to the teachers), the teacher team collaborated in decision making and responsibility for all aspects of program design and operation.

Issues of self-governance were discussed in the second of the two weekly staff meetings. Lack of teacher agreement emerged in many discussions.
The issues that sparked conflict ranged from curriculum planning and
implementation to community rules, infractions, and discipline procedures.

Intervention.   Twice-weekly staff meetings that included real-life
dilemma discussions presented moral conflicts for staff consideration.
These meetings provided the teachers the opportunity to role-take others'
positions and allowed broader perspectives than might be available in
traditional school meetings. One major difference among the teachers
arose concerning a student/teacher discipline committee decision to enforce a community norm with a rigorous penalty. One teacher expressed
her sense that a harsh discipline was appropriate. A second felt that a
harsh punishment did not take into consideration the extenuating circumstances involved in the incident. A third felt that a stiff penalty would
serve as a deterrent for other students in the community. Another felt
that deterrence was less educationally beneficial to the students' learning than understanding that the community's trust had been broken and
should be restored. This example was typical of the type of moral discussion occurring weekly in the teachers' staff meetings. This democratic atmosphere and decision-making process supported the growth of
norms of care, trust, fairness, role-taking, and participation in curriculum writing and policymaking for the program.

Health-Care Facility

Governance.   In the health-care facility, the moral education program consists of the discussion of real-life moral dilemmas and the formation of an "equal-say," quasi-democratic community among the group.
The intervention takes place every other week during regularly sched-
uled business meetings. The meetings on alternate weeks follow an agenda
of department head administrative business. Dilemmas for the intervention are drawn from hypothetical and real-life conflicts of fairness
described by the subjects on their pretest interviews. These dilemmas are
disguised and brought back to the table for discussion.

The intervention model establishes interpersonal relationships among
the department heads based on equity and fairness. At the first meeting,
the intervention strategy—the creation of "equal-say" discussion—is
described to the participants. Specifically, "equal-say" is defined as the
creation of an atmosphere in which each group member is able to have

a say with equal weight. This kind of discussion is described as being part of the process to encourage each person to speak openly.

At first, participants argued that dispensing with the official status of the discussion hour was a violation of the typical medical hierarchical model as well as a violation of the way in which the health-care facility was run. Several professionals did not see the point of having an equal say. One objected: "There's no way to eliminate the hierarchy here nor should there be. The hierarchy is an integral part of the way this place is run." Advocacy for all to speak openly was reaffirmed. It was stated that if the hierarchy was enforced, some people would not speak out. The result of people speaking from positions of power, seniority, or education would be others' sense of intimidation and reticence. The message was: All should be heard, not just those in hierarchical positions.

Norms. Because of the barriers to "equal-say," early discussion was not open and democratic. Over time, each participant espoused that he or she wanted to be fair to others in the group. Those in positions of power spoke less and advocated for more participation from the reticent. Through advocacy for "equal-say," a norm against speaking from a position of power or seniority began to develop. The department head group began the regular use of the quasi-democratic model for discussion of business agenda items. "Equal-say" became a norm with increasing strength. Unaccustomed to thinking about concerns of fairness in business meetings, the group initially addressed procedural issues.

For example, during a discussion concerning the development of performance standards and personnel evaluations, several department heads suggested that it would not be fair to design a long evaluation form. They stated that the department heads, pressed for time, either would not perform an evaluation with care or would manipulate the use of the form. Other department heads claimed that the form should not be too short or it would "short change" the employees. Departing from these procedural issues, discussion moved to concerns of fairness and role-taking, questions concerning the rights of employees. Should the evaluation be a two-way system: department head of employee and employee of department head? Should a discussion be held with the employee? Should space be provided for employee signature and/or comment? Through this discussion, norms of role-taking and fairness began to develop.

Intervention. Early in the intervention, in a conversation outside the dilemma discussion meeting, one participant expressed to another that the tape recorder, used for the transcription of meetings, was inhibiting her from speaking freely. The following week, the problem of the tape recorder was brought to the table for discussion. Advocacy was made for all to have the freedom to speak out. Defense of the tape recorder was made in the name of research and analysis of the intervention. Discussion included the importance of each group member's ability to speak out and have an equal say in the discussions. A proposal was made to keep the recorder running. In the ensuing vote, a veto would indicate that someone felt he or she could not speak openly. A unanimous vote affirmed the status of the recorder in the meetings. A norm of trust and open communication began to grow. In this emerging atmosphere of trust, a discussion of moral conflicts related to patients' rights, patient abuse, doctor–patient relationships, and nursing staff rights began to emerge.

After $3\frac{1}{2}$ months of the intervention, a dilemma of euthanasia was carried over from the treatment meeting to the business operations meeting held the following week. This was the first time a dilemma sparked a topic for the operations meeting. Department heads brought books, magazines, and newspaper clippings on euthanasia. The quasi-democratic style of discussion used in the intervention meetings was incorporated into the business agenda to allow all participants to discuss the facility policy regarding patient death. Although the next operations meeting was conducted in the "old" traditional top–down style, the department heads participated more freely.

One month later in the business meeting, the department heads decided to incorporate a democratic method for creating a facility-wide smoking rule. This agenda item was discussed in a quasi-democratic discussion style. Department heads surveyed all members of the health-care facility and created a ballot for all to vote on concerning where smoking locations would be permitted. Through the success of this discussion of the smoking policy, the department heads started to discuss other facility-wide rules such as coffee break and clean-up responsibility. The norm of "equal-say" and "quasi-democracy" expanded into the heretofore bureaucratic department head meetings. This quasi-democratic work climate and "equal-say" decision making supported the growth of norms of fairness, trust, empathy, role-taking, and participation in policymaking for the organization as a whole.

Scoring of Sociomoral Complexity

Higgins defined five categories of sociomoral complexity levels coinciding with Kohlberg's stages of moral development. The levels of sociomoral complexity are qualitative descriptions of the moral pressures of the work environment (Higgins, 1982, 1983, 1988; Howard, 1984) that describe jobs in terms of their sociomoral complexity. The sociomoral complexity questionnaire is based on open-ended, semi-structured questions. Subjects are asked to describe moral conflicts or dilemmas on the job and others' viewpoints or perspectives that must be considered. Five criteria are used to assess sociomoral complexity. Each is described in turn here.

Role-Taking. The aspect of role-taking helps distinguish between the complexity of occupations and work settings. The ability to take the perspective of another person, group, or society is one of the factors underlying moral reasoning (Kohlberg, 1976, 1984). Role-taking on the job can differ in quantity and quality. Quantitatively, the level of role-taking weighs how many perspectives (e.g., individuals, groups, organizational system) the individual must consider in carrying out the demands of his or her job. The more perspectives an individual must consider, the more complex both the job and the workplace. The qualitative measure describes the differences in the nature of role-taking: One type considers role-taking for those in positions of power within the organization differentiated from their role-taking for clients. For example, a teacher's job may demand a different quality of role-taking for the principal than for the students.

The job can require or encourage the individual to engage in a range of role-taking from strategic/instrumental to empathic. Using strategic role-taking, the worker considers the viewpoints of others only for the extrinsic benefit of the self and does not treat others with respect or as ends in themselves. A higher level of role-taking is empathic, that is, treating others with respect and as ends in themselves through the consideration of others' rights and welfare. Both jobs and workplace organizations differ in the level of role-taking encouraged or required.

Moral Conflicts. This category differentiates the levels of complexity by the type of moral conflicts that arise in the workplace. Some moral conflicts are of greater complexity than others. In health care, the job of a physician who has to consider whether to resuscitate a terminally ill patient represents a more complex moral conflict than the job of a nurse's aide who has to consider how to handle a patient refusing to accept personal care.

Responsibility. This element ranks the complexity of the job and workplace by the degree to which the job role carries responsibility for a fair or morally responsible outcome. At a high level of moral complexity, the jobs of school principal or health-care administrator have responsibilities for moral outcomes that the less complex job of dietary aide at the same institution typically does not have.

Participation. Participation in decisions and policies that affect work is an important feature of the moral environment of the workplace. The moral climate is enhanced when the level of group participation in policymaking is high. Participation on the job can differ in both quantity and quality. Quantitatively, the degree of participation assesses in how many levels the job may allow the individual to participate when carrying out the demands of his or her job. The more positions or levels of the organization in which an individual can participate, the more complex the job and workplace. The second factor in participation is the qualitative factor: When the structure of a job allows full participation, individuals have opportunities to consider the perspectives of others and to assume a greater responsibility for the outcome and consequences of the policies.

Moral Function. Moral function is a description of the levels of congruence between the ethical values of the worker and the objective values of the job duties. In a job with a low level of moral functioning, the worker is expected to carry out job duties even when they conflict with his or her ethical values. An example of a low level of moral function would be a pacifist computer programmer working in a guided-missile engineering laboratory. An example of a high level of moral function is a "pro-choice" social worker working in a planned parenthood clinic.

RESULTS AND DISCUSSION

Findings from this study consist of both quantitative and qualitative analyses. The first section reports the examination of moral judgment scores pretest to posttest. The second section presents a clinical analysis of dilemmas in the moral judgment interview. The final section concerns the relationship of sociomoral complexity of the job and individual moral growth.

Teachers

A quantitative analysis of teachers' moral judgment pretest to posttest indicated that the treatment group changed, whereas the comparison group did not, $t(14) = 3.58, p < .05$. A qualitative analysis of the data showed that 7 of the 10 participating teachers developed over one-third stage.

In the treatment group, 20% exhibited Stage 2 reasoning and none exhibited Stage 5 reasoning on the pretest. On the posttest, there was a complete drop of all Stage 2 reasoning and the addition of a Stage 5 orientation. The comparison group showed similar levels to the treatment group on the pretest, but no significant change pretest to posttest.

Health-Care Providers

For the health-care sample, a quantitative analysis of moral judgment scores pretest to posttest indicated no statistically significant change, although there was a trend in the direction of higher reasoning. A further examination of the health-care group revealed two subgroups: "administrator" and "caregiver." Administrators were those who solely administered the operations of the facility. Caregivers were those who provided both administrative and direct health-care functions. These subgroups were explored separately for further analyses.

Specifically, analysis of the administrator subgroup pretest–posttest scores showed no significant change. In contrast, mean moral judgment change for the caregiver subgroup did reach statistical significance, $t(5)$ = 4.11, $p < .01$. A qualitative analysis of the data showed that 8% of this group were reasoning at Stage 2 and no members of the group showed Stage 5 reasoning on the pretest. Parallel to the results for the teachers, there was a complete drop of all Stage 2 reasoning and an addition of a Stage 5 orientation on the posttest.

**Sociomoral Complexity of the Teachers'
and Health-Care Workers' Jobs**

Examination of the data from the sociomoral complexity questionnaires has suggested that the jobs of health-care administrator and school principal require high levels of role-taking, participation, and responsibility. These positions solicit the maximum level of concern about moral conflict and resolution. These occupations hold high levels of sociomoral complexity (Level 5).

Examination of the pretest to posttest sociomoral questionnaires of the health-care department heads has indicated that the responsibilities of this job fall into a Level 4 job complexity. Specifically, they described being responsible for issues regarding equity in patient care, but not for the consequences of decisions of fairness in the larger organization. In the quasi-democratic dilemma discussions, these workers participated in increased levels of role-taking, decision making, policy determination, and higher levels of responsibility for fair outcomes and value of the group as a group.

Assessment of the sociomoral complexity of teachers' and health-care workers' jobs indicated that these positions, on one hand, showed limited participation in decision making in the traditionally bureaucratic organizational structure and, on the other hand, high levels of participation in the moral education programs. When the teachers and the health-care professionals described their parent institutions, they characterized the role-taking as strategic. They stated that strategic role-taking was both necessary and legitimate for achieving a good evaluation. Teachers and health-care workers alike described the difference between a low level of responsibility for fair outcomes in the larger organization and a higher level of responsibility for the outcomes of the real-life, on-line issues that arose in their moral education forums.

Examination of the sociomoral complexity questionnaires of the comparison group of teachers (who held conventional teachers' jobs) revealed that these traditional teaching responsibilities fall into a Level 3 complexity. In contrast, high levels of complexity are described by all Just Community program teachers. They reported high levels of role-taking, participation in decision making and policy determination, high levels of responsibility for fair outcomes, and a sense of community valuing.

Changes in Reasoning Following Intervention

At the time of the pretest, all of the teachers and health caregivers were reasoning from a lower moral judgment stage than the level of sociomoral complexity of their positions. Seven of the teachers in the treatment group and all six caregivers advanced in moral reasoning so that their reasoning became more similar to the sociomoral complexity of the job.

Employees described being confronted by dilemmas of power, politics, and honesty. When asked to describe a dilemma with which they were confronted, employees reported being faced with such questions as:

> When told to take an action by a superior, should I act if I feel it is wrong?
>
> What can I do about my co-worker's mediocre performance?
>
> Should I do anything about the problem since everyone thinks it's administration's job to catch someone?

On the pretest, workers most often attributed the resolution of their dilemmas to be the responsibility of the organization or another person, often a supervisor or administrator. Through participation in a moral education intervention, these workers were able to understand, take responsibility for, and resolve work dilemmas that they had labelled unresolvable before. Two examples of this are provided.

One teacher, when asked to describe a moral dilemma at school expressed concern about reporting those teachers who were not meeting the competency demands of the teaching role. He stated:

> Even though I know the others don't do a very good job of teaching, I can't do very much about it. I don't have the jurisdiction to do anything about it and even if I did have the jurisdiction, I would not be very effective as others in the school would know that I don't have the authority.

This teacher reasoned at Stage 4 and perceived his responsibility for effective teaching as part of the system of the bureaucracy of the school. He thought that he had no "jurisdiction" nor "authority" to report a fellow teacher. On his posttest, this teacher defined the same moral issues but from his new Stage 4/5 orientation. He stated:

> It was resolved by my addressing the teacher about how I thought several things were not fair to me and to the students, and he listened to me and we discussed the matter and after a rough couple of weeks, it was better and we felt better.

He was speaking from a new position of autonomy, resolving the situation by going to and confronting the teacher. He described making this decision without his original Stage 4 concern for jurisdiction and authority.

One health-care worker, reasoning from Stage 3 on the pretest, described the problem of the faculty's denying admission to Medicaid patients. When asked how she resolved her dilemma, she stated: "I don't resolve that. It's up to the social worker and the hospital to resolve the thing, find a place for that person." She had no idea how to resolve her expressed moral conflict concerning the lack of distributive justice of medical care and attributed the responsibility to others, the social worker, and the hospital.

On the posttest, she defined the same moral issue but from the orientation of her new Stage 3/4 moral reasoning. Rather than perceive that she had no way to resolve the issue, she described a way that a different procedure for admission could be designed. She stated:

> If a patient is a [Department of Welfare] Level 3 and needs some kind of care, it seems to me that there should be a facility for people like that. He needs some place to go, and if he doesn't have the money, Medicaid might pay for him but there isn't a place to send him. It seems to me that perhaps the thing that's unfair is that we're not allowed to take the Level 3s that need the care. I think that Medicaid should take all postoperative patients and indeed, I have found the Welfare team, in particular, has been very generous.

In summary, findings from posttest measures have suggested that a significant number of these teachers and health-care workers were professionals reasoning at a higher moral stage. They appeared to be able to understand, take responsibility for, and resolve their pretest real-work dilemmas. A majority (75%) took action to implement the resolutions.

CONCLUSIONS

The results of this study have suggested that workers' moral maturity can be stimulated through participation in a moral education intervention while they are engaged in on-site work activities. The data also revealed that the democratic teachers' and direct caregivers' jobs were at a higher level of sociomoral complexity than their moral reasoning. The intervention seemed to stimulate their moral maturity to create a match between their moral stage and the sociomoral complexity of their jobs. In order to demonstrate this relationship conclusively, future studies utilizing workplace dilemma discussions with groups working in low complexity jobs would be required.

Finally, these studies have presented the notion that the sociomoral complexity of an individual's job, in addition to its role in the growth of the worker's moral maturity, may have an important function in the relationship between the employee's moral judgment and his or her judgment of responsibility, a precursor to action in the workplace. Specifically, if an individual's level of job complexity is at a higher level than his or her original stage of moral judgment, and he or she participates in a moral education intervention that enhances moral growth, in an attempt to match the job complexity, the employee may make judgments of responsibility and take moral action. This notion has suggested that the interrelation between job complexity and moral maturity may be a mediator between moral judgment and moral action in the workplace.

REFERENCES

Arbuthnot, J. (1984). Moral reasoning development programs in prison: Cognitive-developmental and critical reasoning approaches. *Journal of Moral Education, 13*(2), 112–123.

Candee, D. (1985). Classical ethics and live patient simulations in the moral education of health care professionals. In M. Berkowitz & F. Oser (Eds.), *Moral education: Theory and application* (pp. 297–318). Hillsdale, NJ: Lawrence Erlbaum Associates.

Colby, A., & Kohlberg, L. (1987). *Measurement of moral judgment: Manual and results.* Cambridge, England: Cambridge University Press.

Higgins, A. (1982). *Levels of socio-moral complexity.* Paper presented at the meeting of the Murray Research Center, Radcliffe College, Cambridge, MA.

Higgins, A. (1983). *Adult development*. Paper presented at the meeting of the Society for Moral Education, Boston, MA.

Higgins, A. (1988). *Influence of work on moral development: The socio-moral complexity of a teacher's job*. Paper presented at the International Conference on Politics, Education, and Moral Education, Krakow, Poland.

Higgins, A., & Gordon, F. (1985). Work climate and socio-moral development in two worker-owned companies. In M. Berkowitz & F. Oser (Eds.), *Moral education: Theory and application* (pp. 241–268). Hillsdale, NJ: Lawrence Erlbaum Associates.

Howard, R. (1984). *Adult development in educators: Moral stage and the socio-moral complexity of schools*. Unpublished qualifying paper, Harvard University, Cambridge, MA.

Kanter, R. M. (1977). *Men and women of the corporation*. New York: Basic Books.

Kohlberg, L. (1976). Moral stages and moralization: The cognitive developmental approach. In T. Licona (Ed.), *Moral development and behavior: Theory, research and social issues* (pp. 31–53). New York: Holt, Rinehart & Winston.

Kohlberg, L. (1984). *The psychology of moral development: The nature and validity of moral stages*. San Francisco: Harper & Row.

Kohlberg, L. (1985). The just community approach to moral education in theory and practice. In M. Berkowitz & F. Oser (Eds.), *Moral education, theory and application* (pp. 27–88). Hillsdale, NJ: Lawrence Erlbaum Associates.

Kuhmerker, L., Mentkowski, M., & Erickson, V. L. (Eds.). (1980). *Evaluating moral development*. Schenectady, NY: Character Research Press.

Levering, R. (1988). *A great place to work*. New York: Random House.

Mackin, C. (1984). *The social psychology of ownership: A study of a democratically-owned business*. Unpublished doctoral dissertation, Harvard University, Cambridge, MA.

McPhail, D. (1985). *The effects of socio-moral discussion and role-play on ego development and moral judgement of adult offenders*. Unpublished doctoral dissertation, Boston University, Boston, MA.

Oja, S., & Sprinthall, N. (1978). Psychological and moral development for teachers: Can you teach old dogs? In N. Sprinthall & R. Mosher (Eds.), *Value development as the aim of education* (pp. 117–134). Schenectady, NY: Character Research Press.

Power, C. (1984). *The moral atmosphere of a just community high school: A four year longitudinal study*. Unpublished doctoral dissertation, Harvard University, Cambridge, MA.

Power, C., Higgins, A., & Kohlberg, L. (1990). *Lawrence Kohlberg's approach to moral education*. New York: Columbia University Press.

Ries, S. (1981). *An empirical study of an educational intervention curriculum*. Unpublished doctoral dissertation, Harvard University, Cambridge, MA.

CHAPTER FOUR

Developmental Levels of Entering Medical and Pharmacy Students: Considerations for Admissions Selection Policies and Curriculum Change

Doreen Cleave-Hogg
Linda Muzzin
University of Toronto

Professional schools are established to provide an education leading to particular career paths; mission statements, goals, objectives, and outcomes are designed to meet professional expectations and criteria. Professional school applicants are therefore, in the first instance, self-selecting in that they choose a profession that meets their interests, ambitions, abilities, and so on. However, most professional schools limit (either by choice or fiat) the number of students accepted into a program and must develop criteria to guide selection processes.

Three of the main reasons for generating a selection process are: (a) the need for a reduction in numbers because professional programs are invariably oversubscribed, (b) the need for a method to exclude candidates who are unsuitable, and (c) the need for a method to select candidates with the most desirable qualities (McManus, Powis, & Cleave-Hogg, 1992).

Admissions committees invariably struggle with issues of selection criteria for particular programs. Previous academic achievement is often viewed as the best, sometimes only, indicator of success (however success is defined); selection is made on the basis of applicants with the highest scores whether grades, grade point averages (GPAs), and/or college entrance tests. Yet this notion is questioned as a predictor of professional success (McManus et al., 1992). Further, research carried out by Gough (1978) demonstrated that success in examinations is a predictor only for success in similar examinations. Another issue for deliberation is the length of schooling required before a candidate is considered "ready" for admittance into a professional program. Should minimal educational status be the completion of high school, a number of years in a university program, or after completion of an undergraduate degree?

These issues become more immediate for admissions committees during periods of curriculum development or impending major changes within the system. Questions then center on whether applicants should be selected because they appear to have certain characteristics thought to be necessary to learn effectively within the proposed curriculum. Conversely, do all, or some, of the current students demonstrate these identified characteristics in spite of the lack of attention to these characteristics during the selection process? These questions have led to the present research.

As various committees deliberated on the need to provide curricula based on principles of active, problem-based learning intended to achieve higher level thinking and to deal with professional complexity, the problem of selecting students suitable for the new curricula became more evident. Using extant theories of student epistemological development, we attempted to ascertain the developmental levels of students entering the professional (undergraduate) programs of the Faculty of Medicine and the Faculty of Pharmacy at the University of Toronto. The information gathered is intended to reveal whether current differences in admissions criteria result in disparate profiles of the entering groups. Implications for admissions selection and curriculum design are discussed.

CONTEXT

At the University of Toronto, the Faculty of Medicine and the Faculty of Pharmacy are undergoing major curriculum changes. Concerns have been expressed that students in these programs lack certain cognitive abilities such as critical thinking, problem solving, ethical rationalization, and skills to deal with complex thinking and learning. These concerns reflect those outlined by the Association of American Medical Colleges (1984), Ebert and Ginzberg (1988), The Edinburgh Declaration (1988), the Association of American Colleges of Pharmacy (1991), Strand, Morley, and Cipolle (1987), and parallel general trends in higher education.

Planners developing the new curricula have addressed the need to improve student learning in professional schools. Proposals include such notions as active rather than passive learning, developing complex thinking skills, dealing with uncertainty, expecting students to take more responsibility for their own learning, self-directed endeavours, and lifelong learning. Currently, problem-based learning is viewed as the method central to proposed innovations.

The question of admitting suitable candidates for these programs is one that admissions committees are forced to consider. Should applicants be required to demonstrate the ability to cope with, and benefit from, the new curriculum? Would an undergraduate experience before entrance into these professional programs prepare students to deal more effectively with complex learning tasks and enable them to handle the challenges? It became evident that arguments raised at local levels were presented without any empirical evidence; the polemics were based on "what everyone knows" or "how everyone feels." This generated a need for data to provide a foundation for credible decision making in the admissions procedures.

THE PERRY SCHEME

Integral to this study is the conceptual framework of student intellectual and ethical development devised by Perry (1970). Briefly, Perry postulated that students' conceptions of the nature and origins of knowledge evolve over time and their understanding of themselves as knowers and learners also changes. His studies reveal that students' epistemological development moves from a dualistic position in which a person construes his or her world in unqualified terms of absolute right–wrong, good–bad, through various stages (or positions) during which diversity and uncertainty are gradually realized and accepted. Finally, a relativistic position is reached in which a person assumes responsibility for his or her own learning and makes Commitments (with a capital C, according to Perry) to personal knowing. It is argued that personal knowledge is constructed, not given; contextual, not absolute; and mutable, not fixed.

The principles of the Perry Scheme are that students encounter their educational experiences from a wide variety of conceptual structures. An educator's discourse is received into the frame of reference and conceptual schema of an individual student who then responds to the experience in his or her unique style. Generally, students attempt to assimilate information within their existing schema; when this is impossible, the information is either rejected or a new level or conceptual schema is developed.

Perry delineated nine developmental positions that describe the sequential pattern thought to take place. In addition, three positions of deflection are depicted; these are temporizing, escaping, or retreating from the challenges of life and learning.

The nine positions are described as follows:

Position 1: The student sees the world in polar terms of we-right-good vs. other-wrong-bad. Right Answers for everything exist in the Absolute, known to Authority whose role is to mediate (teach) them. Knowledge and goodness are perceived as quantitative accretions of discrete rightnesses to be collected by hard work and obedience (paradigm: a spelling test).

Position 2: The student perceives diversity of opinion, and uncertainty, and accounts for them as unwarranted confusion in poorly qualified Authorities or as mere exercises set by Authority "so we can learn to find The Answer for ourselves."

Position 3: The student accepts diversity and uncertainty as legitimate but still *temporary* in areas where Authority "hasn't found The Answer yet." He supposes Authority grades him in these areas on "good expression" but remains puzzled as to standards.

Position 4: (a) The student perceives legitimate uncertainty (and therefore diversity of opinion) to be extensive and raises it to the status of an unstructured epistemological realm of its own in which "anyone has a right to his own opinion," a realm which he sets over against Authority's realm where right–wrong still prevails, or (b) the student discovers qualitative contextual relativistic reasoning as a special case of "what They want" within Authority's realm.

Position 5: The student perceives all knowledge and values (including authority's) as contextual and relativistic and subordinates dualistic right–wrong functions to the status of a special case, in context.

Position 6: The student apprehends the necessity of orienting himself in a relativistic world through some form of personal Commitment (as distinct from unquestioned or unconsidered commitment to simple belief in certainty).

Position 7: The student makes an initial Commitment in some area.

Position 8: The student experiences the implications of Commitment, and explores the subjective and stylistic issues of responsibility.

Position 9: The student experiences the affirmation of identity among multiple responsibilities and realizes Commitment as an ongoing, unfolding activity through which he expresses his lifestyle (Perry, 1970, pp. 9–10).

These forms of intellectual and ethical development explain, according to Perry, the various ways students approach a learning situation and make meaning of the experience.

METHOD

Subjects

Subjects were 241 first-year medical students and 114 first-year pharmacy students, attending school at the Faculty of Medicine and the Faculty of Pharmacy, respectively, at the University of Toronto.

The medical students were of three types: (a) those who entered medical school following 2 years of undergraduate school, (b) those who entered medical school after completing their BS or BA degree, and (c) those who obtained some type of postgraduate degree before entering medical school. As far as other admissions criteria are concerned, applicants to the medical school are required to have attained an overall GPA standing of greater than 3.25 on a 4-point scale, passed the Medical Colleges Admissions Test (MCAT) with a score of 8 or more on a 10-point scale, and, in addition, met the established nonacademic criteria. Applicants who have completed a graduate program are assessed on their research and publication accomplishments. Approximately 2,000 applicants compete for 250 places.

Applicants are accepted into the pharmacy program following completion of their high school certification, providing they have at least six senior level credits and pass the Pharmacy Admissions Test (PAT). An overall GPA index is generated from the applicant's high school grades and PAT results and should be greater than 80% to warrant serious consideration for admission. Applicants must also meet established nonacademic requirements. Approximately 500 applicants compete for 165 places. A few students who have completed the first year of a university program with an average of B+ may be accepted into the second year of the pharmacy program if places are available. Of the current sample of students, 1% had more than high school experience.

Procedure

All medical and pharmacy first-year students were asked to complete a Measure of Epistemological Reflection (MER). The questionnaires were distributed and collected during the first 2 months of the term.

The MER was designed and tested by Baxter-Magolda and Porterfield (1985) to measure intellectual and ethical development within the framework of the Perry Scheme. Open-ended questions elicit information on six domains that can be assessed by trained raters. The overall score provides a numerical rating of 0–5 indicating the level of epistemological development at which an individual is functioning. The score parallels the first five levels or positions on the Perry Scheme. For the purpose of this study, the results offer a profile of entering class developmental levels.

RESULTS

Medical Students

Completed questionnaires were received from 241 first-year medical students (96% return rate). Three of these questionnaires were not ratable due to limited data ($N = 238$).

The ratings for medical students revealed that 2% were functioning at Level 1, 27% were functioning at Level 2, 37% were functioning at Level 3, 23% at Level 4, and 10% at Level 5.

However, when the medical students with either a completed undergraduate or graduate degree were omitted from the analysis (35 students), the levels of development appear somewhat lower. The levels for the remaining 203 students were: 2% were again rated at Level 1, 31% at Level 2, 40% at Level 3, 22% at Level 4, and 5% at Level 5. For the medical students, then, most were functioning at Levels 2, 3, and 4.

Pharmacy Students

Of the 114 questionnaires returned from first-year pharmacy students (a 69% return rate), two were not ratable due to limited data ($N = 112$).

Ratings for pharmacy students revealed that 5% were functioning at Level 1, 57% were functioning at Level 2, 25% at Level 3, 7% at Level 4, and 5% at Level 5.

These results suggest that more medical students than pharmacy students were at higher developmental levels. Chi-square tests on the two distributions of medical students (the entire sample of 238) and pharmacy students were used to test this supposition. The results of this test suggested that the distribution of levels among the medical students and the pharmacy students was significantly different, $\chi^{2(4, N = 350)} = 37.42$, $p < .001$. When medical students with completed degrees were omitted from the analysis, the two groups were still significantly different, $\chi^{2(4, N = 315)} = 31.69$, $p < .001$.

Even though the medical students were, in general, reasoning at higher levels than the pharmacy students, it is also important to point out that 33% of them were still functioning at a dualistic level (Levels 1 and 2). Of the pharmacy students, 62% were functioning at a dualistic level. These data warrant attention when planning professional curricula. It should also be noted that some pharmacy students, albeit a small percentage (5%), were functioning at a relativistic level (Level 5) after completion of high school.

DISCUSSION

Overall results indicate that there are differences in the developmental levels between students entering pharmacy after completion of high school and students entering medicine after 2 years at university. It is important to note that, despite these differences, the range of levels attained was from Level 1 to Level 5 for both groups. This seems particularly notable in the case of the medical students. These students met relatively stringent traditional academic criteria for admission. Nevertheless, they show a variety of learning styles that may have an impact on their ability to succeed in their program. Further analysis is needed to determine whether BA and BSc students entering medicine differ in their development and/or if there are gender distinctions.

As professional faculties review their mission statements and curriculum goals, objectives, and methodologies, they are aware that consideration of students' abilities are central to future planning. A curriculum can be designed to accommodate the abilities and aptitudes of students likely to enroll in a particular program. Alternatively, a curriculum can be designed to meet the stated aims of a professional program; students who are thought likely to succeed can then be selected for the program. In reality, there are usually efforts to blend the two approaches. However, when major curriculum changes are anticipated, decisions are typically based on known application numbers and general achievement patterns.

The issues of selection for particular programs become more focused when: (a) the epistemological patterns of current entering medical and pharmaceutical students are studied, (b) an understanding of various learning approaches is achieved, and (c) possible gaps between student learning levels and the epistemological expectations and demands of a particular curriculum are revealed. Resolution of such issues would enable curriculum design to be grounded in the expected abilities and aptitudes of students and would expedite the development of admissions selection criteria to select candidates who are likely to succeed in a particular program.

Thus, data from this study indicate that if the selection processes for pharmacy remain essentially the same, approximately two thirds of first-year students are likely to approach their learning from within a dualistic framework. If they are to be successful in a program designed to elevate cognitive skills and complex thinking, they will need considerable counseling and/or faculty support. When dualistic thinkers are confronted with a curriculum that demands a relativistic approach to learning, they may experience confusion, disorientation and, for some, intellectual chaos as they struggle to make meaning of their educational experiences. This may be expressed as anger toward the professors, militancy regarding what is thought of as "relevant," passivity toward learning, and so on. It may even result in what Perry (1970) termed "escaping, retreating or temporizing from the challenges of life and learning" (p. 10). In addition, approximately one third will approach their learning within a multiplistic mode; that is, they will be struggling to make meaning of their world and will also likely require support to cope with the demands of a curriculum geared to higher level thinking.

After 2 years of university education, students appear to be functioning at slightly higher levels. However, approximately one third of these students are likely to have problems with a more demanding program and could require counseling and/or considerable faculty support. Furthermore, an additional half functioning at multiplistic levels would likely require some support in order to have a successful learning experience.

It was noted earlier that a few of the entering students, in both pharmacy and medicine, are functioning as relativistic thinkers. These students may either be experiencing frustration or may be reluctantly compliant with the traditional, structured program, viewing the end goal of a professional licence as their incentive (cf. Cleave-Hogg & Rothman, 1991); a more self-directed, problem-solving curriculum would probably be appreciated.

Further longitudinal studies are underway that will track the epistemological development of medical and pharmacy students as they progress through the 4-year professional programs. Data on students' academic and clinical performance are required to ascertain links between development and "success" as it is defined in these professional programs. Nonetheless, the current study provides information regarding entering students' epistemological development and offers a different lens for reviewing admissions criteria and resolving issues regarding the selection of students in the context of major curriculum change.

Education planners in the Faculty of Medicine and the Faculty of Pharmacy stated that the new curricula will require students to assume a more active role in the learning process and to become more self-directed and independent. In addition, curriculum goals include educating students to develop problem-solving skills and abilities to deal with complexity and uncertainty, pursue ethical and moral issues, and engage in higher level learning.

In the context of these changing educational environments and the information we have acquired regarding entering students' developmental levels, there are at least four possible approaches to the admissions/curriculum issue. These approaches are discussed next.

Change the Curriculum Without Changing Admissions Criteria. With this approach, the new curriculum is introduced without change in the established admissions criteria for the selection of students. Assuming that the developmental profile of the entering class of students remains relatively constant (as it has for the past 5 years in medicine), it is likely that the majority of students will experience undue anxiety as they try to cope with different learning/teaching parameters. For example, students who are functioning as "dependent learners" (dualistic level) are likely to find it difficult to assume responsibility for their own learning. Another outcome may be an increase in the failure rate if the gap between student ability and curriculum expectations is wide.

Selection of Students for the New Curriculum. This approach uses certain admission's procedures to demonstrate, and select from, students' abilities and/or characteristics thought likely to "fit" the new curriculum. This solution appears practical, but there are innate problems that need to be addressed. One pressing problem, especially in times of fiscal restraint, is that of reduction of base budgets. If selection criteria are changed radically, the outcome may be a lack of suitable candidates and a reduction in the number of registrants. In institutions where formula funding (allocation of $X for each registrant) is applied, underenrollment would have an unwelcomed financial impact.

Another difficulty with this approach is the identification of specific abilities and characteristics that predict success in a particular curriculum (Weiss, Lotan, Kedar, & Ben-Shakhar, 1988). McManus et al. (1992) suggested that careful deliberation is needed to reveal underlying assumptions and agendas as well as conflicting goals. Furthermore, even when admissions committees identify certain attributes, they are then faced with the difficulty of describing these attributes in such a way that they are clearly understood and interpreted by all those involved in the selection process.

A further problem is initiating and implementing reliable and valid processes by which desired attributes can be demonstrated and assessed. Personal references, autobiographies, questionnaires, interviews, psychological and psychomotor tests, academic achievement profiles, job simulation, and group exercises are some of the ways that have been tested, yet each method has disclosed weaknesses. For example, autobiographical information is useful, but needs to be rated by several assessors before interrater reliability can be achieved. The question of who actually writes the autobiography must also be faced unless the writing is carried out under supervision.

It is generally assumed that the utilization of many selection procedures provides a more reliable overall profile of the applicant. In reality, such thinking is tempered by lack of resources, especially faculty, to undertake the time consuming procedures such as interviewing and group exercises.

Matching Model. A third option is to keep current applicant selection procedures and introduce a curriculum that acknowledges the possible gaps in students' aptitudes and abilities to cope with the new curriculum. In this scenario, lack of appropriate learning skills would be addressed by offering opportunities for students to develop certain skills. It has been argued that the requirement "completion of 2 years of university" is intended to provide the necessary experiences but, according to our survey of epistemological development, the goal is not achieved. First-year courses of the new curriculum would be viewed as transitional in that they would be designed to help students move from dualistic, passive, extrinsically motivated postures to active, intrinsically motivated, self-directed, problem-solving learning that views knowledge from a relativistic perspective. This does not necessarily mean a change in content, but rather a shift in methodology and the establishment of a more appropriate learning environment. This approach would allow students time for development, yet there are inherent concerns regarding taking time from a professional curriculum to teach "learning skills."

Two Streams. Another option is to establish two streams within the program: One stream for students who are able to benefit from a self-directed method and who enjoy the challenges of higher level learning, and another stream, the curriculum of which would match student abilities and include methods designed to support student development. The latter stream may include an increase in the number of semesters or more years allocated to complete the undergraduate degree.

In principle, students would gain from streamed programs, but applicants to professional programs are, for the most part, highly competitive (Cleave-Hogg & Rothman, 1991) and selection for the streams would require careful assessment. Applicants invariably look for the fastest way to achieve their goals, that is, passing licensure examinations.

In summary, we suggest that any changes in curricula that aim to introduce students to more complex, higher level learning must change the selection process for admission to a program, or include transitional courses and provide opportunities for students to develop their learning skills and their understanding of the proposed educational objectives.

Achievement of high school certification, university education, or completion of an undergraduate degree do not provide reliable indicators of students' abilities and aptitudes for curricula that demand a shift in students' approach to learning. Our survey suggests that curriculum developers and admissions committees need to address these issues if professional schools are to achieve their aims and objectives.

REFERENCES

Association of American Colleges of Pharmacy. (1991). *Commission to implement change in pharmaceutical education: Special Report.* Washington, DC: Author.

Association of American Medical Colleges. (1984). *Physicians for the twenty-first century: The report of the panel on the general professional education of the physician and college preparation for medicine.* Washington, DC: Author.

Baxter-Magolda, M., & Porterfield, W. (1985). Measure of epistemological reflection. *American College Personnel Association,* N 47.

Cleave-Hogg, D., & Rothman, A. I. (1991). Discerning views: Medical students' perceptions of their learning environment. *Evaluation and the Health Professions, 14*(4), 456–474.

Ebert, H. E., & Ginzberg, E. (1988). The reform of medical education. *Health Affairs,* Supplement 5-38.

The Edinburgh Declaration. (1988). World conference of medical education of the world federation for medical education. *Medical Education, 22,* 481–482.

McManus, C., Powis, D., & Cleave-Hogg, D. (1992). Selection of medical students: The philosophic, social and educational bases. *Teaching and Learning in Medicine, 4*(1), 25–34.

Gough, H. G. (1978). Some predictive implications of premedical scientific competence and preferences. *Journal of Medical Education, 53,* 291–300.

Perry, W. G. (1970). *Forms of intellectual and ethical development in the college years.* New York: Holt, Rinehart & Winston.

Strand, L. M., Morley, P. C., & Cipolle, R. J. (1987). A Problem-based student-centered approach to pharmacy education. *American Journal of Pharmaceutical Education, 51,* 75–79.

Weiss, M., Lotan, I., Kedar, H., & Ben-Shakhar, G. (1988). Selecting candidates for a medical school: An evaluation of a selection model based on cognitive and personality predictors. *Medical Education, 22,* 492–497.

CHAPTER FIVE

Sri Lankan Managers' Leadership Conceptualizations as a Function of Ego Development

Rita Weathersby
University of New Hampshire

Leadership involves defining reality or framing (and often reframing) meaning in organizational situations. That is, what the leader sees or defines as a problem or opportunity is more often than not what is experienced as reality by members of the organization. Defining that reality and creating a "shared reality" that guides others' actions is, in fact, one of the leader's major roles (Morgan, 1986; Smircich & Morgan, 1982). Thus, the exercise of leadership is highly dependent on the leader's frame of reference in making meaning.

This frame of reference is at least partially, and often powerfully, a function of the leader's stage of adult development. Constructive–developmental theory (Kegan, 1982; Kohlberg, 1969; Loevinger, 1976; Piaget, 1967) posits developmental stages in children and adults in which each stage represents a qualitatively different frame of reference for understanding and responding to daily experience. Each successive stage embodies a distinct set of capacities and constraints and reframes earlier elements of personality to create a more complex world view.

The relevance of developmental stage to leadership is obvious when one examines the different strands of development. Progressions in constructive–developmental theories describe movement from simplistic to complex thinking; from power-oriented to principle-oriented ideas of morality; from instrumental conceptions of interpersonal relationships to ideals of mutual responsiveness and common humanity; from faith based on magical or conventional thinking to faith based on chosen commitments; and from limited self-awareness to an increasingly complex understanding of one's own and others' motivations (Weathersby & Tarule, 1980). Individuals at earlier stages are more cognitively simple and concrete (Harvey, Hunt, & Schroeder, 1961; Loevinger, 1976) as well as more stereotypic and dogmatic (McCrae & Costa, 1980). As individuals progress to later stages, their thinking becomes more complex/abstract and also more precise. Further, they become more able to empathize with others who hold conflicting views, to act on perceptions of mutual interdependence, and to tolerate higher levels of stress and ambiguity (Bartunek, Gordon, & Weathersby, 1983). The capacity to reframe situations, to understand multiple points of view, and to understand that "truth" or meaning is at least partially created by the participants in a situation is associated with later developmental stages.

DEVELOPMENTAL PREREQUISITES
FOR EFFECTIVE LEADERSHIP

Recently it has been demonstrated theoretically and empirically that managerial effectiveness implies characteristics of later developmental stages and that transformational models of leadership, in particular, require the capabilities of later stages for implementation (Bartunek et al., 1983; Fisher, Merron, & Torbert, 1987; Fisher & Torbert, 1991; Torbert, 1986, 1991). Smith (1980), for example, in a study of industrial managers, found clear differences in the use of power and personal defense mechanisms among managers at different stages of development. Managers at earlier stages (see Table 5.1) tended to see themselves as enforcing others' decisions rather than making decisions themselves. They used coercive power and handled ambiguous problems by retreating to rules and procedures. At middle stages, managers were more flexible. They made decisions on the basis of conviction and acquired power more through consultation and expertise.

Likewise, in a simulation situation, Merron, Fisher, and Torbert (1987) found differences among managers in approaches to problem solving and collaboration. Managers at later stages were more likely to redefine problems than to accept them as given as well as more likely to solve problems collaboratively rather than unilaterally. Extrapolating from theory, managers at later stages should also be more able to make productive use of dissent, to use oppositional (or assumption testing) models of strategic planning, and to create flexible organizational processes (Bartunek et al., 1983). Thus, they should be better able to guide organizations in times of transition and to provide transformational leadership

TABLE 5.1
Relationships Between Ego Stage,
World View, Leadership Style, and Use of Power

Ego Stage	World View	Leadership Style	Use of Power
Earlier stages: self-protective, conformist	Concreteness, cognitive simplicity, stereotyping, conformity, little empathy, low tolerance for diversity and ambiguity	"Autocratic," "transactional," or "heroic" approaches	Authoritarian, coercive, and reward power, "enforcing the rules"
Middle stages: self-aware, conscientious	Increasing conceptual complexity, self-evaluated standards & self-criticism, awareness of individual differences, concern for communication, reciprocity, long-term goals and ideals	"Mixed bag"—all styles. Implementation reflects degree of personal development, some discrepancy between intention and effect	Increased use of expert and referent power, planning, humor, altruism, "making decisions"
Later stages: individualistic, autonomous	Cognitively complex, broad scope, tolerant of paradox and ambiguity, respect for individuality, inter-dependence, complex causation and communi-cation, concern with self-fulfillment in social con-text, development, change	"Manager as developer," "transformational" approaches	Increased use of collaboration, productive use of dissent, "creating change"

Note: Table is based on the work of Bartunek et al. (1983), Fisher et al. (1987), Loevinger and Wessler (1970), and Smith (1980).

that requires restructuring of organizational policies, objectives, and culture (Fisher & Torbert, 1991).

Powerful correspondences exist between a leader's stage of development and his or her world view, preferred leadership style, and use of power (see Table 5.1). Earlier stage managers tend to have authoritarian or transactional approaches to leadership in which power is a tool to enforce compliance. Later stage managers tend to espouse developmental or transformational approaches; here, power is shared and empowering others is considered necessary to create the organization's capacity for excellence. At middle stages, managers adopt a variety of leadership approaches, often retaining authoritarian or transactional approaches (where the leader remains the locus of control) while espousing aspects of developmental and transformational models. Management education is often aimed at helping managers at middle stages develop the requisite conceptual and interpersonal flexibility to implement the leadership models they espouse.

This research on managers, when combined with the extensive research of constructive–developmental theorists, has profound implications for management education. At the core of management education is a transformational learning process (Bennis, 1989). Management education should therefore, if possible, promote individual human development. Further, learning a new management or leadership style may be difficult because of the requirement to develop new structures for thinking and behavior that represent a fundamental change in developmental level. New management approaches often do not "graft" well, despite focused training. It is entirely probable that this "nongrafting" phenomenon exists because implementing a new approach often requires more than acquiring a new "tool"; it requires greater development on the part of the individual (Fisher et al., 1987).

LEADERSHIP DEVELOPMENT
ACROSS CULTURAL CONTEXTS

This chapter addresses the issue of leadership development in a cross-cultural context, namely, Sri Lanka (an island nation off the southern tip of India, formerly called Ceylon). It explores whether the correspondences between leadership style and adult development documented earlier are meaningful across cultures and whether knowledge of developmental theory can enhance our understanding of cross-cultural leadership development.

Leadership is a cultural phenomenon, heavily embedded in the ways in which meaning is created in particular societal contexts. Leadership models are inherently culturally dependent and, therefore, culturally relative with respect to ideals of leadership behavior and accepted ways to enact those ideals. National cultures, and subcultures within them, differ with respect to the accepted roles of superiors and subordinates, use of power and authority, use of hierarchy and participation, communication style, assumptions about motivation, and basic values in decision-making (Adler, 1991; Hofstede, 1980). The American orientation to pragmatism and to present action (Stewart, 1972), for example, is not universal. Further, research has indicated that, although leadership models can be meaningfully utilized across national cultures, specific elements of the models often need to be reconceptualized. For example, Maslow's hierarchy of needs may apply to the People's Republic of China, but the hierarchy must be reordered so that the highest level is not individual self-actualization but self-actualization in service to society (Nevis, 1983).

Because a leader's role is as creator and keeper of the organization's culture, leaders face several dilemmas with respect to their organization's culture and the management culture of their nation. Recent writing on organizational culture (Frost, Moore, Louis, Lundberg, & Martin, 1985) highlighted the dilemmas of understanding and shaping organizational culture. Leaders are somewhat captive to their organizations as well as potential change agents. Even as they seek change, leaders are obligated to respond to powerful cultural expectations.

In this research, exploration of the correspondences between leadership development and adult development are made more intriguing by the strong contrast in national and organizational cultures between the Sri Lanka and the United States. Sri Lanka and the United States are virtually opposites on the cultural dimensions of work-related values identified by Hofstede (1980, 1984). Sri Lankan culture is *collectivist* (whereas American culture is individualistic), oriented to *high power distance and security* (whereas America's egalitarian values create moderate power distance and promote risk-taking), and concerned with *spiritual and family values* (in contrast to America's greater emphasis on achievement and materialism). Further, Sri Lankan leadership styles are traditionally authoritarian. They have evolved from the ancient practices of able and autocratic kings, upon which the Portuguese, the Dutch, and the British imposed a bureaucratic colonial administration. Social class, caste, religious and educational differences are powerfully present, although their effects are lessened in contemporary workplaces. The work ethic for ordinary workers is greatly relaxed when compared to that of the United States and other industrial democracies. There is also a tradition of political influence in jobs and appointments.

Given these singificant differences, many questions arise. Will American models of leadership be seen as valuable or effective in Sri Lanka?

What allows someone to adopt, or adapt, a leadership model developed in another cultural context? What is the learning process for an individual who is adopting a "foreign" model of leadership? This research provides some provisional answers.

Given the theoretical link between leadership and developmental stage, there are also larger questions relevant to human development. Are there similar patterns of correspondences between developmental stage and leadership style, implying similar or common patterns of leadership development across the two cultures? Will the process of defining leadership be similarly mediated by developmental stage? Will learning new, higher level models of leadership initiate reframings of personality that are steps in developmental stage change?

METHOD

Subjects

Forty-four practicing Sri Lankan managers (from junior- to middle- and senior-level management in public and private sector organizations) served as participants. This group consisted of 38 men and 6 women, ranging in age from late 20s to mid-50s with the majority in their 30s and 40s. All 44 were enrolled in a course on organizational theory taught by the author, who was a visiting professor at the Postgraduate Institute of Management of the University of Sri Jayawardenapura. Thirty-three of these individuals enrolled in the author's subsequent course on organizational leadership.

Course Description

Content for the leadership course consisted largely of American models of management and leadership. A major portion of time was spent on a developmental, transformational model of leadership, the Manager-As-Developer model (Bradford & Cohen, 1984). This model posited that, in complex organizational situations with interdependent and rapidly evolving tasks and a highly educated workforce (e.g., American high technology industries), leadership styles that center on the leader's directive abilities (i.e., "technician" and "conductor" styles) will produce, at best, only adequate performance. High performance is created by a change in the leader's fundamental values and orientation. The leader becomes simultaneously a developer of the organization's vision, its capacity for teamwork (particularly with the leaders' direct associates), and individuals' capabilities for shared management of the organization's priorities. This model has specifically challenged the assumptions of heroic and transactional models in which the leader retains all responsibility and control. Its full implementation requires later stage adult development (see Table 5.1), although elements of the model can be used by managers at the early and middle stages.

Other leadership models were also discussed (e.g., situational and contingency models) and a text on interpersonal processes in leadership assumed American values of participative management. A related course activity was the generation of ideas about leadership models based on the participants' knowledge of the Sri Lankan context. Students wrote papers and/or cases discussing the application of these leadership models to their own sociocultural context.

In important respects, the situational assumptions of the Manager-As-Developer and other participative models are only partially applicable to most Sri Lankan workplaces. With exceptions, notably in the capital city, Colombo, and in some multinational enterprises, organizations are simpler in structure, tasks are less complexly interdependent, and a large proportion of the workforce is unskilled or not professionally skilled. Until recently, management education has also been nonformal, although there is currently great interest among professionals for more training. In most situations, managers are expected to rule by coercive and reward power. Whereas the developer manager is anti-heroic, the Sri Lankan management hero is the hard task master or benevolent dictator.

Procedure

The course was designed to foster an environment that promoted individual and collective reflection and, in that respect, was intended as a developmental intervention. Leadership issues that had no immediate resolution were addressed and dialogue was encouraged (see Bartunek et al., 1983; Weathersby, Bartunek, & Gordon, 1982). The institute's director, who is Sri Lankan, co-taught many of the sessions and provided contrasting opinions to the text and discussions. Conceptual models, case studies, role-plays, personal feedback, and reflection on personal experience all contributed to a challenging learning environment that was—with respect to teaching methods and emphasis on individuals de-

veloping their personal philosophy—at odds with traditional pedagogi-
cal practice in Sri Lanka.

As the core assignment of the course, students were asked to define
their own model of leadership (appropriate to their context), to assess
their strengths and limitations in relationship to their model, and to develop a plan for their self-development as managers. Data were required
for the self-assessment (e.g., questionnaires, interviews, analysis of past
successes and failures, feedback from colleagues, superiors and subordinates, personality measures).

Specifically, students completed Loevinger's Sentence Completion Test
for Ego Development (Loevinger & Wessler, 1970), which was scored
by a reliable scorer alert to cross-cultural bias. Further, the leadership
paper served as the focal measure to assess the effect of developmental
stage on individuals' leadership conceptualizations. Leadership papers
were content analyzed; the content analysis was based on Loevinger's
milestones of ego development, which depict identifying characteristics
and also breakthrough learnings at each successive stage.

Sources of Cultural Bias

There is cultural bias in this study, as there is in all studies, because a
researcher is never without a cultural framework. Similarly, there is potential bias in that the interpretations described here are solely the author's.
However, a conscientious attempt has been made to remain close to the
data and to gain interpretive responses from Sri Lankan students and colleagues.

The universality of Loevinger's developmental scheme and scoring
procedures may also be questioned, particularly with regard to content
items that reflect cultural values (i.e., what "conformists" say in any culture reflects cultural norms). Also, Loevinger's scheme has a western cultural bias in that it differentiates progressions of individual development
more clearly than the development of concepts of community, as one
would do in a collectivist culture such as Sri Lanka. Only a few studies
(Galaz-Fontes et al., 1991; Lasker, 1978; Tietjen & Walker, 1985) have
explored leadership concepts cross-culturally. Similar to this study, they
have used western conceptual schemes. Studies in the constructive–
developmental tradition seem to have established the validity of these
concepts across cultures (Edwards, 1986; Snarey, 1985). Presumably other
patterns are also present and would be apparent if one employed eastern
conceptual schemes, and/or a combination of eastern and western
thinking.

RESULTS AND DISCUSSION

Managers' Stages of Development

Ego stage scores for these Sri Lankan managers are similar to previously published scores of American managers in the range of scores exhibited (see Table 5.2).[1] However, this group of Sri Lankan managers (n = 44) is unusual in that the distribution of their ego stages differed significantly in comparison with the combined American samples, χ^2 (3, N = 428) = 18.8, p < .001. Over all American studies of managerial levels, Torbert (1991) found the following percentages at each ego stage: self-protective, 2%; conformist, 8%; self-aware, 45%; conscientious, 36%; and individualistic and autonomous, 9%. In contrast, in the Sri Lankan sample, there are proportionately more managers at the later stages than in the groups of American managers who have been previously studied.

Loevinger has hypothesized that the median level of the adult population in America is at the self-aware level; the data in Table 5.2 indicate that managers usually match or go beyond the general level of the population. This group of Sri Lankan managers is exceptional in that regard. Given the Postgraduate Institute of Management's mission of providing leadership for the country's economic and social development, this group represents a potential nucleus of managers who are expected to make a significant positive contribution to the country's management practice.

Several reasons can be advanced to explain these high scores. Recent research on uneducated adults in a Mexican setting (Galaz-Fontes et al., 1991) suggested that assuming leadership roles may facilitate higher stage reasoning, particularly among individuals who also have education or work experience outside their own cultures. These findings could explain, in part, why this highly educated Sri Lankan group has such significantly high scores. They are unusual among Sri Lankan managers in that they had completed a college degree (about 1% of Sri Lanka's population is able to attend a university and this is by competitive exam) and had gained admission to the Postgraduate Institute of Management, which offers one

---

[1] Table 5.2 is merely indicative of the range of managers' possible scores. Workplace setting, managerial level, age, and education are obvious variables that influence stage scores. Smith's (1980) study (Study 1), which was conducted among middle level supervisors in an industrial plant, may more accurately represent the majority of people who hold managerial or supervisory positions. Torbert's (1983) study (Study 2) occurred in a managerial population enrolled in an MBA program and is probably more comparable to the Sri Lankan group. However, the Sri Lankan group was on average both more experienced and older. Even though the group included both junior and senior level managers, the data more closely resemble groups of American senior managers.

TABLE 5.2
Distribution of American and Sri Lankan Managers by Developmental Stage
in Five Recent Studies*

Ego Development Stage	Study 1 First Line Supervisors (N = 37)	Study 2 Junior & Middle Managers (N = 177)	Study 3 Senior Managers (N = 66)	Study 4 Executives (N = 104)	Study 5 Sri Lankan Managers All Levels (N = 44)
Self-protective	0.0	5.0	0.0	0.0	2.0
Conformist	24.0	9.0	6.0	3.0	5.0
Self-aware	68.0	43.5	47.0	43.5	25.0
Conscientious	8.0	40.0	33.0	39.5	45.0
Individualistic	0.0	2.0	14.0	11.0	16.0
Autonomous	0.0	.5	0.0	3.0	7.0
	100.0%	100.0%	100.0%	100.0%	100.0%

*Study 1 is by Smith (1980); Study 2 is by Torbert (1983); Study 3 is by Gratch (1985); Study 4 is by Quinn and Torbert (1987); Study 5, by the present author, represents scores of the entering class of managers in the MBA program, June 1987, Postgraduate Institute of Management, Sri Lanka. Of these 44, 33 took the organizational leadership course described in this chapter.

of the two MBA programs in the country. Several had already completed master's work in other fields. Many had education or work experiences outside of Sri Lanka.[2]

Managers' Responses to the Leadership Conceptualization Task

An impressionistic content analysis of the leadership papers ($n = 33$) revealed some possible correspondences between managers' leadership conceptualizations and their developmental stage. Identifiable patterns appeared by ego stage, and ego level appeared to be a mediating variable in influencing an individual's response to the task of developing a personal leadership model.

---

[2]Galaz-Fontes et al. (1991) hypothesized that, among uneducated adults, leadership is the reason for moving up in developmental stages, but only to Piaget's Stage 3/4, or formal operations. The same reasons advocated for leadership as facilitating higher stage reasoning along with cross-cultural contact can be advanced in relation to the highest stage individuals in this Sri Lankan group. Most of the highest stage individuals, at Loevinger's individualistic and autonomous stages (Piaget's postformal operations), had undertaken major managerial responsibilities, often in difficult economic and social situations; most had education and/or work experience outside Sri Lanka. These findings corroborate the Galaz-Fontes et al. study in a different nonwestern context.

Despite cultural differences, the American participative models, and especially the Manager-As-Developer model, were well received. Managers at all levels adopted combinations of situational, participative, and developer models. Several created their own composite models. Most commented on factors in the Sri Lankan context that would affect implementation. As predicted, managers at the later stages placed more emphasis on the importance of the leader's role as an agent of cultural change.

Also, as expected, possible differences related to ego stage may exist in conceptual complexity, degree of reliance on external versus internal authority, depth of self-knowledge, use of data (including information and feedback gathered from others), and perceptiveness of recurring patterns in personal experience.

Managers' Conceptualizations of Leadership by Ego Stage

Effectiveness requires leaders to adapt to complex situations and select courses of action within their personal repertoire of strengths and limitations. Managers at all ego stages struggle to develop the requisite complexity. The following paragraphs describe group differences in the Sri Lankan managers' leadership assessments and include quotations for illustration.

Conformist Stage. "I followed what my predecessor did. . . . Now I realize it is not the right model." Theory suggests that conformist managers would rely on external authorities in determining their leadership styles. These managers observe protocol and are concerned to follow established standards. They avoid conflict and seek status; loyalty is to one's immediate organizational group (Torbert, 1987). Conformist managers conceptualize in generalities; course texts and other references are adopted as "truth." Self-assessment is often based on personal opinion with little use of corroborating data.

For example, a senior manager in a public sector corporation reported coming to a new conceptualization of leadership as the course progressed. He essentially used one reference, the course text. In describing his leadership style, he presented himself as a former authoritarian who was now a "technician" manager. In discussing why he adopted the Manager-As-Developer model as his goal, he spoke in terms of right and wrong, as though he had essentially replaced the expectations of an earlier set of authorities for those presented in the course.

> I followed what my predecessor did. He ruled with an iron hand. Performance had to be achieved at any cost. Deadlines have to be met. There was no time to develop subordinates. . . . Now I realize it is not the right

model. . . . These concepts [the developer model] appear to be the ideal ones for me to adopt. But I have a long way to go from where I stand.

This manager's ego development score was noted as "high" conformist by the scorer. His experience in writing the leadership paper appeared to show breakthroughs in his thinking that were indicative of movement to the self-aware stage.

Self-Aware Stage. "I had the courage to decide my own style and practice same. . . . By writing this paper I have acted as a leader to myself. . . . I have raised questions on myself, found solutions for these problems, and presented to myself for approval." Managers at this stage present their ideas well, although somewhat generally. Contradictory data and lack of comprehensiveness (e.g., details of implementation) sometimes appear unnoticed in self-assessments. Theory posits that managers at this stage are engaged in asserting their uniqueness in relation to others and to social norms; consequently, they are sometimes dogmatic in their thinking and generally need to gain greater awareness of the impact of their behavior on others and on the organization. Because of this lack, they sometimes fail to realize their ideals. Managers at this stage are interested in problem solving and see contingencies and exceptions. Perfectionistic, they seek efficiency and choose it over effectiveness (Torbert, 1987).

One noteworthy self-analysis was completed by an engineering manager who was scored as moving toward the conscientious stage. The leadership norms at his workplace were extremely authoritarian. Characteristically, he noted that he had chosen to go against the culture. "Although the dockyard management wants engineers to act as technician leaders and always promoted that style, I had the courage to decide my own style and practice same." He selected a situational model in which he preferred to use the developer style with subordinates, but did not rule out authoritarian behavior.

Mine is mostly a situational model. The leadership role may vary from one situation to the other depending on the circumstances such as the nature of the problem, the superiors involved, the subordinates involved, etc. Sometimes I may take the role of a developer–leader if I find there is time and resources to develop the subordinates. However, if I have limited time and the situation was more critical, I would take a different approach and take the role of a technical leader. Similarly, there are occasions I have to follow the power model and act as an authoritarian.

In self-assessment, he identified important general strengths ("I was very successful in achieving results with my own model of leadership in a better way than my colleagues who follow different models") and also identi-

ficd personal limitations (e.g., excessive worry, difficulty changing decisions once made, impatience over career ambitions). His self-development
plans emphasized self-management qualities characteristic of the conscientious stage.

Conscientious Stage. "I believe that I possess the necessary mental
framework to meet the demands placed by the developer model on my
self-ego." Managers at this stage are effectiveness- and results-oriented; they
appreciate systems and strive to realize long-term goals and personal standards (Torbert, 1987). Typically they evolve their leadership conceptualizations in tandem with a comprehensive synthesis of theories. Their self-
assessments are databased and thorough. Many select some version of the
developer or participative models; in doing this, they show fuller understanding of these models than did individuals at earlier stages. Communication and feedback in the development of interpersonal competence to
implement their ideals emerge as a central point of learning for this group.

A case analysis written by one manager at this stage reveals an ability to
use theory to reframe one's understanding of a situation. He described the
situation of a severely problematic employee in his department whose
behavior was finally corrected, in Sri Lankan style, by threat of a sacking
by a high-level superior. The employee's behavior was clearly deficient,
yet this manager acknowledged his own complicity in creating the conditions that allowed the poor performance. In hindsight, it was his contention that some of his failings as a manager had contributed to the severity
of the problem. "The only management style I knew was the heroic style
'take command over your department.' Hence the shared responsibility
team was absent." Using concepts of motivation, attribution, and the developer manager's responsibility to communicate shared goals, develop
subordinates on the job, and foster shared responsibility among co-
workers, he ultimately constructed a more ideal management scenario.

Individualistic and Autonomous Stages. "A deeper understanding of self and environment to develop capacity to manage my own destiny." Individuals at these stages are process- as well as goal-oriented and
place high value on principle and judgment (not just rules and customs)
in making decisions. They think relativistically and place a high value
on individuality (Torbert, 1987). Most, in tracing their work history, see
themselves as moving toward more developmental and participative styles
as a function of experience and maturity. Leadership is viewed as a process
with attention paid to the learning and consolidating of a new style over
time. Leadership models are consciously self-chosen in alignment with
personal visions and values. Inner conflict is highlighted as individuals
question personal values in relation to their career. Classroom incidents,

conversations, and role-plays are often used to illustrate points of self-assessment. Increased mention is made of individual, social, and economic linkages and of the importance of personal and societal transformation. Strong commitment to change and growth is expressed.

One experienced senior manager traced his work history in successive organizations and his evolution, as a result of increasingly complex challenges, from an authoritarian manager to the technician and conductor styles and finally to the Manager-As-Developer model. This is illustrated by an extended example of his strategic use of a shared responsibility team to improve financial accountability in a troubled public sector corporation. His self-assessment focused on the necessity for increased self-examination to consolidate the developer style.

> My choice of a leadership model stems from a personal mission in life and the vision for its means-to-end. . . . It needs courage and determination to literally "come out of myself," to appreciate short-comings mirrored and shed the residual latent heroic attitudes, and as to restructure the correct emphasis for personal development.

Evidence of Developmental Reframing

A person's developmental stage, similar to one's culture, constitutes an unnoticed frame of reference. Like culture change, change in developmental stage requires dissonance, intensity of experience, self-awareness, and commitment. Exposure to alternative ways of thinking is important as are experiences that create a need or desire for new styles of behavior. Stage change requires a significant period of time (e.g., several years or more) and seemingly occurs through successive changes (microsteps) that cumulatively create a new infrastructure for thinking and behavior. It is helpful to conceptualize two dimensions of movement, one horizontal and one vertical. Horizontally, there is a "filling in" process where new ways of thinking and reacting acquired in relation to one set of experiences are transferred, under favorable conditions, to other situations. Vertically, there are "perspective transformations" that usher in a substantially different world view (see Bartunek et al., 1983; Kegan, 1982).

In this study, stage change was not measured or expected. However, there was ample evidence that the leadership development process initiated by the course stimulated reframing of both the "filling in" and "perspective transformation" dimensions of development. The task of framing a leadership philosophy and of assessing one's strengths and limitations against it, particularly across the differences in assumptions made by Sri Lankan and American cultural contexts, required repeated reframing of leadership ideas. Reframing was also present as people traced patterns in their past work experience to identify their implicit models of practice. This process of reframing one's conceptualization of leadership appears to be enhanced by ego level and seems to follow the direction of greater development. Roughly one third of the managers revealed reconceptualizations that not only changed or consolidated aspects of leadership, but also reflected steps in the process of stage change. With advancing ego levels, a manager's capacity to implement transformational and developer models appeared to increase as did his or her capacity to adapt the American models to the Sri Lankan context.

Examples of Reframing Leadership at Conformist and Autonomous Ego Stages

Implications of ego stage differences in the reframing process can be illustrated by contrasting two individuals who are four steps apart in ego stage.

Mr. Wijesinghe. In his mid-50s, Mr. Wijesinghe (described earlier to illustrate conformist managers' responses to the leadership conceptualization task) is a senior finance manager of a large public sector corporation responsible for a large department. He illustrates a reframing of leadership that reflects movement from the conformist to the self-aware stage. He described his realization that his older model of leadership was inadequate and that newer, more flexible models would be more effective. In his writing, one sees a change in stage-related thought structures. In describing the basic assumptions of autocratic, technician, and developer models, Mr. Wijesinghe found a need to revise his past assumptions. His thinking shows the understanding of choices and possibilities that is indicative of the self-aware stage. "Now I realize that I have to change the style of leadership for I have been using an inappropriate style. The different models of leadership have to be examined and the most suitable model has to be adopted."

This manager's self-assessment confirms that he is undertaking a fundamental change in perspective. Frequently, his self-set recommendations indicate reframed ways of understanding supervisory situations. This changed thinking is apparent in his learning priorities; for example, learning to give negative feedback without discouraging subordinates:

Now I have learned that *I should not say* to a subordinate who has not performed well that "I know that you did not have the ability to do it" but *I should say* "There is more that you can do and I have confidence" (e.g., About learning to give up heroic control). Now I see change as a step at a time that moves the issue beyond giving up control to expanding control.

Other learning priorities include using daily problems as opportunities to bring change, creating more shared responsibility ("I have to get them to join me in figuring out what has to be done and how to do it"), correcting misperceptions of people based on initial impressions, and increasing two-way communication in the organization. In these statements, one sees a clear movement away from unexamined behavior to self-chosen behavior based on greater self-awareness, increased awareness of the effect of one's behavior on others, and also more flexibility.

Will he be more effective if he changes his authoritarian style? Mr. Wijesinghe argued that it is necessary and gave examples of potentially improved supervisory situations in his work setting. However, learning new behavior without role models in a nonreinforcing context is difficult. Changing his management style will require simultaneous personal development and change in organizational norms.

> When I start along the path of managing as a developer, I may find some subordinates not cooperative, suspicious, resistant, dependent or unable to work together. I have to change slowly. I must build up confidence of my subordinates and eliminate their fears.

Although he did not discuss it, Mr. Wijesinghe will necessarily become, in adopting the Manager-as-Developer model, an agent of cultural change in the organization. Quite probably, his effectiveness will increase, although his ability to change others in his organizational context will be an important factor in actualizing his new vision.

Mr. Perera.   A manager at the autonomous stage responded to the leadership conceptualization task by adding a third dimension of "caring" to situational leadership models emphasizing task- and relationship-oriented behavior. His response illustrates the capacity of individuals at later stages to reframe leadership very complexly, very personally, and in broad cultural perspective. He created his own model and specifically addressed its cross-cultural dimensions.

In his model, "caring" refers to behavior that affirms that followers are not merely resources to achieve results, but that they have intrinsic value. This adaptation is argued as necessary in Sri Lanka to balance the western focus on results. The importance of caring is traced to religious values and also to the collectivist nature of Sri Lankan culture in which obligations to others are strong and mutual indebtedness between employer and employees must be expressed in caring. "Surely, leaders in a country steeped in Buddhist culture, with its central concept of 'universal kindness,' or 'maithri,' must affirm the concept of caring in their leadership style." *Balance* in this model is achieved by consistent, long-term caring, independent of situational variables. Subordinates' needs for security, as well as the traditional high power distance characteristic of Sri Lankan superior–subordinate relationships, are taken into account; however, long-term effectiveness requires the leader to seek to change subordinates' expectations. The goal is high relationship, and appropriate task-oriented behavior within a context of consistent caring.

Culturally based objections to the model (e.g., the showing of excessive caring and, therefore, the possible creation of lax discipline) are discussed in terms of the paradox that caring sometimes requires more discipline than autocratic behavior. The objection that subordinates may take advantage of a "soft" management style is countered by the idea that being soft requires a toughness in interpersonal communication that is beyond most autocratic managers.

The leader's role as a creator of contexts and an agent of change is stressed. If the followers are not ready to be challenged, the leader must initiate the change. Further, the leader needs to be somewhat independent of cultural factors while taking them into account.

> The leader must not be passive in his interaction with cultural factors. Cultural values are not sacrosanct. At times the leader may have to act counter to cultural norms. Ultimately, the leader must judge the appropriateness of his actions in terms of how those actions are consistent with his philosophy of leadership; not in terms of what is culturally appropriate. . . . The manager should view sociocultural factors as the context within which he must operate. Some of these factors will be opportunities to express his leadership style while others will be constraints that need to be removed or circumvented. . . . The leader has to "sell" a new set of values in place of the old.

In this leadership model, the characteristics of someone at the autonomous stage are apparent: cognitive complexity, ability to identify complex patterns and interrelationships, ability to see things from multiple perspectives, ability to recognize and deal with paradox, a perspective both inside and outside of one's role and culture, reliance on internal authority, and a compelling concern for learning, change, and development. Additionally, Mr. Perera has been inventive in framing a leadership philosophy that consciously addresses both his personality (he described himself as having a natural inclination to be people-oriented) and Sri Lankan culture.

In this conceptualization, there is no evidence of stage change, as is the case with Mr. Wijesinghe. The evidence is of a greatly expanded ability to adapt foreign leadership models to local circumstances—an ability that is stage-related. Mr. Perera is eloquently effective at framing a response that adapts the situational leadership model to the Sri Lankan situation. His unique contribution lies in conceptualizing a model that other Sri Lankan managers can utilize and that westerners can use to understand the culturally dependent dimensions of their leadership ideas.[3]

Both Mr. Wijesinghe and Mr. Perera can be effective managers in contexts where their strengths match their organization's needs. Further, each reveals how the interaction of developmental stage change and cultural change makes reframing leadership complex and difficult. Sri Lankan managers adopting western leadership models are required to change their organizational cultures as well as aspects of themselves. Thus, for this group of managers, the developmental crucible, already accelerated, may be stronger and more apparent.

Reframing Leadership Across Cultural Differences

Throughout this chapter, it has been demonstrated that the context for leadership is strongly different in Sri Lanka than it is in the United States and other western or developed nations. However, on the dimension of human development, it appears that the process of reframing one's leadership capabilities follows similar patterns despite cultural differences. Moreover, this capacity to reframe ideas is what appears to allow for cross-cultural synthesis. Individuals at later developmental stages are more able to adapt foreign models of leadership practice and also to create individual models suited to their specific situation. At earlier stages, theories are either adopted uncritically or experienced as "not fitting." At later stages, people are more likely to reframe or modify theory, retaining essential elements, but discarding or changing assumptions that are counter to one's circumstances. In some instances, one's current assumptions are questioned and revised. A vital activity in this adaptation process is examining one's assumptions and reframing the basis for "fit."[4]

---

[3]Basseches (1984), in describing work as a context for adult development, discusses the structural characteristics of jobs in relation to adult development stages. In Basseches' classification, Mr. Wijesinghe, at Loevinger's conformist stage, represents Stage 3, the "coal miner," in which conflicts are resolved by promoting conformity to shared norms and adjudicating between one's own perspective, others' perspectives, and those of norm-bound social groups. However, Mr. Wijesinghe is moving toward Stage 4, the "executive stage," in which the organizational system is prominent. Mr. Perera, discussed as representative of managers at Loevinger's autonomous stage, represents Basseches' Stage 5, or "social theorist," whose goal is transforming existing systems toward more ideal ones. The social theorist adopts the additional perspectives of the ideal, the universal, and those of an observer and becomes a transformational leader through his ability to integrate multiple, disparate realities.

[4]Argyris and Schon (1974) have developed a methodology to increase managerial competence by asking managers to generate case incidents involving their behavior and examine them for discrepancies between their espoused values and the values implicit in their actual behavior. The process of discovering these incongruities, and searching for actions that are congruent, stimulates personal development. A similar process of questioning assumptions can occur when cross-cultural differences are made salient.

The range of these managers' responses to western leadership models illustrates this adaptive process with regard to cultural context. One manager who found the developer model personally appealing commented that he could not practice it in Sri Lanka because of the educational level of the workers, but could practice it outside the country and had done so. Others believed that it could be practiced in Sri Lanka and that it was needed. Some viewed traditional Sri Lankan assumptions of supervisor and subordinate roles as responsible for keeping Sri Lankan workers passive and inefficient. For these managers, Sri Lanka was seen as an extreme case of "fit" for which the more participative western models, with opposite cultural assumptions, were the cure.

Others rather straightforwardly found ways to apply the essential ideas, adapting them stylistically to Sri Lankan settings. For example, a manager-owner who had the opportunity to establish teamwork and the shared responsibility concept at a newly established coconut factory did so and reported success. At the groundbreaking ceremony, he consciously deviated from cultural norms to emphasize the employees' importance at the event, in addition to acknowledging high status guests who expected recognition.

Cultural Synergy in Management Thinking

One way to explain why so many of these Sri Lankan managers found value in western participative models, and in the Manager-As-Developer model in particular, lies in these middle and later stage individuals' abilities to adapt leadership ideas despite a divergent context. A second explanation lies in the possibility and the importance of culturally synergistic thinking in management practice (Nanayakkara, 1989; Weathersby, 1989).

Important Sri Lankan values create synergy or "fit" with the developer concept. The developer model insists on a fundamental shift of perspective, making a manager's primary value the development of co-workers and subordinates through collective vision, teamwork, and continuous skill development on the job. This mindset taps deeply into the Sri Lankan belief that a well run enterprise should function, in part, like a family to promote the collective welfare of employees and society. The developer model also builds on the honored role of the teacher in eastern cultures. It mitigates the high power distance in the society. It allows expansion of caring, using the workplace as an extended family. It promotes productivity through two-way communication and mutual problem solving. Essentially, spiritual values and management effectiveness are merged.

One illustration of this cultural difference in emphasis was found on the cover of the Postgraduate Institute of Management's (PIM) program brochure, depicting the profile of a mother instructing a small child:

> An expression of PIM's management philosophy of "holism and humanism in our cultural context" which is characterized by the Fivefold Path in organizational life: Vision, Effort, Harmony, Restraint, and Caring. It is illustrated in the parallel between the role of the mother in taking the children through such a fivefold path and that of a top manager of an organization in Sri Lanka. The Father's role in the family is parallel to that of an entrepreneur in management.

It is ironic that a model designed for highly technical, "cutting edge" organizations in America is perhaps just as suited, although for different reasons, to the practice of management in a South Asian nation with a developing economy. These different values in Sri Lankan culture enable managers to understand developmental leadership in ways that go beyond the understanding of managers in the United States. Given their more "masculine" achievement-oriented values (Hofstede, 1980), it may be more difficult for American managers to develop the mentality suggested by this framework. It is certain that, for these Sri Lankan managers, the fit with their situation engages their culture's collectivist and spiritual values in addition to the American concern for creating excellence through harnessing individual productivity.

There is opportunity here for mutual learning. No culture has a monopoly on the universals of leadership. The path of synergy requires the combining of different perspectives to produce "something new" or "something more" that is not found in either perspective. It is this thoughtful engagement with difference that will allow international managers to understand and use the strengths of diverse cultures in promoting organizational goals.

CONCLUSIONS

Constructive–developmental theory suggests that later stage managers would be better implementers of developmental and transformational leadership models and, thus, better able to guide organizations in times of fundamental restructuring. Sri Lanka's need to advance economically in an increasingly interdependent world economy would seem to require more managers at the later stages of adult development. The responses of this high stage group of managers indicate that potentiality.

Yet transformation occurs at all levels, from where people are to where they can go next. Change is frequently incremental and one person's abandoned assumptions may be someone else's newly acquired insights. No one group has a monopoly on transformation. Implementation can occur at all levels. It simply works differently given different contexts and implementers. Because constructive–developmental theories make a convincing case that higher is better (and the percentage of individuals at the later stages in any society is relatively rare),[5] it is important to make the case that good managers at *all* levels are needed, in Sri Lanka and elsewhere.

Reframing leadership is a global concern. We all have a stake in enhancing everyone's capacity to enhance productivity and, finally, to collaborate across widely divergent philosophies, economies, technologies, and degrees of wealth. Cultural synergy in views of leadership and the common dynamics of human development are critical factors in framing a world system based on assumptions of complementarity.

In that spirit, this study has:

1. Demonstrated that this group of Sri Lankan managers' leadership conceptualizations reflect developmental patterns characteristic of their ego stage scores.
2. Indicated that, for this group, the process of reframing a personal conceptualization of leadership appears to be enhanced by higher ego level and, frequently, to follow the dynamics of developmental stage change.
3. Suggested that individuals at later stages are more able to modify and implement foreign leadership models and to create appropriate synergy within their cultural context.
4. Highlighted the role of the leader as an agent of cultural change with prerequisite personal development as an important factor in that role.

ACKNOWLEDGMENTS

The author is grateful for the ongoing friendship, collaboration, and inspiration extended by the faculty, staff, and students of the Postgraduate Institute of Management of the University of Sri Jayawardenapura, Sri

---

[5]It cannot be said frequently enough that the intrinsic value of being human is independent of stage. In specifying that higher stage is better the reference is to probable managerial outcomes. The case that higher stage individuals are more *likely* to be managerially effective and more able to practice transformational leadership is well conceptualized (Bartunek et al., 1983; Fisher & Torbert, 1991; Fisher et al., 1987; Torbert, 1991). However, other influences, especially a match with one's context and historical situation, also determine an individual's effectiveness in any given situation. Each person's and each stage's strengths thus are needed.

Lanka. Special thanks go to Dr. Gunapala Nanayakkara, Director of the Postgraduate Institute of Management, and to Professor Robin Willits of the University of New Hampshire, whose continued efforts created many fruitful exchanges.

Appreciation is also extended to the United States Information Agency for funding the Partnership in Management Education Program that created 3 years of cooperative faculty exchanges between the Whittemore School of Business and Economics at the University of New Hampshire and the Postgraduate Institute of Management of the University of Sri Jayawardenapura, Sri Lanka.

REFERENCES

Adler, N. J. (1991). *International dimensions of organizational behavior* (2nd ed.). Boston: PWS-Kent.

Argyris, C., & Schon, D. (1974). *Theory in practice: Increasing professional effectiveness.* San Francisco: Jossey-Bass.

Bartunek, J., Gordon, J., & Weathersby, R. (1983). Developing complicated understanding in administrators. *Academy of Management Review, 8,* 272–284.

Basseches, M. (1984). *Dialectical thinking and adult development.* Norwood, NJ: Ablex.

Bennis, W. (1989). *On becoming a leader.* Reading, MA: Addison Wesley.

Bradford, D., & Cohen, A. (1984). *Managing for excellence: The guide to developing high performance in contemporary organizations.* New York: Wiley.

Edwards, C. P. (1986). Cross-cultural research on Kohlberg's stages: The basis for consensus. In S. Modgil (Ed.), *Lawrence Kohlberg: Consensus and controversy* (pp. 419–430). London: Falmer Press.

Fisher, D., Merron, K., & Torbert, W. (1987). Human development and managerial effectiveness. *Group & Organization Studies, 12*(3), 257–273.

Fisher, D., & Torbert, W. R. (1991). Transforming managerial practice: Beyond the achiever stage. *JAI Press, 5,* 143–173.

Frost, P. J., Moore, L. F., Louis, M. R., Lundberg, C. C., & Martin, J. (1985). *Organizational culture.* Newbury Park, CA: Sage.

Galaz-Fontes, J. F., Hernandez Morelos, I. G., Sierra Morelos, I., Miranda-Romero, B. E., Commons, M. L., & Morse, S. J. (1991). *Leadership may provide the means of moving up in adult moral developmental stages.* Paper presented at the Sixth Adult Development Symposium, Society for Research on Adult Development, Suffolk University, Boston, MA.

Gratch, A. (1985). *Managers' prescriptions of decision-making processes as a function of ego development and of the situation.* Unpublished manuscript, Teachers College, Columbia University, New York.

Harvey, O. J., Hunt, D. E., & Schroeder, H. M. (1961). *Conceptual systems and personality organization.* New York: Wiley.

Hofstede, G. (1980, Summer). Motivation, leadership and organization: Do American theories apply abroad? *Organizational Dynamics,* 42–63.

Hofstede, G. (1984). *Culture's consequences: International differences in work-related values* (abridged edition). Beverly Hills, CA: Sage.

Kegan, R. (1982). *The evolving self.* Cambridge, MA: Harvard University Press.

Kohlberg, L. (1969). Stage and sequence: The cognitive-developmental approach to socialization. In D. A. Goslin (Ed.), *Handbook of socialization theory and research* (pp. 347–502). Chicago: Rand McNally.

Lasker, H. (1978). *Ego development and motivation: A cross-cultural cognitive-developmental analysis of achievement.* Unpublished doctoral dissertation, University of Chicago, Chicago, IL.

Loevinger, J. (1976). *Ego development: Conceptions and theories.* San Francisco: Jossey-Bass.

Loevinger, J., & Wessler, R. (1970). *Measuring ego development* (Vol. 1 and Vol. 2). San Francisco: Jossey-Bass.

McCrae, R., & Costa, P. T. (1980). Openness to experience and ego level in Loevinger's sentence completion test: Dispositional contributions to developmental models of personality. *Journal of Personality and Social Psychology, 39,* 1179–1190.

Merron, K., Fisher D., & Torbert, W. (1987). Meaning making and management action. *Group & Organization Studies, 12*(3), 274–286.

Morgan, G. (1986). *Images of organization.* Newbury Park, CA: Sage.

Nanayakkara, G. (1989, Winter). Synergy and alternatives. *Whittemore Review, 5* (Whittemore School of Business and Economics, University of New Hampshire).

Nevis, E. (1983). Using an American perspective in understanding another culture: Toward a hierarchy of needs for the People's Republic of China. *Journal of Applied Behavioral Science, 19*(3), 249–264.

Piaget, J., (1967). *Six psychological studies.* New York: Random House.

Quinn, R., & Torbert, W. (1987). *Who is an effective transforming leader?* Unpublished manuscript, University of Michigan, School of Business, Ann Arbor.

Smircich, L., & Morgan, G. (1982). Leadership: The management of meaning. *Journal of Applied Behavioral Science, 18*(3), 257–273.

Smith, S. (1980). *Ego development and the problems of power and agreement in organizations.* Unpublished doctoral dissertation, George Washington University, Washington, DC.

Snarey, J. R. (1985). Cross-cultural universality of social-moral development: A critical review of Kohlbergian research. *Psychological Bulletin, 97*(2), 202–232.

Stewart, E. C. (1972). *American cultural patterns: A cross-cultural perspective.* Yarmouth, ME: Intercultural Press.

Tietjen, A. M., & Walker, L. J. (1985). Moral reasoning and leadership among men in a Papua New Guinea society. *Developmental Psychology, 2*(6), 982–992.

Torbert, W. R. (1983). *Identifying and cultivating professional effectiveness: "Bureaucratic action" at one professional business school.* Paper presented at the annual meeting of the American Society of Public Administration, New York.

Torbert, W. R. (1987). *Managing the corporate dream: Restructuring for long-term success.* Homewood, IL: Dow Jones Irwin.

Torbert, W. R. (1991). *The power of balance: Integrating power and justice, inquiry and productivity.* Beverly Hills, CA: Sage.

Weathersby, R. (1981). Ego development. In A. W. Chickering (Ed.), *The modern American college.* San Francisco: Jossey-Bass.

Weathersby, R. (1989, Winter). Culture and management thinking. *Whittemore Review,* 4–5 (Whittemore School of Business and Economics, University of New Hampshire).

Weathersby, R. (1991). *Leadership and ego development: A study of Sri Lankan managers' leadership conceptualizations.* Paper presented at the Sixth Adult Symposium, Society for Research in Adult Development, Suffolk University, Boston, MA.

Weathersby, R., Bartunek, J. M., & Gordon, J. R. (1982). Teaching for "complicated understanding." *EXCHANGE: The Organizational Behavior Teaching Society Journal, 7*(4), 7–15.

Weathersby, R. P., & Tarule, J. M. (1980). *Adult development: Implications for higher education.* Washington, DC: American Association for Higher Education, AAHE-ERIC/Higher Education Research Report No. 4.

CHAPTER SIX

Issues of Maturation in the Seasoned Psychotherapist

Carl Goldberg
Albert Einstein College of Medicine
New York City

Mature clinical practice is the time in our career when we can most wisely reflect on our own experience. I have been a psychotherapist for the past 25 years. I have reached a point in my career and personal life at which people generally ask themselves some vital questions about where they have come in their lives and what is still realistically attainable in the time they have left. This crucial inquiry about how we will design our life structure has to do with the vital tasks of mid-life that adult developmentalists (e.g., Levinson, 1978) have told us each individual has to undergo in mid-life in order to appropriately direct one's life toward the requirements of constructive maturity.

Reflecting on my own life and professional career, I wondered what other experienced practitioners have had to report about how the developmental issues of mid-life and the years beyond affected their lives and practices. For example, in what ways have they found their daily existence to be subjectively and qualitatively different from that of a younger and less experienced person?

In extensively searching the psychological literature on the lives and practices of mature practitioners,[1] I found little empirical data or sub-

---

[1] Who the "seasoned" practitioner is cannot be calculated by simply the number of years of clinical practice. Each practitioner will phenomenologically experience his or her therapeutic maturity in his or her own particular way. Generally, however, we can operationally define the experienced practitioner as someone who has had a serious commitment to being a practitioner for at least a decade.

stantial research on how psychotherapists handle the issues of mid-life and the years beyond. It is curious that a profession that purportedly holds empirical research in the highest regard has not scientifically investigated the subject of practitioner maturity, which is of crucial and direct consequence to the lives of both therapists and patients.

My own need to have a perspective from which to view and understand my own mid-career issues would be addressed by even a few insightful self-reports from senior practitioners, responding to the issue of whether or not mature therapists are similar to other mature people who are not healing practitioners. Their personal accounts would help to answer the central questions that I have tried to address in my recent book (Goldberg, 1992) from which this chapter has been distilled: "Do mature psychotherapists face the same developmental concerns as other people or do they have unique issues?" and "Does being a well trained and experienced examiner of the human psyche lead to richer, wiser, and more mature lives than they would have been capable of living had they not become a psychotherapist?"

In self-reflective exploration, these questions seem to be the kinds of inquiry that thoughtful practitioners would periodically ask themselves in trying to understand their relationships with their patients. Nevertheless, my search of the psychological and psychoanalytic literature unearthed few personal vignettes (or even statements) about how mature practitioners have dealt with such life issues. What I found the most astounding, however, was that the largest source of information about the lives of experienced practitioners was found in popular literature rather than in social science publications. The impression that these popular accounts give about the practice and personal character of psychotherapists is almost entirely virulent. Many of these short stories and novels appear to be thinly disguised accounts of the authors' personal experiences as patients with therapists, who are most often presented as undergoing personal crises or bedeviled by unusual abnormalities. This stress or deviance leads the therapists to commit questionable or unethical behavior with their patients. The best known of these stories is F. Scott Fitzgerald's (1977) *Tender is the Night*.

A few senior practitioners have themselves written novels about the practice of psychotherapy. The best of these are the early novels of Allen Wheelis, an eminent San Francisco psychoanalyst, who portrays the perils of mature therapeutic practice in his novels. Such literature on psychotherapeutic practice compels the experienced practitioner to walk alone into the night. It provides the unmistakable impression that the vast material on therapeutic practice focuses almost exclusively on understanding the neophyte practitioner.

Yet, the task of maturation is continuous, never finally secured. Each stage of life imposes new demands and re-examination of previous life satisfactions and solutions. Nonetheless, those who write on the subjects of psychoanalysis and psychotherapy have made the tacit assumption that, once the practitioner acquires clinical skills, he or she should be able to maintain these skills with facility over a lifetime (Goldberg, 1990). Those who make this assumption serve their colleagues poorly. As senior practitioners, we can no longer afford to disregard the process of *disillusionment* that comes about through aging and maturation, a troubling disillusionment that has seriously afflicted a considerable number of practitioners (if not every practitioner of psychotherapy) at some point in his or her senior years of practice.

Clearly, serious dissatisfactions in one's practice and/or private life will reduce clinical effectiveness. No less significantly such dissatisfactions will concomitantly jeopardize the practitioner's physical, emotional, and spiritual well-being (Goldberg, 1990). Each vocational career has its own particular limitations and perils. There are some careers, however, that are downright dangerous at times. The practice of psychotherapy is one of these. The work in which we are involved has profound effects on our health and well-being.

As senior practitioners, we might learn from the mentoring of inspired role models who have struggled with these significant developmental issues before us. Unfortunately, our profession has fostered a mystique. As a result of the uniform unwillingness of experienced practitioners to supply information about themselves, we know less about the lives of psychotherapists than about members of any other prominent profession (Henry, Sims, & Spray, 1973). It would be, at best, a slight exaggeration to submit that most seasoned practitioners know little more about the issues of mature practice than what has actually happened in their own lives and practices. We probably know more about the private lives of our accountants, attorneys, and physicians than we do about our own colleagues.

As psychotherapists, we recognize that the serious personal issues of practice require open and frank discussion. However, as Burton (1972) indicated in his book about the lives of therapists, there is "a natural repugnance in man that militates against revealing the innermost details of his life" (p. 186). This reluctance for self-revelation is supported by scholarly tradition that maintains that the personal aspects of the scientist's or practitioner's life have no place in professional, let alone, popular publications.

This state of affairs is represented by the model of Sigmund Freud. In the introduction to Jones' (1961) biography, we are informed that "On several occasions Sigmund Freud expressed himself strongly against being made the subject of biographical study, giving as one of his reasons that the only important thing about him was his ideas—his personal life, he said, could not be of the slightest concern to the world'' (p. vii).

Freud was mistaken in his disregard for the biography of the psychotherapist. His endorsement of the obscurity of the clinician's private life has furnished an unfortunate mystique behind which psychotherapists (perhaps overly concerned that their patients would be adversely affected by learning intimate details about their clinicians' lives) have remained hidden. However, if my findings (Goldberg, 1992) accurately represent the current practice of psychotherapy, it would appear that the healing endeavor has become an increasingly less secretive process than it once was. Hopefully, by bringing out into the open experienced psychotherapists' personal concerns, this research will help to promote a greater understanding of psychotherapeutic practice as well as of the lives of the men and women who are involved in the task of healing the wounds of the human psyche.

REVIEW OF WHAT EXPERIENCED PSYCHOTHERAPISTS HAVE SAID ABOUT MATURE PRACTICE

What do we know about the old masters of psychoanalysis and psychotherapy that can help us with the way we practice and conduct our lives as senior practitioners today? An extensive search of the psychoanalytic and psychological literature clearly reveals that the master practitioners who came before us, although leaving us with a rich legacy of theory and technique, have written very little about the personal effect of their middle and senior years on their practices. This information, most definitely, would be of help to us in our own coming to terms with issues of mature practice.

Three of the most prominent practitioners of the past—Freud, Jung, and Rogers—seemed to have increasingly lost interest in conducting psychotherapy when they reached senior maturity. They spent more of their time writing theoretical rather than clinical papers and applying what they had learned from their clinical experiences to broad social issues.

For example, in his autobiography, Freud (1952) related the following about his last contributions to psychoanalysis: ''I myself find that a significant change has come about. Threads which in the course of my development had become intertangled have now begun to separate; interests which I had acquired in the later part of my life have receded, while the older and original ones become prominent once more'' (pp. 136–137). Freud also appeared to have been rather disheartened by what he regarded as the lack of importance of his later work. He indicated that, after 1923, "I have made no further decisive contributions to psychoanalysis; what I have written on the subject since then has been either unessential or would soon have been supplied by someone else" (p. 137).

The physical fatigue of aging may be a factor that wears down practitioners, contributing to their despair in finding meaning in the sunset of their lives. In her collaborative biography of Jung, Jaffe (1989) wrote of his last years: "No bounds could ever be set willingly to his questioning and inquiring spirit, but his body was tired, too tired to stand up to the demands of another round of creative work" (p. 115). Rogers (1975) also wrote of the physical strain of his own aging in reporting on his 46 years as a practitioner: "I am no longer actively engaged in individual therapy or empirical research . . . I am finding out as one passes 70, there are physical limitations on what one can do" (p. 143).

Physical health alone, however, does not explain the changes in the master practitioner's activities and interests. Jaffe indicated, in preparing Jung's autobiography with him, that: "During the years in which the book was taking shape a process of transformation was also taking place in Jung. With each succeeding chapter he moved, as it were, farther away from himself, until at last he was able to see himself as well as the significance of his life and work from a distance" (p. vii).

Rogers added to the perspective on the master practitioner, namely, that although his whole approach to people and their relationships only slowly changed as he aged, his understanding of how to apply his values and beliefs changed markedly. Similar to Freud and Jung, he became more interested in the ways that the educational principles of his therapeutic system could be taught to many more people through a well-conceived education program rather than in the individual benefits derived from being a psychotherapy client.

All three of these master practitioners expressed considerable disappointment in how few of their own cherished ideas were well received by their colleagues at the time of their conception. They also expressed reluctance in frankly discussing these disappointments. For example, Freud (1952) precipitously ended his autobiography by indicating that the public had no right to learn more of his personal struggles and disappointments than he had openly and frankly written about earlier. This is understandable because Freud felt that the earlier reporting of his own self-examination had not been well treated by many of his colleagues. Jung (Jaffe, 1989), however, took a more historical and universal perspective on the reception of his work in his lifetime: "If I ask the value of my life, I can only measure myself against the centuries and then I say, 'Yes, it means something. Measured by the ideas of today, it means nothing' " (p. xii).

The disappointment of Freud, Jung, and Rogers at the time of their contributions is somewhat understandable. They were highly innovative and creative theorists as well as longtime practitioners. It is an unfortunate but frequent occurrence that creative thinkers are misunderstood and underappreciated in their lifetimes. But what of less exceptional senior practitioners?

Whereas there are numerous studies of the satisfactions and disappointments in the careers of younger practitioners (e.g., Farber & Heifetz, 1981, 1982; Henry, Sims, & Spray, 1971, 1973), I uncovered only one empirical study measuring issues and concerns of the senior practitioner. Specifically, Kelly, Goldberg, Fiske, and Kilkowski (1978) provided data from a long-term follow-up study of those who interned as clinical psychology trainees at veterans administration hospitals (assessed in 1947, surveyed again in 1957, and then again in 1972). As a group, scholarly production was minimal; satisfaction with career choice, which was low at the 10-year mark, was even lower after 25 years. Therapists and researchers were the least satisfied, whereas diagnosticians and teachers were the most satisfied with their careers.

In that the master practitioners of the past have not reported extensively on the issues of mature practice, have senior practitioners in recent times provided more pertinent information? Hardly! The only empirical study I found that examined the clinical work of experienced practitioners was conducted by Whitehorn (1960). He demonstrated that, at different ages, psychiatrists with different personality structures related differently to patients. Specifically, some of these age-related therapeutic styles were found to "click" better with some patients than with others. In other words, not every patient in Whitehorn's study related best to the most experienced therapists.

Even impressionistic reports on mature practice are difficult to find. The few in the literature that there are usually report the influence of illness on the aging practitioner. For example, Weiner (1990) found, from interviews with 15 older psychiatrists, that they—similar to other older people deeply involved in their work—continue to practice as long as they possibly can and that poor health is the main factor for their retirement. In this regard, Maeder (1989) maintained that many psychotherapists seem unwilling to leave their practices when they have reached retirement age because of their need to be needed.

Dewald (1981), in discussing personal illness on mature practice, has suggested that countertransferential narcissism is involved in much of the adverse effect of illness on the aging practitioner. He points out that the anxiety and conflict aroused by personal illness is generally handled by denial and the enactment of the wish to avoid taking the topic seriously. Eissler (1977) is consistent with Dewald's view. He indicates that the analyst's narcissistic involvement in patients' clinical material heightens with age. However, he suggested that there may also be some positive consequences of the aged analyst's narcissism (see Goldberg, 1992).

The only book written on aspects of mature practice was edited by Burton (1972). This book provided autobiographic accounts of the lives of 12 prominent psychotherapists. Since these stories covered their entire careers and were written while each therapist was still practicing, only minimal aspects of senior practice were described.

RESEARCH PROJECT

Because no empirical data have been published on the crucial issues in the personal and professional lives of experienced psychotherapists, I decided to collect this information myself. Specifically, my overall research interest was embedded in the question, "What do seasoned practitioners do in their work and how do they feel about themselves and their patients that differs from when they were beginners?"

To answer my research question, I adopted five investigatory strategies:

1. In my sample I included members of the four prominent mental health disciplines: psychoanalysis, psychiatry, psychology, and social work.
2. I sought out practitioners both from throughout the United States and Canada.
3. I tried to include representatives of diverse cultural and ethnic groups. Previous investigators (e.g., Burton, 1972; Henry et al., 1971) concluded that their findings are representative of a highly circumscribed cultural–ethnic grouping rather than generalizable across cultures.
4. I decided that the most efficient method to collect information about how highly articulate, self-examined people conduct their lives was to employ a combination of questionnaires and in-depth personal interviews.
5. I compared my findings to those of two previous empirical studies on satisfying and stressful aspects of psychotherapeutic practice (Farber & Heifetz, 1981, 1982). I did this to evaluate my findings vis-à-vis what is already empirically known about the personal concerns of psychotherapists.

Despite these strategies, I make no claim that my findings are representative of the entire senior psychotherapist population in the United States or elsewhere. Questionnaires that probe people's private lives, no matter how well formulated, generally do not have high rates of returns. This may account for why surveys are sent out in large numbers.

In planning my study, I was faced with a related concern. Because of funding limitations, I needed to ensure the largest possible return of completed questionnaires relative to the number sent out. Mailing questionnaires to a randomly selected group of senior practitioners was, therefore, not cost efficient. I assumed that I would obtain a considerably higher rate of return from practitioners who knew me personally and believed that I would not misuse the information provided. Second, the study was limited by a self-selection process inherent in using volunteers. As I report later, a large number of practitioners sent questionnaires did not return them.

I also do not assume that my findings are representative of experienced psychotherapists of all different theoretical orientations. The information collected (see Goldberg, 1992) is probably more representative of those with psychoanalytic, psychodynamic, or existential/humanistic perspectives because these are the practitioners with whom I have the closest personal association. The ways in which behavioral and/or cognitive psychotherapists live and practice their profession may well be different from those of my respondents.

On the other hand, it is possible that my data actually represent the most seasoned practitioners. There is something about being a healer—regardless of the precise way that one's clinical practice is theoretically formulated—that draws practitioners together and suggests that we probably have some crucial core values in common. This is most likely true of experienced practitioners with different theoretical points of view than it is of beginners. The empirical research of Fiedler (1950) verifies this contention. He showed that, as therapists become more experienced, they tend to work more similarly to other senior therapists of different theoretical orientations than they do with less experienced therapists of their own theoretical persuasion.

Theoretical Assumptions

My questionnaire on mature practice (see Goldberg, 1992) was based on the following assumptions. First, I assumed that there are important issues and concerns that practitioners encounter in their mature years of practice that they do not anticipate when they start their careers. For instance, Rogers (1975) indicated that, when he looked back over nearly 50 years of practice, the major element of his reaction was "surprise" at what the work consisted of and how it was received by his colleagues. The significant issues of psychotherapeutic practice, when recognized, can be of critical value to all practitioners, not only experienced ones.

Further, Wheelis (1956) lamented that it is usually at mid-career that practitioners decide that their profession was chosen for the wrong reasons and come to believe that it is too late to do much about their commitment of the last two or three decades. Obviously, the practitioners' health would be far better served if the student and the beginning clinician had some reliable information to guide them in the assessment of whether they were embarking on the right career path.

Second, I also was interested in the ways that practitioners' views about neurosis and human nature had changed over their years of practice. I assumed that one of the most important factors to learn about mature practice concerned whether there was any significant change in the way that the practitioner now regards and responds to human suffering from the way he or she did in the past. I also assumed that, whatever the source of his or her own personal psychic pain, this angst would be significant in understanding the practitioner's current functioning as a psychotherapist. Correspondingly, I set out to query about life issues that may have decisively modified their youthful values, including their perspectives on neurosis and human nature.

In my experience as a psychotherapy educator, young practitioners seem to believe that psychoanalysis and psychotherapy are finely tuned rational tools that can successfully resolve all types of emotional conflict. Many of them view psychotherapy as an art that can be steadily and finally mastered from experience and perseverance. From my own clinical experience, I have found that, over time, my faith in psychological insight and in my own expertise has been replaced with more trust in my patients' inner wisdom and in the healing capacities of compassion, decency, and common sense. I was curious about the extent to which this experience was true of other seasoned practitioners.

Third, I also was curious about the most important lessons that seasoned psychotherapists had learned from their patients. Those who are called to the profession of psychological healer generally do so with an intense interest in finding out about themselves. They find a career that provides them with a continuous means for examining their own lives. I inquired about their personal analysis or psychotherapy as well as their own self-examination (self-analysis). I assumed that, unless practitioners are still interested in examining their own lives after completing their apprenticeships, they will feel restive and bored. In contrast, practitioners who are still available for further personal growth will be curious about the inner happenings of their patients in terms of what they can learn about themselves.

A well-known line from a poem by William Butler Yeats tells us that: "A man must choose perfection of the life or the work." Yeats was referring specifically to the life of the creative person. I was curious as to whether his statement held true for therapists as well as for artists. I assumed that the source of creative wisdom derives at least as much from the practitioner's private life as from his or her clinical practice. Therefore, I expected that those who currently experienced distress in their professional practice would also currently experience disappointments in their private life. I anticipated that the sources for both disappointment and satisfaction in practice could be tapped by asking practitioners about their "personal myth" or prototypic story that has direct implications for how one regards the world (e.g., its resources, opportunities, and impediments to the achievement of one's desires).

Background Information

Questionnaires were sent to 200 experienced psychotherapists. Fifty-three (26.5%) questionnaires were returned. In addition to these questionnaire data, I held in-depth interviews with 12 eminent psychotherapists. Demographic information on the subjects is provided in Table 6.1.

Due to space limitations, I discuss in this chapter only one overall impressionistic finding culled from the data thus far. This finding, which has important implications for understanding the developmental issues of the mature psychotherapist, serves as the basis for the remainder of this chapter.

A MULTIDIMENSIONAL THEORY OF MATURATION

Toward addressing the limitations of current theories of adult development (see Goldberg, 1992), the theoretical model that I posit consists of five existential polarities. These polarities have been conceptualized to exist in dialectic interaction with one another and have been posited in positive terms so as to provide a logical sequence for the crucial interrelationships of adult issues.

The idea that the conflictual struggles of seasoned psychotherapists might be usefully conceptualized through a multidimensional dialectic process initially came from my interview with a Boston analyst. Specifically, he spoke with acrimony about the vicious political battles in which many of his senior colleagues were involved. When I asked about the effects of their destructive power ploys on the ways they practiced psychotherapy, he stopped and thought for awhile. Then he told me:

> I hadn't thought of this before. But, perhaps, the way these power-driven guys practice clinically has nothing to do with how they conduct the other business in their lives. I say this because I have heard from a number of

TABLE 6.1
Background Information on Questionnaire Respondents

Number of questionnaires mailed	200
Number of returned questionnaires	53
Number of psychologists	34
Number of psychiatrists	15
Number of social workers	4
Number of men	37
Number of women	16

Nationality

U.S.A.	48
Canada	4
Switzerland	1

Theoretical Orientation

Psychodynamic	10
Existential–humanistic	5
Psychoanalytic	9
Object relations	4
Sullivanian	5
Eclective	4
Self-psychology	3
System theory	2
Ego psychology	1
(Erik) Eriksonian	1
Symbolic experiential	1
Modern psychoanalytic	1
Cognitive psychoanalytic	1
Horneyian	1
Bowen family systems	1
Crisis mobilization	1
Psychosynthesis	1
Gestalt	1
No designation	1

Prominent Analysts Interviewed

Men	8
Women	4

Theoretical Orientation

Psychoanalytic	12

101

different patients of many of these practitioners that these men are quite compassionate and sensitive analysts in their own offices.

I would not agree that the ways in which these men conducted their personal and professional lives are unrelated—no more than the kind of civilized private demeanors of Nazi doctors were unrelated to their inhumanity as concentration camp physicians (see Lifton, 1986). However, what is relevant is the necessity to disregard explanation of complex people (as most psychotherapists undoubtedly are) simply in terms of their psychological types. That is, it is erroneous to assume that any one of us is either essentially power driven or, actually underneath, a kind and caring person. All of us are many-sided.

The complexity of our personalities results from the *tension of opposites* in our attempts to come to terms with who we are and how best to articulate our sense of our personal identity to others. In many ways, Jung (1986), rather then Freud, has been the most helpful in understanding the conflictual issues in the lives of therapists as a dualistic struggle between creative and constructive forces. Indeed, the novel, *Tender is the Night*, was a literary exploration by Fitzgerald of Jung's thesis that a person in conflict is strongly attracted to a powerful force in another person that is sensed as a potential counterbalance to one's own overwhelming desires. The coming together of these magnetically drawn people, as Fitzgerald implied, results in the destruction of the apparently stronger, but actually weaker, personality.

I believe that Fitzgerald misread Jung in this regard. Based on the central doctrine of the ancient Greek philosopher, Heraclitus, it is the necessary tension between opposites that is the basis of harmony. Jung (1986) wrote that the striving for wholeness and self-realization requires a dialectic process within the personality. These speculations about the role of a dialectic process in self-realization seem similar to Jones' (1961) attempt to explain Freud's genius. Jones characterized Freud as motivated by an obstinate dualism that pervaded both his thinking and the way that he conducted his personal life. According to Jones, Freud was forever fighting pulls between scientific discipline and philosophical speculation as well as a number of other contradictory tendencies, including the capacity for both brilliant critical insights and facile gullibility.

Specifically, Jones (1961) explained the dualities in Freud's personality as follows:

> Now Freud had inherently a plastic and mobile mind, one given to the freest speculations and open to new and even highly improbable ideas. But it worked this way only on the condition that his ideas came from himself; to those from the outside he could be very resistant, and they had little power in getting him to change his mind. I was at first puzzled by this resis-

tiveness to outside opinion until I hit on what I consider to be the explanation of it. An intuition, soon confirmed by evidence, told me that side by side with Freud's great independence of mind and skeptical criticism of ideas was also a concealed vein of the very opposite—his restiveness was a defense against the danger of being too readily influenced by others . . . this curious strain in Freud's nature, far from being an unfortunate weakness or deficiency, constituted an essential part of his genius. He was willing to believe in the improbable and the unexpected—the only way, as Heraclitus pointed out centuries ago, to discover new truths. It was doubtless a two-edged weapon. It led Freud at times into making serious misjudgments, possibly even ridiculous ones, but it also enabled him dauntlessly to face the unknown. (pp. 379–380)

Following my rereading of Jones' account of Freud, I interviewed a New York analyst and asked if his notions about neurosis and human nature had changed over the course of his career. He told me the following:

I do a lot of writing so I am always reformulating my ideas about myself and my work. It is difficult to give you any one direction that characterizes my work. As I finish one paper I am already criticizing that position in another. I used to be tough on myself. I used to say to myself, I no longer believe that nonsense. How could I have ever thought that way! I no longer do that myself. I now know that I am going to change my views about my work and my life and I feel good about that. It is quite exciting to me. I have increasingly come to believe that it is the novelty of the situation rather than a truth buried deep in the unconscious that makes for constructive therapeutic action. If you start to think about things differently you can go on from there and you need not stop growing.

Similar in some ways to Jones' description of Freud's creative process, this analyst was alluding to the intricacies of the *dialectic process* as the receptive epigenetic crucible of interaction between stability and change that is essential to natural growth and maturity. Thus, the language of dialectics provides us with a vibrant and complex explanatory set of processes, a fertile context from which to understand human behavior and experience.

For example, it is perhaps more accurate to describe people who have lived deeply as moving between positions of having known deep love as well as intense hatred, rather than trying to determine whether they are a warm, kind person or an angry, hostile one. I take the position that a person is not really one "true self"—hidden intrapsychically, there to be discovered only by sophisticated psychological inquiry. Metaphorically, each of us may be described as consisting of many "selves." This concept is similar, but not identical, to what Jung has described as an *archetype*. It is instructive to our understanding of psychodynamics to

regard these selves (as Jung did with archetypes) as more or less elastical-
ly interrelated patterns of behavior existing between two significant life
forces.

For the most part, each of these selves, in the Jungian sense, expresses
itself at any one time in terms of a "manifestly operative polarity" and
a "latently potentially operative polarity." From this frame of reference,
ambivalence and personal conflict have two major sources. Most often,
these are moments in the life cycle in which both sides of one of these
selves are vying for dominance to express their dispositional needs. For
example, patients in psychological treatment vacillate between intense
personal curiosity about their own motivations and a morbid fear of what
they might discover and believe that they cannot accept about themselves.
Our times of greatest crisis are when two or more of these selves operate
antagonistically toward each other. This conflict may, in a devastating
manner, threaten the integrity and survival of one's personality as exemplified by Sid Fallon's case (discussed in Goldberg, 1992). Fallon's need
for feeling professionally competent was in violent conflict with that of
allowing himself to respond compassionately to a highly disturbed patient, who was derisive of his professional competence.

In the Eriksonian sense, the side of the polarized-self that is most likely to take dominance, at any particular time in our lives, is ordered by
the way in which we have negotiated specific identity issues earlier in
our lives. However, were this the only operating force in our personalities, behavior would remain largely constant. We cannot understand human growth and creativity unless we recognize that intrinsic to human
intentionality is not only a curiosity about the external world but, just
as impellingly, a curiosity about the other polarized-selves in our personality and a desire to interact intimately with and participate in the lives
of our other selves.

The nature of these interactions are heavily influenced by the developmental issues in our lives at the moment. As common sense tells us, these
developmental issues are best handled by a person who has the most flexible access to both sides of each polarized-self and has the resources (e.g.,
courage and trust in oneself) to enable these selves to interact construc-
tively and creatively. Moreover, at any stage of our lives in which a dialectic issue is denied or circumvented, serious problems in psychological
growth will likely arise. It should also be pointed out that external crises
are not the only causes of tension among the selves. These aversive feelings will ensue even following successful resolution of developmental
issues because a growthful personality never remains integrated in the
same way for long.

I believe that Freud's (1937) recommendation that practitioners "enter analysis once more at intervals of, say, five years and without any feeling of shame in so doing'' was based on his intuitive recognition of the sequence of developmental crises in the lives of psychotherapists. As may be deduced from earlier discussion, Freud's advice in this matter has largely been ignored.

My view of what constitutes these polarized-selves differs in some ways from what I understand to be Jung's conceptualization of an archetype. People differ, in Jung's view, as to which specific archetypes are available and operative in their lives. In contrast, everyone shares the same existential issues that comprise the polarized-selves. Therefore, according to my theoretical position, the question is not: what is the dominate force(s) in that person's life (an inquiry about archetypes), but rather under what conditions and circumstances does one side of a polarized-self dominate rather than another, and what are the potentially constructive and creative energies of the interacting selves that are being fostered at that stage of the person's life? Both resolution of tension and creative expression come from the successful cooperation of a well articulated side of two or more polarized-selves.

POLARITIES DERIVED
FROM BASIC EXISTENTIAL ASSUMPTIONS

I approach the question of what are the forces in the human condition that determine the issues that need to be addressed in mid-life and the years beyond from a small number of existential assumptions. These assumptions are consonant with Kelly's (1963) personality theory. Specifically, Kelly indicated that the dichotomizing of experience is not necessarily a product of the individual's conflictual relation to the world nor to oppositional instincts within his or her psyche. According to Kelly, duality is an essential attribute of thinking itself. An individual creates his or her own way of perceiving the world by formulating experience in terms of *constructs* with varying degrees of predictive efficiency. The cardinal principle that guides the use of one construct rather than another one is that the need to make sense of one's being-in-the-world organizes all our other needs and motives. These constructs are, of course, not passive speculative beliefs. They are implicit strategies for taking action in such a way to live most meaningfully vis-à-vis how the individual has come to understand and master his or her world. Therefore, those constructs that offer an individual what is to him or her the best predictive option for understanding one's experience will be the most attractive among the opposing alternatives in any given situation. Some of these options are transient and represent only the convenience of the moment. Still others are more enduring in terms of their roles in presenting options for living one's life meaningfully and well.

My theoretical system implies that the overriding task for the individual at each stage of the life cycle is to make sense of one's existence in terms of one's *personal identity*. An individual's personal identity is a complex enterprise. It consists not only of the sense of who one currently is. It also includes beliefs and desires about who one should be and what one can become. From this context, every action and interaction on one's part may be judged in terms of the information it provides for either substantiating, or disconfirming, the self that one desires to be. Where there is a congruent fit between the experiences of the tested self (e.g., the import of one's senses about the circumstances of one's life) with the images, fantasies, and intentions of one's desired self, a feeling of competence and well-being accompanies these experiences. A lack of congruence results in shame and discontentment (Goldberg, 1991). The existential task of monitoring one's personal identity involves five basic questions to be answered in dialectic fashion in terms of five spheres of possibility in human existence. Each of the existential polarities are profiled in Table 6.2 and discussed extensively in Goldberg (1992). In previewing these dialectic issues, it is important to bear in mind, not only the specific contexts in which these issues are being enacted, but also how they interact with the other polarized-selves.

TABLE 6.2
Issues of Self-Realization in Adulthood: Five Existential Spheres

Developmental issue	Sensory-cognitive
Existential question	"What kind of person do I believe myself to be?"
Dialectic process	Certainty versus curiosity
Developmental issue	Courageous–creative
Existential question	"What experiments, exercises and ways of being will help me become the person I intend to become?"
Dialectic process	Discovery versus industriousness
Developmental issue	Intuitive–emotional
Existential question	"What fears and conditions are interfering with my experiencing all aspects of my existence directly?"
Dialectic process	Vulnerability versus power
Developmental issue	Passionate–social
Existential question	"How do I use my relationship with myself and with others to become the person I intend to become?"
Dialectic process	Self-awareness versus peer influence
Developmental issue	Volitional–spiritual
Existential question	"If I am the person I intend to be, how do I put my values into action?"
Dialectic process	Compassion versus emphasis on being accountable

REFERENCES

Burton, A. (1972). *Twelve therapists*. San Francisco: Jossey-Bass.

Dewald, P. A. (1981). Professional profile. When the analyst is seriously ill. Roche Report. *Frontiers of Psychiatry, 11,* 12–13.

Eissler, K. (1977). On the possible effects of aging on the practice of psychoanalysis. *Psychoanalytic Quarterly, 46,* 182–183.

Farber, B. A., & Heifetz, L. J. (1981). The stresses and satisfactions of psychotherapeutic work: A factor analysis study. *Professional Psychology, 12,* 621–630.

Farber, B. A., & Heifetz, L. J. (1982). The process and dimensions of burnout in psychotherapists. *Professional Psychology, 13,* 201–293.

Fiedler, F. (1950). The concept of an ideal therapeutic relationship. *Journal of Consulting Psychology, 14,* 239–245.

Fitzgerald, F. S. (1977). *Tender is the night*. New York: Macmillan.

Freud, S. (1937). *Analysis terminable and interminable* (standard ed.). London: Hogarth Press.

Freud, S. (1952). *An autobiographical study*. New York: Norton.

Goldberg, C. (1990). *On being a psychotherapist*. Northvale, NJ: Jason Aronson.

Goldberg, C. (1991). *Understanding shame*. Northvale, NJ: Jason Aronson.

Goldberg, C. (1992). *The seasoned practitioner—Triumph over adversity*. New York: Norton.

Henry, W. E., Sims, J. H., & Spray, S. L. (1971). *The fifth profession: Becoming a psychotherapist*. San Francisco: Jossey-Bass.

Henry, W. E., Sims, J. H., & Spray, S. L. (1973). *Public and private lives of psychotherapists*. San Francisco: Jossey-Bass.

Jaffe, A. (Ed.). (1989). *Memories, dreams and reflections*. New York: Random House.

Jones, E. (1961). *The life and work of Sigmund Freud*. New York: Basic Books.

Jung, C. G. (1986). *Symbols of transformation*. New York: Pantheon Press.

Kelly, E. L., Goldberg, L. R., Fiske, D. W., & Kilkowski, J. M. (1978). Twenty-five years later. *American Psychologist, 8,* 746–755.

Kelly, G. (1963). *A theory of personality*. New York: Norton.

Levinson, D. J. (1978). *The seasons of a man's life*. New York: Ballantine.

Lifton, R. (1986). *The nazi doctors*. New York: Basic Books.

Maeder, T. (1989, January). Wounded healers. *The Atlantic Monthly Magazine*, pp. 37–47.

Rogers, C. (1975). In retrospective: Forty-six years. In R. I. Evans (Ed.), *The man and his ideas*. New York: Dutton.

Weiner, M. F. (1990). Older psychiatrists and their psychotherapy practice. *American Journal of Psychoanalysis, 44,* 44–49.

Wheelis, A. (1956). The vocational hazards of psychoanalysis. *The International Journal of Psychoanalysis, 37,* 171–184.

Whitehorn, J.C. (1960). Studies of the doctor as a crucial factor for the prognosis of schizophrenic patients. *International Journal of Social Psychiatry, 6,* 71–77.

CHAPTER SEVEN

Life Themes Manifest Through Artistic Creativity

Lorraine Mangione
Antioch New England Graduate School

LIFE THEMES

Developmental theorists have differed over the nature of development as continuous or discontinuous, as well as whether it is more akin to a model emphasizing stages, straight lines, or dialectics (Wrightsman, 1980). In this chapter, the construct of *life themes* is suggested as one way in which both the seemingly radical changes and the repetitions over time can be understood and explored. Life themes is a useful construct for seeing, describing, understanding, and working with the consistencies, inconsistencies, coherencies, patterns, changes, and development of a whole person throughout his or her life span.

A major question that animates certain developmental theorists is the following: What changes, internally, as a person progresses through life and what does not change (Bee, 1987; Fiske & Chiriboga, 1990)? For example, Erikson (1950) emphasized a basic internal conflict at each stage of development; Levinson (1978) focused on the ways in which a person adapts internally to the external world at each stage; and Gould (1978) explicated the idea of identification with and giving up of myths. In this discussion of life themes, the focus is also on the internal world of the person and the attempt is to respond to the question of what does and does not change internally as a person develops.

When one sets out to examine a life (e.g., in psychotherapy, in an elderly person's life review, through one's personal soul searching, or in the

109

writing of a biography or autobiography) one often does find a thematic unity and a pattern to that life. There are links and leitmotifs weaving in and out of the different stories and events, changes and feelings, weaving through the years and decades. These links may be obscured to the person living them out but operative nonetheless. One of the ways the linkages are lived and expressed is through the psychological organizing principle of life themes.

If there were no life themes, daily living would have the feel of a concatenation of disparate, almost random events. The events would seem to have little coherency or connectedness other than that of time sequence and identity of the person. We would experience them as occurring one after the other and as happening to the same person, oneself, over time. Other than that, however, the choices, relationships, decisions, opportunities, difficulties, and situations of 5 years ago would have little bearing on and little relationship to those of today or the possibilities 5 years hence. It is suggested here that life themes are what keep most of our lives and selves from this daily experience of fragmentation. When this fragmentation and loss of connectedness to the self do occur, it is a signal that something is wrong and the person has become alienated from the ongoing, deeper meaning of his or her life.

Life themes and similar constructs have been decribed by personality researchers and theorists throughout the years. Murray (1938), from his elaborate studies of individual people and their needs and motivations, spoke of "unity themas":

> Experience was to teach us that, though the reasons for many of the subject's responses were mysterious and much of his past entirely out of reach, it was possible to find in most individuals an underlying reaction system, termed by us *unity-thema*, which was the key to his unique nature. I say "key" because if one assumed the activity of this unity-thema many superficially unintelligible actions and expressions became, as it were, psychologically inevitable. A *unity-thema* is a compound of interrelated—collaborating or conflicting—dominant needs that are linked to press to which the individual was exposed on one or more particular occasions, gratifying or traumatic, in early childhood. (p. 604)

G. Allport (1961) used the terms *cardinal* and *central traits* to describe the coherency and consistency of a person's life:

> In every personality there are p.d.'s [personality dispositions] of major significance and p.d.'s of minor significance. Occasionally some p.d. is so pervasive and so outstanding in a life that it deserves to be called a *cardinal* disposition. Almost every act seems traceable to its influence. . . . No such disposition can remain hidden, an individual is known by it, and may become famous for it. Such a master quality has sometimes been called the

eminent trait, the *ruling passion*, the *master-sentiment*, the *unity-thema*, or the *radix* of a life.

It is an unusual personality that possesses one and only one cardinal disposition. Ordinarily the foci of a life seem to lie in a handful of distinguishable central p.d.'s. How many is the question we shall ask presently. Central dispositions are likely to be those that we mention in writing a careful letter of recommendation. (p. 365)

. . . A *cardinal disposition*, for example, is, by definition, a mark of unity. Tolstoy's passion for the "simplification of life," or Schweitzer's guiding ideal of "reverence for life," like all cardinal traits, are unifying to a high degree. (p. 378)

Spotts and Shontz (1980) used life themes as a construct to organize their data and guide their understanding about people's lives. In an intensive study of several individuals who are serious cocaine users, they speak at length about life themes and their place in the personality organization of the men:

As the research progressed it became apparent that each participant's life style was organized around only a few (usually no more than five or six) underlying *life themes*. . . . Life themes are not to be thought of as traits or motives, for a theme is not an entity or force. Rather, life themes are the organizing principles that make a person's traits and motives understandable. For example, Arky L. has traits of gregariousness and rebelliousness, motives of hostility and revenge, and feelings of rejection and isolation. What gives these coherence is the recurrent theme in Arky's life that he is an alien in a complex and challenging world.

Choice and Inevitability

Several men seem to have made deliberate choices of life themes, and often it seems that their commitments were made very early. For example, Arky L. is aware of his commitment to being a robber and his reasons for making it. George's determination to make himself into a machine or fortress was probably deliberately made, perhaps at a specific moment. In the course of extensive work with business executives, one of the authors (J. V. S.) has noted that many of them can precisely identify the times when they decided to shape their lives in particular ways. Once adopted, a life theme has a fate-like or entelechial quality that makes it seem to have a destiny of its own. (pp. 487–488)

Thus, life themes are seen as significant and powerful in a person's life. For this chapter, life themes encompass several aspects:

1. They are *psychological* organizing principles of a person's life and experience and express an underlying order or coherency to a person's existence.

2. They occur with some degree of regularity in one's life because they represent issues of existence or ways of being in the world rather than problems that get solved once and for all.

3. Life themes include both content such as the issue of, for example, freedom, recurring in a person's life as well as process such as the tendency to take a confrontational approach toward others.

4. Themes do not *make* a person grow or change, but can be expressions of development (or stagnation) and signposts to further development.

5. A core of basic themes for most people probably exists, although there certainly can be infinite variety in the ways in which people live these themes out in their lives.

We do, in fact, live themes out in our daily lives. Themes are not merely abstractions; they are the foundations of everyday experience and infuse the manner in which a person gives meaning to or construes his or her existence, relationships, work situations, choices, and encounters. These themes exist even if the person is not aware of them. Becoming aware of them changes one's relationship to the themes and certainly elaborates them in the process, but talking about the person's life is not what *creates* the themes. They are there, not articulated, but affecting the person nevertheless. A person's relationship to his or her life themes can evolve and develop over a lifetime.

Life themes and their development are intimately involved with the concept of the self and the changes in the self over time. In keeping with some of the newer notions of a self that evolves over time and is more open-ended and in process (Kegan, 1982; Sampson, 1985), the life themes point to the ways in which the self changes over time. The periods of change and discontinuity are just as significant as the times of seeming stability. Sampson's (1985) model of personhood as one "whose very being hinges on its continuous becoming" (p. 203) is both exciting and unsettling in its ramifications for development. For the life themes to develop, they must be connected to a self that has, at the same time, both a stable core and great capacity for mutability. (See Mangione, 1990, for a more in-depth treatment of the relationship between life themes and the self.)

ARTISTIC CREATIVITY

Life themes are involved in many facets of a person's life and, thus, they can be studied through any one of their several avenues of expression. In this chapter, life themes are viewed in conjunction with artistic creativity.

Artistic creativity is one very important process through which a person works to create him or herself as well as the object of art itself. Having a significant creative project is a way for a person to work on and work out his or her issues of existence as embodied in the life themes and to create the self that one is to become. This same process occurs with other people who are not working as artists. One's self-creating project can be undertaken in many ways, particularly including one's vocation or avocation, if it is something to which the person is deeply committed and it involves risk-taking or challenge. A person profoundly involved in teaching science to high school students or on a quest to climb the Himalayas may be engaged in a personal project of the level described here. (A more complete description of "the self-creation project" can be found in Mangione, 1990.) For the artist, there is a special relationship between his or her work and vocation, as eloquently expressed by Rank (1932):

> Compared with the average professional man, the artist has, so to say, a hundred percent vocational psychology . . . One can say of the artist that he does not practise [sic] his calling, but is it, himself, represents it ideologically. For whereas the average man uses his calling chiefly as a means to material existence, and psychically only so far as to enable him to feel himself a useful member of human society—more or less irrespective of what his calling is—the artist needs his calling for his spiritual existence, just as the early cultures of mankind could not have existed and developed without art.
>
> For the artist, therefore, his calling is not a means of livelihood, but life itself. . . . (p. 371)

The artist represents a special case of the ultimate interconnection between psychological development and vocation. However, the intimate connection between life themes and one's "project" is posited to exist for other people as well. In this chapter, the manner in which life themes and artistic process are intertwined, and how understanding themes elucidates the artistic process and vice versa, are demonstrated and discussed.

METHOD

Representative Case Method

Since the 1980s, there has been an increasing and insistent voice in psychology arguing in favor of an expanded epistemology and methodology to either supplant or complement psychology's traditional emphasis on positivism and laboratory experiments. Some of these speakers include:

Gergen (1982, 1985) and the social constructionist movement in which the idea of one truth and one way is abandoned in favor of the concepts of interpretation and multiple viewpoints; Polkinghorne (1983; Hoshmand & Polkinghorne, 1992) and his emphasis on the need to create a human science that does not merely mimic the hard sciences; and various feminist thinkers (e.g., Flax, 1983; Harding, 1987; Keller, 1985) who question the biased, political, and patriarchal basis of the science of psychology as it now stands and push for the inclusion of relationship and subjectivity in research.

"Qualitative" research has gained stature alongside more traditional quantitative research, especially as psychologists have more seriously considered the idea of suiting the methodology to the problem at hand, rather than allowing one's choice of problem to be dictated by methodological limitations (Trierweiler & Stricker, 1992). Although laboratory-oriented quantitative research may provide general laws of human behavior, qualitative research with its emphasis on individual experience provides greater understanding of the ways in which general principles are lived out in the world. There is not one way of doing qualitative research, but an array of methods suitable to an array of problems (Patton, 1990). Case study research is one set of methods that has been reintroduced to mainstream psychology as a viable research tool (Yin, 1989).

The emphasis on narrative and what it can teach us about people's lives has also added to this discussion (Polkinghorne, 1988; Sarbin, 1986). Polkinghorne views narrative schemes as "ubiquitous in our lives" (p. 14) and basic to our sense of making meaning of our lives both as individuals and as a culture. He sees the possibility of a life-span psychology based on a "retrospective narrative understanding of individuals' pasts" (p. 118). He noted that "People use self-stories to interpret and account for their lives. The basic dimension of human existence is temporality, and narrative transforms the mere passing away of time into a meaningful unity, the self. The study of a person's own experience of her or his lifespan requires attending to the operations of the narrative form and to how this life story is related to the stories of others" (p. 119).

It is in the spirit of these visions and ideas that this project evolved. For this study, I was interested in finding a way to investigate the process of artistic creativity and the questions of the personality, development, and personhood of the artist with all of the depth, complexity, and contradictions inherent in such large questions. Previous research had addressed these questions in a more limited manner or, if it looked at the artist in a wholistic sense, it did so in more clinical or broadly theoretical treatises (see Mangione, 1984, for a description of this literature). Thus, a qualitative methodology—that would sacrifice a certain amount of neatness, specificity, quantitative rigor, and cause–effect relationships for the purpose of providing an in-depth portrait of the artist in conjunction with the process of creating art—was chosen.

The methodology used is the representative case method as developed by Shontz (Gordon & Shontz, 1990a; Shontz, 1965, 1976; Spotts & Shontz, 1980). It has been philosophically linked (Gordon & Shontz, 1990b) to: personology (Murray, 1938), with an emphasis on studying whole human beings in depth; human sciences (Polkinghorne, 1983; Ricoeur, 1981) and the need to create a more interpretive, dialectical science; phenomenological psychology (Giorgi, 1970; Mangione, 1984), in which the experience of the subject is considered of major importance; and feminist epistemologies (Mangione, 1991a), with the call for alternative methodologies that respect relationship, context, and meaning.

The case study is known as a familiar hypothesis-generating and teaching tool in psychology and especially in clinical work. Case studies are usually viewed as rich sources of ideas and stimulating dialogue, but certainly too impressionistic and retrospective to be considered "science." The representative case method, however, is purposefully designed to be a more rigorous kind of case study. It is planned in advance and can be exploratory, hypothesis testing, or both. It is always guided by specific ideas or questions from the literature or the researcher's own thinking, but with enough flexibility to allow for reworkings and modifications as the study proceeds.

This method constitutes an intensive study of one or a series of individuals who embody the process of interest, such as artistic creativity. It has been used to study diverse populations and issues, such as cocaine abusers, adjustment to spinal cord injury, the experience of being HIV positive, values in psychotherapy, and reminiscence in old age. Shontz (Gordon & Shontz, 1990b) described it as "well suited to learning about how individuals deal with critical human decisions and experiences" (p. 63).

Certainly the subject matter of the field of adult development is replete with human beings dealing with critical decisions and experiences as well as how these processes do or do not change over time. The representative case method is one way of allowing the individual, in all of his or her nuances and complexity, to enter into psychological research and theory. It can "flesh out" the general laws and hypotheses one has generated from aggregate, large N research to help illuminate if and how these processes happen in relation to real individuals.

A study of this type begins with a problem that the researcher, here called the principle investigator, wants to explore. The co-investigator, a person who embodies the process to be studied, is chosen. The co-investigator is considered a collaborator and expert consultant. Thus, the research is usually framed with the statement "I wish to study a person who . . . ," which is followed by a description of the condition, experience, or circumstances of interest (Gordon & Shontz, 1990b). The principle investigator has to set certain criteria, which may be derived from the empirical or theoretical literature, to help assure that the co-investigator will indeed be "representative." In an intensive study of cocaine addicts, the principle investigator would certainly not include weekend recreational users and then might narrow the field to include only males and, therefore, come up with findings that may be more suitable to other men.

Once a suitable co-investigator is found, the two collaborators can begin to work using whatever procedures the principal investigator has chosen as a means of studying the person. Although some procedures must be decided on beforehand, there has to be room in this methodology for the co-investigator to help devise or suggest ways to gather data and to comment on the principle investigator's tools and findings. In this project, the co-investigator offered journal writings as another means of learning about her creative process and was not able to do one particular procedure, devised by the principle investigator, that the artist found too intrusive.

Thus, the relationship between the two investigators is similar to that between an anthropologist acting as participant-observer and the people with whom the anthropologist is involved and studying. Owing to the nature of this relationship, it is important for there to be a supervisor and set of advisors monitoring the work. Gordon and Shontz (1990b) elaborated on this procedure.

What exists at the end of this intensive study of an individual or a series of individuals? The principle investigator has the responses to many questions and situations that will elucidate the process under investigation and help to create an in-depth model of a given arena of human functioning. This model, although certainly not generalizable to all human beings in all contexts, can provide the field or a clinician or anyone involved with that particular process a great deal to learn and think about and use as a basis for decisions, further study, and theory building. Although one person can never be truly representative of all people, the study of one person in sufficient detail and depth can open many doors to and illuminate many corners of a psychological question or quandary.

Present Study

The major questions guiding this study were: Who is the artist and what happens to his or her internal world when involved in creating art? These questions were broken down into exploratory, open-ended research questions and specific hypotheses, including some about the role of life themes in the artist's experience and art. The artist chosen to be co-investigator was a 35-year-old female painter who had been painting and drawing since childhood and considered art a very significant part of her life and identity. I call her Grete.

The two investigators met for several hours each week over a period of 10 weeks and engaged in different types of interviews, filled out and discussed daily experience audits, examined journal writings, utilized a Q-Sort that was designed to elicit the artist's changing self-concept, answered questions on rating scales, did some psychological testing, and in general the principle investigator observed Grete as they worked together. Specifically, to elicit themes and encourage Grete to think on the more global level of patterns and meaning in her life, the following questions and directives were used:

1. Do you feel there are certain themes, ideas, or feelings that recur in your life, your psychological processes, or your work?
2. Complete the statement: "The most important thing for me to do in my life is . . ."
3. Sum up the major concerns of your life.

RESULTS

The data presented and discussed here are a small fraction of the data collected. Rather than a summary of the data, this presentation should be viewed as a representative sampling of the relevant results regarding life themes. Large portions of Grete's responses and conversation are included in an attempt to remain true to the narrative quality of an intensive case study and to the richness and nuances of the data. In keeping with the spirit of a representative case study and the collaborative nature of the research relationship, the artist's own self-report is valued and considered valid. The principle investigator certainly commented on and at times interpreted the artist's statements, but the intent was to understand her world view and sense of self. The manner in which the themes were extracted by the principal investigator relied on the judgments of two research assistants, the principle investigator, and the supervising psychologist. The research assistants, equipped with a list of questions to be answered (including "What are Grete's themes?" and "How are the themes changing?"), read through the interviews and categorized them according to their questions, as did the principal investigator. If two of the three readers agreed on a statement, it was included. When the principle investigator strongly disagreed with the two research assistants, the matter was taken to the supervising psychologist for discussion and a decision. For the most part, the categorization was fairly straightforward, and all readers were instructed to try to consider and understand the artist's viewpoint rather than become interpretive or look for deeper meanings in the data. Overall, there was a 69% agreement rate between all three raters.

Overview of Themes

The themes Grete articulated include strength, freedom, flowing and observing, understanding and learning, the relationship between her spiritual and physical aspects, and restlessness. She spoke of "strength" as the major theme and described it as "love of self. Understanding of the magnitude of yourself . . . not allowing interference that causes pain." She said of freedom: "It's strength. It's being free to do what you want to do, to live how you want to live, to be with the people you want to be with and to be away from those you want to be away from. . . . Freedom is riding on a horse galloping across a field." Another is flowing and with it goes observing. She spoke about them in this way: "to just . . . move with it [life] and flow with it and watch it and feel it and observe it but not stop." Understanding is what she feels she is constantly trying to do; it is her attitude toward life and herself and she called it the major concern of her life. The relationship between her spiritual and physical aspects has often been an issue for her, especially in that she can become too involved in the spiritual side of life or herself and have difficulty with the physical side. Restlessness is something she has often felt; what it means to her is "It says that I, that physical part of me, does not yet know what it's gonna be doing but another part knows. You know, it's restless because I'm not, I don't seem to have a direction but yet I'm, not settled either." Learning is a theme I supplied for her for it had seemed to be such a basic part of her life and who she is, and somehow it seemed different than understanding. After I suggested it, she said "That's the basic theme—to learn, whatever it is you need to learn." If strength is the overarching theme, learning is perhaps the underpinning of them all.

In the following sections, narratives about some of the themes are presented, focusing on an elucidation of the theme, its history in Grete's life, and its relationship to her life, self, and art.

Strength

Grete discussed her reactions to being robbed the night before this interview:

G: Yeah. . . . And today, I feel a lot that I also, I feel that intimidation that comes from people asking more of you than you have to give. Or demanding it, even. . . . And that's a really heavy lesson to learn too. Well, to know when it's too much and be able to say "sorry." No, not even sorry, you know just, "No, I don't have it."

R: What do you think is the thing that up 'til now blocks you from saying that to somebody? That last night blocked you from saying No to that man.

G: I think it's, in that case it's fear, it's fear of, uh . . . that if I'm, I want to be able to say No but not in a hostile way because if I'm hostile . . . then I'm going to receive hostility back and I'm afraid of that. If I say "No, Fuck you, just leave me alone" then it's, you know, that's it. . . . But it's really hard sometimes to communicate on that level— "No, not me," you know.

R: Because what might result is that physical hostility?

G: Yeah. I think just a, not an understanding of that whole sort of personal space thing. "No, you're invading on my space, man. I wanna go home. I'm tired, I need my space" [exaggerated voice, both laugh].

R: So what do you think, what's going to happen with you with this whole incident?

G: . . . Well, I don't know exactly but I do know something has already happened. . . .

R: In terms of?

G: Oh . . . I think I can't be intimidated. I think it's a lesson in strength. That's one of my themes.

Strength changes over the years and it shows in her paintings:

R: So is it that over the years things have kept coming up that help you to work on that theme?

G: Yes, because when I *don't* follow through with strength, inevitably something happens to me, in one form or another, that I don't want to happen. . . . It comes through in the Motherhood painting, the mother figure is somehow strong even though she's surrounded by draining forces. . . . But she's aware of them, for what they are.

R: When you painted her did she feel strong?

G: Yes.

R: Is that something that maybe 5 years ago you would have had trouble painting?

G: Yes.

R: Why is that?

G: Because I don't think I understood at that point. At that point I was still afraid of strength. I was thinking, I think a lot of conditioning leads people to believe that strength is something to fear.

R: . . . How do you think you've grown in strength?

G: I've *done* things that I've wanted to do that I didn't do before. I'm living the way I want to live. And I wasn't doing that.

Freedom

R: How do you think freedom has changed, the theme of freedom, throughout the years of your life? Or has it not changed?

G: It's probably changed, uh, it's changed and it's not changed probably. Like—"freedom" was getting away, getting my independence, being free from parents, leaving the nest, and then leaving the mate, leaving the child. You know, it's like—leaving. Leaving the roots, the homeland.

R: Do you find freedom easier now or harder now?

G: I find it easier.

R: Do you feel like you've done most of the *work* on that theme?

G: I've done a lot of it. But I still have more to do, because I still have more to do on strength. Like—I was not *free* last night and someone entered my space, took part of me. You know, that leather pouch was part of me. They ripped it off of me so—literally you know. It's real obvious. So, I allowed that, on one level I *allowed* someone to do that. So I'm still working on being free. . . . But I think it is easier. It doesn't come up as often.

R: When I look at your life it seems like maybe, maybe a number of years ago that was more *pressing* a theme than it appears to be now.

G: . . . I was more a prisoner. I was more confined. Well I was *allowing* myself but nevertheless I was held under people and I don't feel as much, you know, people that I spend time with now are people I want to be with all the time. And, even though some of those people that I felt uh . . . imprisoned by I loved. They were demanding and I can't be around demands.

A painting of people intertwined with each other speaks about freedom:

G: The people entangled has something to do with freedom. Freedom from those people. Freedom from that way of relating . . . I am no longer a part of that. That's why it was really important to me to visualize it. It's like it is a separate thing from me. That love by entangling.

R: So by painting it you got free of it?

G: Yes.

Flowing and Observing

R: The most important thing for me to do in my life is . . .

G: Well dancing is a good thing . . . Is dancing . . . Dance through my life.

R: What does it mean to "dance through life"?

G: To just . . . move with it and flow with it, and watch it and feel it and observe it but not—stop. You know, it's when we stop that we get too involved. Then we freak out and try to understand what's going on on the physical level. And the physical level is really, doesn't show all that much you know as far as, well it does but if you *just* have the physical level. . .

G: . . . Just if you stop dancing and get involved in it it gets painful, because you're not dancing anymore, you're stopped. And you're, you know, you're trying to . . . figure it out but you're not moving with it, you're not flowing with it. You're stopped.

R: Would you say that's what happened to you last night [with the robbery]?

G: . . . Yes. . . . Somebody *knocked me down* on the dance floor. . . .

Flowing is linked with her paintings:

R: Is there one of your paintings that you feel manifests the flowing theme, the idea of flowing?

G: Well, there's one that manifests the idea of *not flowing*. That's the figure that's suspended.

R: The one between the levels?

G: Yes. That's not flowing. That's suspended in the vacuum. It's like caught in the middle. Flowing? Maybe would be the sun worshiper.

R: How about some of your new figures?

G: The dancers . . . yes. That's flowing.

R: Okay. So, if—if you had to look at the dancers next to the figure caught between the levels—

G: Yes, . . . and . . . the sun worshiper. . . . It's like the figure caught between the levels would come first, and it did chronologically. The figure between the levels is the first one. Just, just considering those three. Then—

R: And what's that one doing as far as flowing?

G: That one's stopped. It's caught. Which probably brings about awareness, just the awareness of being caught.

R: So it maybe makes the theme conscious in a sense?

G: Yes. And then the sun worshiper: In the center is that figure of the meditating sun worshiper at peace but surrounding her are all of these things going on . . . and that's [the painting] like in the middle because she's at peace but still sort of being caught. And the dancers are just *dancing*.

R: So what's she still being caught by?

G: By emotions I think.

R: And so she's not flowing. If she were always flowing, what would she be flowing with?

G: Herself. Flowing with um, with the whole process, with the whole, flowing with understanding. Yeah, flowing with understanding.

R: Okay. And the dancers are?

G: Nothing's interfering. It's just the dancers.

R: And they're moving.

G: Yes. And things are still happening but they're *moving with* the things rather than moving in the middle of the things caught. Like the sun worshiper is still, it's almost like you could see the same, it would be interesting to see it—[that painting was not there] even visually that figure is in the center with things around it.

R: The dancers are different.

G: Yes.

R: How would you describe that?

G: The difference?

R: Yeah, because you just pointed out the way the other two are—

G: Oh, well there's not, the dancers aren't caught. There's not things going on around them. They're just, ah, dancing and flowing, it's all a part of them. They're more harmonious than the other two.

R: Would you say that that parallels a development in you over the years?

G: I would imagine.

R: Can you describe that, like in other parts of your life? Or—describe it with reference to yourself.

G: That's why I paint so [laugh]. I did in the paintings.

R: Oh, okay.

G: Um . . . just, I think what we've been talking about. You know, learning to flow. One of the biggies of the "Here and Now" is observing, you know, realizing that my strength lies in my ability to stand back and watch, and observe. And that way—nothing interferes as much as [instead] it *shows* you, so that you can "do a new step," you know. A new step in the dance.

Understanding

Some themes seem to take on a larger than life proportion almost as if they constitute the person's mission in life. For Grete, understanding and learning had that quality. They infused all of who she is and seemed to be a basic motivating factor for her. She was always looking for what the things in her life were teaching her. She sees troubling situations in her life as lessons to be learned rather than crises. When requested to sum up the major concern of her life she replied:

G: In my life, I am concerned with . . . ah . . . understanding.

R: Can you say a little bit more about that?

G: I am concerned with growth. I am concerned with the Death Flow, learning to flow, learning to accept. But no, just, not accept in the way of um, I don't know that word sounds like "accept blindly." But I mean, accept in terms of seeing it all as . . . all that happens to me is showing me something. And it all seems to fit, it all seems to work you know. Whenever I apply that, it uh, it's right there.

R: Whenever you apply the idea that "everything seems to fit" then everything seems to work?

G: Yes, it all is for, that it's all manifestation maybe, okay—in my life I am concerned with "manifestation." You know it's all manifestation and it's right there.

R: It's all a manifestation of what?

G: Of, a higher level. Of, like we're here in this physical world right now, on this plane, to learn certain things that are really, uh, the physical is a good way to learn them because it's a good manifestation. It shows us a lot, that might be more difficult somewhere else.

DISCUSSION

Although Grete had not specifically thought in terms of life themes before, she was able to find and discuss several themes that were quite important to her and seemed to organize disparate events and time periods in her life. Several properties of life themes become apparent in reading these discussions. The first is that life themes are intimately connected with who the person is. They are not peripheral, accidental aspects of the person, but rather represent core issues or conflicts within the person. "Strength" is a theme for Grete partly because she sometimes has trouble responding with enough internal strength and can find herself in difficulties because of that. Thus, themes can represent a tension to be confronted in order for the person to grow. Themes appear in a person's life in ways that challenge the person and one's sense of self can often be shaken by the reappearance of an old theme. The way in which the person responds to his or her life themes is crucial in determining who the person will become. They are part and parcel of how a person makes meaning of his or her life, a process that is emphasized by Kegan (1982) and Polkinghorne (1988) and lies at the heart of the human capacity for creating narratives. Life themes weave throughout the self and narratives about the self and the person's life.

Life themes, although they can involve other people and external aspects of one's life, are ultimately private, internal experiences and constructs. As such, they represent a somewhat different view of development (and in this case, female development) than has been recently promulgated by the emphasis in women's development on relatedness and the relational context (e.g., Chodorow, 1978; Gilligan, 1982; Surrey, 1984). Life themes ultimately involve the person as person. Although life themes are manifest in the world of relationships and work, the more important and prior relation is between the self and the life themes. That aspect of development that is highlighted in a discussion of life themes is what Kegan (1982) referred to as "that side of the person that is individuated, the side of differentiation" rather than that side that is "embedded" in relationships and the culture (p. 116). The individuated side of a woman's development and the complex nature of her relationship to herself, her past and future, the domain of work, and her life themes must be recognized.

For the artist, life themes can be manifest through artistic production, as was seen when Grete talked about the Motherhood painting as an expression of strength. In the artist's work, the themes are especially salient because the artist is working on him or herself. The creating of art can also help the artist in working out a theme that is embodied in a specific life issue through a painting. The Entangled painting is a graphic visualization of a situation involving relationships and freedom, or lack of freedom, which showed Grete something very important about herself and that difficult situation. Raw experience is transformed into understanding through the creative process and, when the theme comes around again, as it surely will, the artist will be able to respond with a bit more self-knowledge and awareness. Thus, the artist learns about his or her life themes through the process of creating, just as the mountain climber can learn about his or her life themes through each mountain and blizzard, and the tedium and excitement, involved in a life dedicated to climbing. It has been suggested (Mangione, 1991b) that one of the ways creating art helps a person to learn and grow is through the particular type of consciousness into which the artist enters when painting. This type of consciousness, labeled *creative consciousness*, has been linked to states of mind described by meditators and those involved in Eastern religious and philosophical practices (Csikszentmihalyi, 1979; Ornstein, 1986; Pelletier, 1985; Wilber, Engler, & Brown, 1986). It may be that those activities that encourage people to engage in a type of being, thinking, and experience different from our usual Western rational ways are ones that encourage internal growth and the development of life themes. Consciousness has been a somewhat neglected topic in adult development research per se, although work on the development of cognitive structures and thinking has been prominent. Wilber et al. (1986) argued that Western science has ignored what Eastern religious practices have developed to an extremely high degree—namely, the understanding of consciousness—and, thus, our psychology is truncated.

Themes do not remain static over a lifetime. They are expressed in different ways, from varied angles perhaps, at different points throughout a person's life-span. They may become salient at times of crisis and great change, times when a new response may be needed and is ripe to occur. Grete could show three paintings that all involve the theme of "flowing," but from distinct time periods of her life and each representing a diverse piece of the internal journey she has taken with regard to this theme. Because life themes embody issues of existence rather than problems to be solved, they cannot disappear entirely. We do not find a solution to them and put them to rest once and for all. Rather than finding answers to them, we have responses to the life themes, and at progressive stages of life and learning, one's response reflects who one has become at that point.

A person's life themes are interconnected. Although Grete was able, with the help of the researcher's questions, to speak of them separately, they are ultimately quite intertwined. They can involve a person's relationship with the self, others, work, or the physical world, but often the underlying themes running through these seemingly separate domains of life are few and inextricably woven together. Thus, for Grete, freedom is almost a subset of strength and is part of what she needs to understand. Flowing and observing help her to stand back and take a more detached position from which she can learn and reach a greater level of understanding.

Finally, understanding and working with a person's life themes is a way of learning about a person's unconscious, history, and future and, thus, his or her particular developmental path. Most people are not conscious of their life themes and the tension that makes themes important is often out of people's awareness. Thus, the process of examining one's life through this lens can open doors to what has been significant but heretofore unrecognized in the person. Working with the themes and the specific memories, feelings, decisions, and so on, that constellate around them is a way of developing a relationship with the unconscious aspects of the self. The naming of the themes can provide a guide for thinking about how the person is developing and where he or she might be headed. For Grete, it seems clear that strength is still a very alive and potent theme for her and she will have more situations in which she will once again be challenged in that realm.

Life themes weave in and out of a person's life. They provide for and represent two important psychological functions in the person: continuity and coherency over time, and internal disequilibrium that is the impetus to growth. A person is not just a collection of random events and reactions. Nor is a person a finished product who can coast through life untouched by internal or external challenge. Life themes are met and worked out in all aspects of life. The focus here has been on the manifestation of such themes through a specialized form of work or vocation, that of artistic creation. However, any person's life could be understood in terms of life themes and many people's work—be it as a chef or a psychologist or an entrepreneur—could be seen as an arena for the interaction of the person and his or her life themes.

REFERENCES

Allport, G. W. (1961). *Pattern and growth in personality.* New York: Holt, Rinehart & Winston.

Bee, H. (1987). *The journey of adulthood.* New York: Macmillan.

Chodorow, N. (1978). *The reproduction of mothering.* Berkeley: University of California Press.

Csikszentmihalyi, M. (1979). The flow experiece. In D. Goleman & R. J. Davidson (Eds.), *Consciousness: Brain, states of awareness, and mysticism* (pp. 63–67). New York: Harper & Row.

Erikson, E. (1950). *Childhood and society.* New York: Norton.

Fiske, M., & Chiriboga, D. A. (1990). *Change and continuity in adult life*. San Francisco: Jossey-Bass.

Flax, J. (1983). Political philosophy and the partiarchal unconscious: A psychoanalytic perspective on epistemology and metaphysics. In S. Harding & M. Hintikka (Eds.), *Discovering reality: Feminist perspectives on epistemology, metaphysics, methodology, and philosophy of science* (pp. 245–282). Boston: D. Reidel.

Gergen, K. J. (1982). *Toward transformation in social knowledge*. New York: Springer-Verlag.

Gergen, K. J. (1985). The social constructionist movement in modern psychology. *American Psychologist, 40,* 266–275.

Gilligan, C. (1982). *In a different voice: Psychological theory and women's development*. Cambridge, MA: Harvard University Press.

Giorgi, A. (1970). *Psychology as a human science: A phenomenonologically based approach*. New York: Harper & Row.

Gordon, J., & Shontz, F. C. (1990a). Representative case research: A way of knowing. *Journal of Counseling and Development, 69,* 62–66.

Gordon, J., & Shontz, F. C. (1990b). Living with the AIDS virus: A representative case study. *Journal of Counseling and Development, 68,* 287–292.

Gould, R. (1978). *Transformations: Growth and change in adult life*. New York: Simon & Schuster.

Harding, S. (Ed.). (1987). *Feminism and methodology*. Bloomington: Indiana University Press.

Hoshmand, L. T., & Polkinghorne, D. E. (1992). Redefining the science-practice relationship and professional training. *American Psychologist, 47,* 55–66.

Kegan, R. (1982). *The evolving self: Problem and process in human development*. Cambridge, MA: Harvard University Press.

Keller, E. F. (1985). *Reflections on gender and science*. New Haven, CT: Yale University Press.

Levinson, D. J. (1978). *The seasons of a man's life*. New York: Knopf.

Mangione, L. (1984). Artist and artistry: A representative case study of creativity. *Dissertation Abstract International, 45,* 26925B.

Mangione, L. (1990). *The art of self creation*. Manuscript submitted for publication.

Mangione, L. (1991a, January). *Feminist epistemology and the representative case method*. Paper presented at the National Council of Schools of Professional Psychology, Mid-winter Conference on Women in Professional Psychology, Tucson, AZ.

Mangione, L. (1991b, August). *Creating art and creative consciousness*. Paper presented at the American Psychological Association annual meeting, San Francisco, CA.

Murray, H. A. (1938). *Explorations in personality*. Oxford: Oxford University Press.

Ornstein, R. (1986). *The psychology of consciousness*. New York: Viking Penguin.

Patton, M. Q. (1990). *Qualitative evaluation and research methods*. Newbury Park, CA: Sage.

Pelletier, K. (1985). *Toward a science of consciousness*. Berkeley, CA: Celestial Arts.

Polkinghorne, D. (1983). *Methodology for the human sciences: Systems of inquiry*. Albany: State University of New York Press.

Polkinghorne, D. E. (1988). *Narrative knowing and the human sciences*. Albany: State University of New York Press.

Rank, O. (1932). *Art and artist: Creative urge and personality development*. New York: Tudor.

Ricoeur, P. (1981). *Hermeneutics and the human sciences: Essays on language, action, and interpretation*. Cambridge, England: Cambridge University Press.

Sampson, E. E. (1985). The decentralization of identity: Toward a revised concept of personal and social order. *American Psychologist, 40,* 1203–1211.

Sarbin, T. R. (Ed.). (1986). *Narrative psychology: The storied nature of human conduct.* New York: Praeger.

Shontz, F. C. (1965). *Research methods in personality.* New York: Appleton-Century-Crofts.

Shontz, F. (1976). Single-organism designs. In P. M. Bentler, D. J. Lettieri, G. A. Austin (Eds.), *Research issues: 13: Data analysis, strategies, and designs for substance abuse research* (pp. 25–44). Rockville, MD: DHEW Publications # (ADN) 77-389.

Spotts, J. V., & Shontz, F. C. (1980). *Cocaine users: A representative case approach.* New York: The Free Press.

Surrey, J. L. (1984). Self-in-relation: A theory of women's development. *Works in Progress.* Wellesley, MA: Stone Center.

Trierweiler, S., & Stricker, G. (1992). *The core curriculum in professional psychology* (Vol. 1). Washington, DC: American Psychological Association.

Wilbur, K., Engler, J., & Brown, D. (1986). *Transformations of consciousness.* Boston: New Science Library.

Wrightsman, L. (1980). *Personal documents as data in conceptualizing adult personality development.* Presidential address to the Society for Personality and Social Psychology, American Psychological Association annual meeting, Montreal, Canada.

Yin, R.K. (1989). *Case study research: Design and methods.* Newbury Park, CA: Sage.

CHAPTER EIGHT

Effects of Work and Leisure-Role Salience on Career Development

Peter D. Bachiochi
Suffolk University

Work and leisure have been defined in several ways in previous research. Kabanoff (1980) compiled a very thorough review of the research conducted on work and nonwork, including models and definitions of both work and leisure. For purposes of this study, Blocher and Siegal (1981) defined *work* as relatively structured and continuous activity that provides extrinsic material rewards and intrinsic psychological satisfactions. Kabanoff (1980) defined *leisure* as "activities primarily carried out in the pursuit of personally valued goals or in the expectation of fulfilling individual needs rather than in return for monetary rewards" (p. 69). Much of the early research defined leisure as any activity that was not work or personal maintenance functions (Kelly, 1972; Parker, 1965; Wilensky, 1961). However, most of the recent research conducted on the work–leisure relationship has found the two spheres to be more closely related than first hypothesized.

That is, past research has offered several hypotheses as to how work and leisure (or nonwork activities) interact. Most of these hypotheses have fallen into one of three general categories: segmentation, compensation, or spillover. The segmentation hypothesis states that the two spheres have little or nothing in common. There has been little if any empirical support for this proposition, however.

The compensatory hypothesis states that one attempts to fulfill needs in one sphere that are not satisfied in the other. For instance, if one is not able to satisfy important needs in the work situation, he or she will attempt to satisfy or compensate for these needs in another area of life (e.g., leisure). However, demands from one sphere (e.g., family) may be too great to allow one to enjoy such work–leisure compensation (Brief & Nord, 1990).

The spillover hypothesis proposes that effects from one domain generalize to other areas of life. This hypothesis is based on the premise that the values, interests, and skills that lead one to participate in certain activities in work, for instance, also lead one to participate in similar nonwork activities. Therefore, the spillover hypothesis asserts that work activities are inherently similar to nonwork (or leisure) activities. In addition, and perhaps as a result, satisfactions (and dissatisfactions) from work carry over to the nonwork sphere.

SUPER'S LIFE-SPAN, LIFE-SPACE APPROACH TO CAREER DEVELOPMENT

Most relevant to the theme of this volume, Super's (1980) view on career development across the lifespan is consistent with the spillover hypothesis. Specifically, Super has proposed that people play a variety of roles (child, student, leisurite, citizen, worker, spouse, homemaker, parent, and pensioner) as they mature, often playing several roles concurrently.

Super defined roles in terms of expectations (both of the actor and of the observer) and performance. Performance is viewed in terms of enactment of the role and shaping of the role. Roles may be shaped by the actor to suit better "the developing conception of the role" (p. 285) by redefining the role itself as well as the expectations of others. Through this process of redefinition, "the individual acts as the synthesizer of personal and situational role determinants" (p. 285). For instance, workers may go through a training program that prepares them for additional job duties. By training themselves to do more in their job, they have changed the role of worker for themselves as well as having changed the expectations of the person(s) for whom they work.

In addition, Super proposed that these roles are played out in four principal contexts or "theaters": the home, the community, the school, and the workplace. There is not necessarily a direct role-to-theater connection. For instance, every theater may not be entered, a role may be played out in several theaters, and/or several roles may be played in a single theater. One of the secondary purposes of this study is to explore the intermingling of these roles and theaters and to examine the effect each may have on the others.

Also relevant to the theme of this volume, Super has integrated the concept of life stage into his model. The five stages he referred to are growth, exploration, establishment, maintenance, and decline. The growth stage corresponds to the childhood years, whereas the exploration stage covers the teen years and early 20s. During the exploration stage, one examines options, evaluates information, determines lines of action, and weighs potential outcomes. The establishment stage covers the years from the mid-20s through the 40-year point and is marked by a pursuit of a plan, be it a career or a lifestyle. The maintenance stage covers the 40s through the 60s and is generally marked by a certain plateauing. The decline stage corresponds to the "retirement years" from the 60s and on. The boundaries of each stage have been left intentionally fuzzy because the start and end of each stage vary from person to person and depend on the area to which they are applied (e.g., career vs. lifestyle).

Super also pointed out that roles change their behavioral definitions with age. For instance, the role of worker changes through the lifespan as other roles take on or lose significance. One's first job has a very different meaning than a job one holds when becoming a parent. Not only does the worker role take on new significance (i.e., breadwinner), but it changes as the expectations of the parent role impinge upon the worker role. Super also proposed that occupation, family, community, and leisure roles have an impact on each other and success in one role often facilitates success in another. Such a holistic approach to work, nonwork, and career has become increasingly popular in the study of work-related development (Brief & Nord, 1990).

In fact, the field of leisure counseling currently relies on just such an approach. In leisure counseling, one's leisure activities are used as tools to facilitate development or to manage conflicts in other areas of life. For example, several authors have examined the use of leisure as a career development tool (Bloland, 1984; Hesser, 1984; McDaniels, 1984). For instance, leisure may be used as a means of vocational exploration, developing vocational competencies, or as a vocational apprenticeship. As Bloland (1984) stated: "If we think of leisure in terms of its potentiality for personal development and as an integral component of career, then leisure becomes as important for its own sake since both work and leisure are then seen as complementary and essential constituents of career" (p. 123).

PURPOSE OF THIS STUDY

The purpose of this study was to investigate empirically the work–nonwork relationship. The specific work attribute studied, relevant to this volume, was career development and the nonwork attribute studied was leisure-role salience. Career development, in this context, can be viewed as the taking of the necessary steps to define one's career path more clearly. More specifically, two dimensions of career development—career planning and career exploration—were examined. This study investigated the simultaneous involvement in multiple roles (e.g., leisurite and worker), at a particular stage of development (exploration), and the effects of these roles on one's career development.

Hypothesis 1a: The Salience of One's Work Role Will Significantly Predict Career Planning Activity. More specifically, subjects who perceive work to be important (the role of worker is central to their identity) will take part in activities that help them to define more clearly their role of worker. Career planning (a measure of career development) is one such activity. As a result, people with higher work-role salience will report participating in significantly more career planning activity.

It is also hypothesized that this relationship will generalize to other measures of career development; more specifically, career exploration.

Hypothesis 1b: The Salience of One's Work Role Will Significantly Predict Career Exploration Activity. Subjects who perceive work to be an important life role will participate in significantly more career exploration activity.

Brief and Nord (1990) stated that "To understand the connections among work and other life domains, we must adopt an orientation to the whole of life—that is, to the total collection of roles a person plays" (p. 182). The primary focus of this study was to investigate the tie between leisure and work and to identify some of the developmental activities in which people participate that underlie this tie.

Leisure is often indirectly (and sometimes directly) related to one's work experiences. In this sense, leisure can be viewed as a developmental activity with effects on various life domains, particularly work and more specifically, career development. As a result, the following two hypotheses have also been proposed.

Hypothesis 2a: The Salience of One's Leisure Role Will Significantly Predict Career Planning Activity. Subjects who perceive leisure to be an important life role will participate in more career planning activity.

Hypothesis 2b: The Salience of One's Leisure Role Will Significantly Predict Career Exploration Activity. Subjects who perceive leisure to be an important life role will participate in more career exploration activity.

METHOD

Subjects

Fifty-six undergraduate students at a small liberal arts university participated in the study in return for experimental credit for psychology classes.
Their ages ranged from 17 to 29 years (M = 19.9 years) and students
from freshmen through senior levels were represented. Of the subjects,
28 were male, 27 were female, and 1 subject failed to report gender. This
latter subject was removed from any analyses involving gender, but included in all other analyses. The average number of years worked by the
students was 5.1 and the type of work varied considerably. In general,
subjects worked part-time jobs, but many of the jobs were precursors to
full-time employment. The type of employment is not critical because
the instruments used explicitly measured the relative importance of work
to the subjects.

Subjects came from working-class/middle-class backgrounds. The combined income level of parents averaged $50,000 and education levels of
parents ranged from high school level to advanced degrees, with most
reporting some college or a college degree.

Instruments

Subjects responded to the Salience Inventory (SI; Super & Nevill, 1986)
and to the Career Development Inventory, College and University Form
(CDI; Super, Thompson, Lindeman, Jordaan, & Myers, 1981). The following descriptions of the inventories are taken from Nevill and Super
(1988).

The SI is a 170-item inventory that measures the relative importance
of a number of life roles. It consists of three parts: (a) participation in
the roles of student, worker, citizen, homemaker, and leisurite; (b) commitment to each of these roles; and (c) value expectations in each role.
The roles of worker and leisurite were examined in this study. The Participation scale is behavioral in content and asks ''what you actually do
or have done recently'' in each role. The Commitment scale is affective
in content and assesses attitudes toward roles by asking ''how you feel
about'' them. The value expectations scale is also affective in content and
assesses attitudes toward roles by ratings of the degree to which major
life satisfactions or values are expected to be found in each role. It consists of 14 values such as ability utilization, achievement, autonomy,
creativity, and physical activity.

The CDI is a 120-item inventory that measures five specific dimensions of career development. The dimensions of career planning and career exploration were used in this study. Career Planning is a 20-item scale that measures the amount of career-planning activity undertaken by a student. The Career Exploration scale is a 20-item scale that asks the student to rate the use of various sources of career information and the usefulness of the information received from each of these sources. On each scale, higher scores reflect greater levels of the career development dimension measured.

Procedure

The SI and CDI were administered to small groups (5–20) by a research assistant. Subjects also indicated their year in school, age, gender, years worked, and parents' combined income and education levels. The procedure took between 45 and 75 minutes to complete.

RESULTS

Multiple regression analyses were conducted to test each of the hypotheses. The SI measures of Participation, Commitment, and Value Expectations for the appropriate role (work or leisure) were used as predictors in each analysis (see Table 8.1). Career Planning measures from the CDI were used as the dependent variable in Hypotheses 1a and 2a, and Career Exploration scores were used in Hypotheses 1b and 2b. No meaningful intercorrelations between these variables and the demographic variables measured were revealed.

TABLE 8.1
Means, Standard Deviations, and Intercorrelations of Predictors
and Dependent Variables

Variable	Mean	SD	1	2	3	4	5	6	7
1. PW	26.70	5.5							
2. CW	33.20	5.8	.53**						
3. VW	45.78	6.2	.34**	.60**					
4. PL	29.10	6.7	.09	.16	.36**				
5. CL	31.80	6.1	.06	.33**	.45**	.70**			
6. VL	41.30	8.3	.06	.27*	.38*	.43*	.68**		
7. CP	70.60	12.6	.22*	.48**	.27*	−.08	.00	.27*	
8. CE	157.58	23.6	.21	.42**	.48**	.04	.13	.22*	.46**

Note: PW = Participation in Work, CW = Commitment to Work, VW = Value Expectations in Work, PL = Participation in Leisure, CL = Commitment to Leisure, VL = Value Expectations in Leisure, CP = Career Planning, CE = Career Exploration

$*p < .05. ** p < .01.$

Hypothesis 1a. The three components of work role salience significantly predicted Career Planning scores (adjusted R^2 = .18; p < .01). Commitment to the work role (emotional attachment to work) was the strongest predictor variable (see Table 8.2).

Hypothesis 1b. The three components of work-role salience significantly predicted Career Exploration scores (adjusted R^2 = .21; p < .01). Value expectations from work (the extent to which major life satisfactions and values are found) was the strongest predictor variable (see Table 8.2).

Hypothesis 2a. The three components of leisure role salience significantly predicted Career Planning scores (adjusted R^2 = .09; p < .05). Value expectations from leisure (the extent to which major life satisfactions and values are found) was the strongest predictor variable (see Table 8.3).

Hypothesis 2b. The three components of leisure role salience failed to predict significantly Career Exploration scores (see Table 8.3).

DISCUSSION

The results of this study lend support to the hypothesis that work and leisure are related in interesting ways. The findings of Hypotheses 1a and 1b, that the work role-related measures were significantly related to career development, are consistent with previous research (Nevill & Super, 1988). It was expected that someone who was interested in work or looked to work to fulfill important life satisfactions would have developed attitudes and behaviors consistent with career development.

Of greater interest were the findings regarding leisure-role salience and career development. Subjects who felt leisure was a valid means by which

TABLE 8.2
Multiple Regression Results for Work Hypotheses 1a and 1b

	Career Planning		Career Exploration	
	Beta	Adj. R^2	Beta	Adj. R^2
Partic. in Work	−.046	.18**	−.003	.21**
Commitment to Work	.524**		.205	
Value Expect. in Work	−.039		.349*	

*p < .05. **p < .01.

TABLE 8.3
Multiple Regression Results for Leisure Hypotheses 2a and 2b

	Career Planning		Career Exploration	
	Beta	Adj. R^2	Beta	Adj. R^2
Partic. in Leisure	−.107	.09*	−.075	.00
Commitment to Leisure	−.257		.010	
Value Expect. in Leisure	.491**		.248	

*$p < .05$. **$p < .01$.

to satisfy important life values were more likely to have reported taking part in career planning activities. Only this measure of career development was related to leisure-role salience. However, this finding lends further support to the contention that work and leisure worlds are related. Similarly, the spillover hypothesis of work–nonwork relationships, when viewed in this context, receives additional support.

The relationships hypothesized in this study could be reversed. It could be argued that those who have participated in various career development activities have taken steps to define more clearly the various roles that they play in life. Regardless of the perspective one takes on this relationship, it is apparent that career development and leisure are related to one another.

Several potential explanations for this relationship can be considered. The explanation that best supports these findings is that there is consistency across various life roles. Brief and Nord (1990) proposed that this consistency results at a process level: that "people are consistent in the reasons why they choose their work and their diversions" (p. 182).

In this sense, work does not necessarily influence the choice of leisure activities, or vice versa, but each is a means by which one acts out a particular self-image, a particular combination of roles. Although people may act somewhat differently in different roles, particular knowledge, skills, and abilities carry across the different roles, thus maintaining a level of underlying consistency.

Brief and Nord (1990) proposed that this consistency is a result of the acting upon of similar values in the different roles (i.e., values that are important to one in work are also important to one in leisure). To the extent that the same values are important and applicable in different domains, these domains will be perceived as being similar. It is hypothesized that just this sort of consistency of skills or values was potentially at work in this study as well.

Brief and Nord (1990) argued that to understand the connections among work and other life domains, we must adopt an orientation to the total collection of roles a person plays. Also, by looking at career development as taking the necessary steps to define more clearly one's life roles, particularly work and leisure, a better understanding of work and leisure may be attained.

SUMMARY

Although the participants in this study were predominantly in the exploration life stage, conclusions do not necessarily need to be restricted to only this stage of development. Super (1980) argued that steps or actions taken in early stages of career development facilitate movement into subsequent stages or roles. Thus, it could be suggested that leisure activities can be used as career development tools, even before a specific career has been settled upon. Leisure activities that help to develop future work-related skills and abilities may have a positive impact on career development.

It will be interesting for future studies to explore how the work–leisure relationship changes (if it does) from one life stage to the next. However, this study demonstrates that, by viewing careers in a more holistic sense similar to Super (1980) and Brief and Nord (1990), consistency in one's various life roles is much more easily understood and explained. This more holistic approach will allow researchers and practitioners to address more thoroughly issues of work, home, leisure, and career as well as to integrate these different spheres of behavior into a cohesive whole, rather than to separate them into unrelated fragments.

ACKNOWLEDGMENT

I would like to thank Janice Latoszek for her assistance in collecting and entering the data for this study.

I am now located at Personnel Research, IBM Corporation, Management Development Center, Old Orchard Road, Armonk, NY 10504.

REFERENCES

Blocher, D. H., & Siegal, R. (1981). Toward a cognitive developmental theory of leisure. *The Counseling Psychologist, 9,* 33–44.

Bloland, P. A. (1984). Leisure and career development: For college students. *Journal of Career Development, 16,* 119–127.

Brief, A. P., & Nord, W. R. (1990). Work and nonwork connections. In A. P. Brief & W. R. Nord (Eds.), *Meanings of occupational work: A collection of essays* (pp. 171–199). Lexington, MA: Lexington Books.

Hesser, A. (1984). Leisure and career development: For adults. *Journal of Career Development, 16,* 129–144.

Kabanoff, B. (1980). Work and nonwork: A review of models, methods, and findings. *Psychological Bulletin, 88,* 60–77.

Kelly, J. R. (1972). Work and leisure: A simplified paradigm. *Journal of Leisure Research, 4,* 50–62.

McDaniels, C. (1984). The role of leisure in career development. *Journal of Career Development, 16,* 64–70.

Nevill, D. D., & Super, D. E. (1988). Career maturity and commitment to work in university students. *Journal of Vocational Behavioral, 32,* 139–151.

Parker, S. R. (1965). Work and non-work in three occupations. *Sociological Review, 13,* 65–75.

Super, D. E. (1980). A life-span, life-space approach to career development. *Journal of Vocational Behavior, 16,* 282–298.

Super, D. E., & Nevill, D. D. (1986). *The Salience Inventory.* Palo Alto, CA: Consulting Psychologist Press.

Super, D. E., Thompson, A. S., Lindeman, R. H., Jordaan, J. P., & Myers, R. A. (1981). *Career Development Inventory.* Palo Alto, CA: Consulting Psychologist Press.

Wilensky, H. L. (1961). Orderly careers and social participation. *American Sociological Review, 24,* 522–529.

PART TWO

DEVELOPMENT OF THE DYAD/GROUP IN THE WORKPLACE

Contextual Variables That Enhance/ Inhibit Career Development Opportunities for Older Adults: The Case of Supervisor–Subordinate Age Disparity

Janet L. Barnes-Farrell
University of Connecticut

The "graying" of the American workforce has produced an increased awareness of the impact of an individual's age upon the manner in which he or she is treated in work situations. One outcome of this awareness was the 1967 Age Discrimination in Employment Act which recognized formally, for the first time, what Sheppard (1971) called "the older worker problem." The substantial amounts of age-related litigation that have ensued since the early 1970s make it clear that this is a problem for organizations as well as for individual workers. As such, it is important that we develop a clear understanding of the manner in which personnel policies and procedures can permit a worker's age to interfere with his or her opportunities for success in the workplace.

It can be documented that employers discriminate against older employees and older job applicants in a wide range of areas (Doering, Rhodes, & Schuster, 1983). For example, it has been demonstrated that older workers, once unemployed, have a more difficult time securing new employment (Axelbank, 1972; Belbin, 1965; Harris & Associates, 1975). Furthermore, skill obsolescence and age discrimination appear to be major factors in the "voluntary" withdrawal of middle-aged men from the workforce (Parnes & Meyer, 1972). Not only are older workers less successful in becoming re-employed, but those who are re-employed have reduced upward mobility (Smith, 1967). Age discrimination has also been reported in the recruitment of workers for training programs, even though it has been clearly shown that problems with training older workers reflect shortcomings in the training programs themselves (Belbin, 1965; Havighurst, 1973; Sheppard, 1971). Beyond documentation of the objective difficulties of older workers in obtaining job and career development opportunities is evidence that older workers, as a group and as individuals, *perceive* that they are discriminated against in employment situations (Kasschau, 1976; McCauley, 1977), a finding that has implications for the motivation of employees and job seekers alike.

On the other hand, there is a body of evidence that suggests that there is no general decline in skills with age. In addition, indices of work performance such as productivity, absenteeism, accidents, turnover, and trainability do not support the notion that older workers perform at lower levels than younger workers. The weight of empirical evidence supports the position that age per se is not a particularly useful or valid predictor of job competence (Avolio, Barrett, & Sterns, 1984; Doering et al., 1983).

It is often suggested that one of the major factors perpetuating the existence of age bias in the treatment of workers is the negative stereotype of the aging worker prevalent in our society. The existence of an "older worker" stereotype has been documented by a number of researchers (Bennett & Eckman, 1973; Douse, 1961; O.E.C.D., 1967; Rosen & Jerdee, 1976). In particular, a frequently cited study by Rosen and Jerdee (1976) concluded that age stereotypes do exist for such work-related dimensions as performance capacity, potential for development, and stability, even though the accuracy of such stereotypes is generally unsupported by research. These stereotypes depict the older person as generally less employable than a younger person, particularly for jobs requiring high performance and potential.

When supervisors are responsible for making salary and promotion recommendations, their subjective evaluations of an employee's work performance and potential have a major impact on a worker's ability to gain recognition for achievements and opportunities for organizational advancement. For this reason, it is particularly important to understand the conditions under which worker age is likely to influence such judgments. It has been argued that negative stereotypes about the aging process produce age bias in subjective evaluations. However, recent research suggests that contextual variables may play an important role in determining whether worker age hinders career development. Such variables as the amount of relevant information about an applicant (Lee & Clemons, 1985), accountability for decisions (Gordon, Rozelle, & Baxter, 1988), rater age (Cleveland & Landy, 1981; Ferris, Yates, Gilmore, & Rowland, 1985; Schwab & Heneman, 1978), and the age-type of an occupation (Arvey, 1979; Cleveland & Landy, 1983) have been proposed as contextual variables that may affect the presence and/or direction of age bias in the work setting.

It is argued here that disparity in age between supervisors and subordinates, rather than worker age per se, influences supervisors' evaluations of subordinate work performance and promotability. Specifically, it is argued that age disparity and supervisors' perceptions of age disparity will produce negative bias in subjective evaluations of worker performance and worker promotability. An examination of performance judgments within the framework of social cognition approaches to person perception suggests why this might be so.

Current conceptions of the performance judgment process depict performance appraisal as a specific instance of person perception (cf. DeNisi, Cafferty, & Meglino, 1984; Feldman, 1981; Landy & Farr, 1980). Theoretical and empirical work in the field of person perception has long recognized that social cognitions do not occur in a vacuum; they are colored by our social milieu and anchored in terms of the reference groups to which we belong and to which we aspire. As Sherif (1976) pointed out, our social perceptions and social behaviors are affected in important ways by whether the individual being perceived is defined by the perceiver as "my kind of people" or "that kind of people." The particular similarities or differences among people that are salient in defining "my group" versus "those people" vary from culture and from situation to situation. However, the occurrence of age discrimination in social judgments in the work context (e.g., hiring and recruiting decisions) suggests that, in our society, age may be a salient cue in performance appraisal contexts. Thus, a supervisor may react to a worker's age in terms of its perceived similarity or disparity to his or her own age. Subordinates who are similar in age to the supervisor are likely to be categorized as "my kind of people"; subordinates who are disparate in age are likely to be perceived as "that kind of people." Work that has examined the formation of social impressions in work contexts provides evidence of a bias known as "similar-to-me" error (Rand & Wexley, 1975), which suggests that judges evaluate individuals who they perceive to be similar to themselves more positively than individuals who they perceive to be dissimilar to themselves.

This chapter examines evidence for the age-stereotype hypothesis and the age-disparity hypothesis from a pair of field studies that focused on appraisals of the work performance and promotability of managers in a large manufacturing organization. Study 1 was essentially a replication of the work on age stereotypes reported by Rosen and Jerdee (1976), adapted to the conditions of a performance appraisal setting. In a field experiment, worker age was manipulated in descriptions of the work behaviors of a hypothetical worker; evaluations of work performance and promotability were examined for evidence of a negative age stereotype that is reflected in performance ratings.

Managers who completed Study 1 were invited to participate in a second study. Study 2 was a correlational field study that measured the relationships between a variety of age-related variables and actual evaluations of work performance and promotability for 87 supervisor–subordinate dyads in the organization. The relative ability of an age-stereotype explanation and an age-disparity explanation to account for variability in the performance evaluations of managers was examined.

STUDY 1

Method

Subjects

Subjects were drawn from all managerial employees of a large manufacturing organization who participated in a corporation-wide performance appraisal training program. There were 163 managers ranging in age from 21 to 63 years (M = 39.2 years, SD = 9.5 years) who participated in the study; 97% were male. The occupations of participants fell into three basic categories: general managerial, professional/technical managerial, and sales managerial. Participation in the study was voluntary and anonymous.

Procedure and Design

Study 1 was a field experiment that utilized a between-subjects design to test the hypothesis that there is a general stereotype of the older worker that operates independent of rater age. Managers attending a performance appraisal rater training program participated in a performance appraisal exercise, during which they were asked to use the new appraisal form to evaluate the performance of a hypothetical worker. The training program consisted of a half-day workshop, during which the performance appraisal form was introduced and explained in detail. In addition, a 1-hour lecture on rating errors was presented. Traditional rating errors were defined, examples of these errors were given, and suggestions for reducing rater bias were provided. Each participant in the study was randomly assigned to Condition A (old worker) or Condition B (young worker) and asked to complete the age-stereotyping measure described here.

Measures

Age-Stereotyping Measure. A brief written description of a hypothetical employee was presented to each subject. Included in this description was the kind of information that managers would typically have at their disposal: basic background information (age, job tenure, and job title) as well as observations and comments about on-the-job performance. Observations and comments were selected to describe an employee performing at average levels in the job. Each subject received a description of a 60-year-old employee (Condition A, n = 90) or a description of a 30-year-old employee (Condition B, n = 73). The stimulus materials for Condition A and Condition B were identical in all other respects. Subjects were asked to assume the position of supervisor, and to rate the performance of the stimulus employee, using the performance appraisal form.

Performance Rating Forms. A performance rating form developed specifically for managerial employees in the organization was introduced during the performance appraisal training sessions that all participants attended. The rating instrument introduced during training and used for the annual performance reviews was composed of 23 performance items comprising six subscales: Use of Time, Problem Solving, Interpersonal Relations, Interpersonal Problem Solving, Cost Effectiveness, and Communications Skills. Performance was rated on a 6-point scale for each item. In addition, overall work performance and promotability rating scales were included in the instrument. Overall work performance was evaluated on a 4-point scale ranging from *marginal performer* (1) to *outstanding* (4). Worker promotability was evaluated on a 6-point scale ranging from *doubtful* (1) to *immediately promote* (6).

Results

Subscale scores were computed for each of the six performance categories on the performance evaluation form. Means and standard deviations for subscale scores, overall ratings, and promotability ratings were computed for Condition A and Condition B. The means and standard deviations of performance ratings assigned under Condition A and Condition B are shown in Table 9.1.

Eight t tests for the difference in means between independent groups were used to test the hypothesis that performance ratings assigned in Condition A are significantly lower than performance ratings assigned in Condition B. Because eight t tests were performed, the Bonferroni technique was used to control the Familywise Type I error rate, which was set at .05. Tests for the difference in mean ratings assigned were not significant for any of the dependent measures. Thus, the hypothesis that subjects will assign significantly lower ratings to an older employee than to a younger employee was not supported for any of the performance dimensions rated.

TABLE 9.1

Mean Performance Ratings Assigned in Condition A (n = 90)
and Condition B (n = 73): Study 1

Dependent Variable		Condition A (60 years)	Condition B (30 years)
Use of time	M	3.51	3.40
	SD	.66	.71
Problem solving	M	3.90	3.85
	SD	.57	.66
Interpersonal relations	M	3.97	3.94
	SD	.83	.79
Interpersonal problem solving	M	2.97	2.87
	SD	.83	.72
Cost effectiveness	M	3.61	3.56
	SD	.91	.95
Communication skills	M	4.00	4.35
	SD	.75	.98
Overall performance	M	3.65	3.62
	SD	.59	.57
Promotability	M	3.78	4.11
	SD	1.12	1.23

Discussion

At first glance, these findings appear to conflict with the results of earlier studies documenting an existing negative older worker stereotype. In particular, the work of Rosen and Jerdee (1976) appears to directly conflict with the results obtained here. A closer examination of the two studies suggests several possible explanations for these differences, however. In both the current study and the Rosen and Jerdee study, subjects were asked to describe a 60-year-old employee and a 30-year-old employee. Both studies were simulations that utilized hypothetical "paper people" as stimulus objects. However, there were two major differences in the design and intent of the two studies.

First, Rosen and Jerdee used a within-subjects design that required subjects to describe both a 30-year-old employee and a 60-year-old employee. It is a distinct possibility that some of the differences observed in the description of the two employees may have been an artifact of the demand characteristics of such a design; the nature of the task may have implied to subjects that there were differences between the two employees. Study 1 was specifically designed to eliminate this possibility. A between-subjects design was used, with each subject describing the performance of only one employee.

A second major distinction between the two studies lies in the nature of the task that was presented. Rosen and Jerdee's subjects were asked to imagine an employee of a particular age and to describe the characteristics of that person. In other words, subjects were given very limited information about the stimulus person: Employee age was the only informational cue provided. Rosen and Jerdee's results imply that, given limited information, subjects use age as a cue, and that subjects have differential expectations about the abilities and skills of employees of different ages. This may be relevant in situations, such as employment screening, where only minimal information about a job applicant is available. However, the current study addressed a somewhat different question: In the presence of job-related information, is worker age used as a cue to the differential perception and evaluation of that information? The answer appears to be no. Although an older worker stereotype may exist, it does not appear to be reflected in performance evaluation when behavioral information relevant to the performance dimensions being evaluated is available.

The thesis of this research was that *disparity* in age between rater and ratee is the variable that affects the treatment of workers in the context of performance evaluation. The results of Study 1 do not contradict such a proposition. Because Study 1 considered only ratee age and not rater age (or differences between the two), it tends to support the proposition that ratee age per se is not a cue that affects the evaluation of worker performance and potential; it does not rule out the possibility that ratee age may affect performance evaluations in other ways (e.g., via relative age or via age disparity).

STUDY 2

Method

Subjects

Participants in Study 1 were invited to take part in Study 2 on a voluntary basis; 87 managers who had completed Study 1 also provided usable data for Study 2.

Procedure and Design

A field study utilizing a correlational design was used to examine the relationship between perceived and actual age disparity and two dependent measures: ratings of overall work performance and ratings of promotability assigned to subordinates.

During Phase 1, managers who had attended the appraisal training program were asked to complete the perceived age-disparity measure for each of their current subordinates. During Phase 2, which took place over the course of the following year, performance ratings assigned to subordinates by each subject during the annual performance review were paired with responses to the perceived age-disparity measure gathered during Phase 1. In addition, chronological ages of subjects and their subordinates, and ratee time in job title (in years) were obtained from company records.

Measures

Performance Rating Forms.   The actual performance ratings assigned by each supervisor to each of his or her managerial employees, after participation in the training session, were obtained using the performance rating form described in Study 1. Recorded evaluations of overall performance and promotability were used as dependent measures in Study 2.

Perceived Age-Disparity Measures.   Each subject was asked to provide the names of all managerial employees for whom he or she had direct supervisory responsibility. For each of these people, the subject was asked to indicate how old that person is, on a 5-point scale ranging from *much younger than I am* (1) to *much older than I am* (5).

The measure of perceived age disparity was defined and coded in two different ways.

1. Nondirectional disparity: Perceived age disparity was defined as the value of the perceived age-disparity rating, recoded so that high scores corresponded to a high degree of perceived disparity. This resulted in a 3-point scale, ranging from *about the same age as I am* (1) to *much younger than I am/much older than I am* (3).
2. Directional disparity: Perceived disparity was defined in terms of the perceived ''oldness'' of the ratee relative to the rater. This was based directly on the ratings that supervisors provided on a 5-point scale, ranging from *much younger than I am* (1) to *much older than I am* (5).

Actual Age-Disparity Measures.   The difference between supervisor age (in years) and subordinate age (in years), was used to create two indices of actual age disparity that are conceptually parallel to the measures of perceived age disparity described earlier.

1. Nondirectional actual age disparity: Large perceived age differences (positive or negative) were coded as large positive scores. Thus,

the minimum possible score of zero represented no difference in age: the maximum score recorded (32) represented an age difference of 32 years.

2. Directional actual age disparity: Differences in which the subordinate was younger were coded as negative scores (the minimum recorded score was −32 years); age differences in which the ratee was perceived as older were coded as positive scores (the maximum recorded score was 28 years).

Results

Performance ratings of 114 managerial employees were obtained from the 87 raters who participated in Study 2. Some subjects rated the performance of two or more employees, whereas others rated the performance of only one subordinate. In order to avoid biasing the dependent variables with uncontrolled individual rater effects, one ratee was randomly selected from among those identified by each rater to be the target ratee in the formation of supervisor–subordinate dyads. The number of cases on which the analyses were based was thus equal to the number of *raters* from whom performance ratings were obtained for each measure of perceived age similarity. Age distributions for selected and unselected ratees were compared, to ensure that the selection process did not alter the age composition of the ratee sample for whom performance ratings were examined. The age distribution of subordinates included in the final sample of 87 supervisor–subordinate dyads (range = 23 years to 64 years; M = 36.9 years) was highly similar to the age distribution for the full sample of 114 subordinates (range = 22 years to 64 years; M = 35.2 years). A t test for the difference in mean ages between the two groups was not significant ($p < .05$). The job tenure of target ratees (number of years in current job title) ranged from 0 to 15 years (M = 2.1 years).

Means and standard deviations for all predictors, dependent measures, and control variables measured in the study are summarized in Table 9.2. It can be seen that the supervisor sample, as a group, was slightly older than the target subordinate sample, which is certainly not surprising. However, an examination of the distributions of responses to the directional perceived age-disparity measure and the directional actual age-disparity measure indicated considerable variability in the size and direction of age disparities among the supervisor–subordinate dyads. Of the 87 dyads included in the study, 32 represented dyads in which the subordinate's chronological age exceeded the age of his or her supervisor; 54 represented dyads in which the supervisor's age exceeded the age of his or her subordinate; 3 dyads were the same age. Supervisor's perceptions

TABLE 9.2
Means and Standard Deviations of Predictors, Dependent Measures,
and Control Variables in Study 2 (N = 87)

Predictors	Mean	Standard Deviation
Nondirectional age disparity		
Perceived (1–3)	2.09	.73
Actual (years)	9.84	8.12
Directional age disparity		
Perceived (1–5)	2.74	1.29
Actual (years)	– 2.42	12.57
Ratee age (years)	36.94	10.62
Rater age (years)	39.24	9.45
Dependent Measures		
Overall performance (1–4)	3.05	.65
Promotability (1–6)	4.42	1.49
Control Variable		
Job tenure (years)	2.12	3.06

of the relative age of their subordinates showed similarly wide variability. Subordinates were categorized by supervisors as *much younger than I am* (21%), *slightly younger* . . . (26%), *about the same age* . . . (22%), *slightly older* . . . (21%), and *much older* . . . (10%).

The primary concern in this study was the impact of age disparity on variables that affect a worker's access to career improvement opportunities, independent of worker skills. Job tenure, which is related to ratee age (r = .51), affects the likelihood that ratees will have acquired the experience and skills necessary to be promoted. For this reason, it was used as a control variable in assessing the correlation between age-related predictors and the dependent variables. To test the hypothesis that age disparity is negatively related to assessments of overall work performance and promotability, partial correlations controlling for ratee job tenure were calculated between all age-related variables and ratings of overall work performance and promotability; these are presented in Table 9.3.

The data provide some support for the hypothesis that age *disparities* may interfere with opportunities for advancement. As shown in Table 9.3, when worker job tenure was controlled, both nondirectional indices of supervisor–subordinate age disparity were negatively correlated with ratings of worker promotability, as predicted. On the other hand, none of the indices of ratee "oldness" (i.e., ratee age, perceived directional age disparity, and actual directional age disparity) were significantly correlated with ratings of worker promotability. Furthermore, none of the age-related variables measured in this study were related to ratings of overall work performance.

T tests for the difference in magnitude between two dependent corre-

TABLE 9.3
Partial Correlations Between Predictors and Dependent Measures,
Controlling for Job Tenure

	Dependent Measure	
Predictor	Overall Performance	Promotability Rating
Nondirectional age disparity		
Perceived	– .07	– .21*
Actual	– .02	– .20*
Directional age disparity		
Perceived	.01	– .13
Actual	.01	– .13
Ratee age	.10	– .18
Rater age	.06	– .03

*$p < .05$

lation coefficients were used to test the hypothesis that nondirectional age disparity is a significantly better predictor of promotability ratings than other age-related variables are. None of the comparisons tested were significant. As noted earlier, however, none of the other age-related variables were significantly correlated with promotability.

A multiple regression analysis to select the combination of predictors that provided the best explanation of variance in each of the dependent variables did not yield any new information. The only dependent measure that was significantly predictable was promotability. It has already been observed that nondirectional age-disparity measures each accounted for a significant proportion of the variance in ratings of promotability. The inclusion of additional variables in the prediction equation did not significantly increase the amount of variance explained beyond that in the simple partial correlations.

Discussion

The failure to find evidence of a negative age stereotype that is reflected in appraisals of current work performance is echoed in Study 2. In fact, none of the age-related variables measured in the study accounted for significant variance in evaluations of overall work performance. Furthermore, direct measures of worker age, and measures of worker "oldness" relative to supervisor age were not able to account for significant variance in judgments about worker promotability. Thus, little support was found for an age-stereotype explanation of the impact of worker age on subjective evaluations of employee performance and potential.

However, the results of Study 2 provide some support for the proposition that age disparity between supervisors and subordinates may have an impact on opportunities for career advancement. Although age disparity was not related to evaluations of current work performance, both indices of nondirectional age disparity exhibited significant negative correlations with judgments of worker potential in the form of promotability ratings. This would suggest that subordinates who are substantially different in age from their supervisors (younger or older) may encounter more barriers to career advancement than subordinates in similar-age supervisor–subordinate dyads. To the extent that supervisors' judgments regarding promotability are used as the basis for decisions regarding promotions and other career advancement opportunities, this may be a legitimate concern.

GENERAL DISCUSSION

The results of this pair of field studies suggest that, among managers, the performance appraisal process can serve to help or hinder a worker's opportunities for career advancement in ways that relate to worker age. However, the best way of explaining the relationship between worker age and career advancement prospects does not rely on negative stereotypic expectations about the relationship between advancing age and work performance.

The practical implications of these findings are twofold. First, the good news. At least in the context of managerial occupations, the results of both studies imply that advancing worker age does not necessarily intrude upon evaluations of a worker's worth and potential within the organization. On the other hand, they should alert us to the importance of recognizing contextual variables, such as the nature of the supervisor–subordinate dyad, that may introduce subtle inequities into the treatment of equally qualified workers. Although it is certainly not practical or sensible to consider assigning subordinates to supervisors on the basis of age similarity, supervisor and rater training programs can help to minimize the impact of age disparities on the treatment of workers through the explicit recognition of the influence that age disparity can have in subjective assessments of employee potential, and recognition of the long-term consequences of such biases for employee career development.

REFERENCES

Arvey, R. (1979). Unfair discrimination in the employment interview: Legal and psychological aspects. *Psychological Bulletin, 86,* 736–765.

Avolio, B., Barrett, G., & Sterns, H. (1984). Alternatives to age for assessing occupational performance capacity. *Experimental Aging Research, 10,* 101–105.

Axelbank, R. (1972). The position of the older worker in the American labor force. In G. Shatto (Ed.), *Employment of the middle-aged* (pp. 17–27). Springfield, IL: Charles C. Thomas.

Belbin, R. (1965). *Training methods for older workers.* Paris: Organization for Economic Cooperation and Development.

Bennett, R., & Eckman, J. (1973). Attitudes toward aging: A critical examination of recent literature and implications for future research. In C. Eisdorfer & M. P. Lawton (Eds.), *The psychology of adult development and aging* (pp. 575–597). Washington, DC: APA Task Force on Aging.

Cleveland, J., & Landy, F. (1981). The influence of rater age and ratee age on two performance judgments. *Personnel Psychology, 34,* 19–29.

Cleveland, J., & Landy, F. (1983). The effect of person and job stereotypes on two personnel decisions. *Journal of Applied Psychology, 68,* 609–619.

DeNisi, A., Cafferty, T., & Meglino, B. (1984). A cognitive view of the performance appraisal process: A model and research propositions. *Organizational Behavior and Human Performance, 33,* 360–396.

Doering, M., Rhodes, S., & Schuster, M. (1983). *The aging worker: Research and recommendations.* Beverly Hills, CA: Sage.

Douse, H. (1961). Discrimination against older workers. *International Labor Review (Geneva), 83,* 349–368.

Ferris, G., Yates, V., Gilmore, D., & Rowland, K. (1985). The influence of subordinate age on performance ratings and causal attributions. *Personnel Psychology, 38,* 545–557.

Feldman, J. (1981). Beyond attribution theory: Cognitive processes in performance appraisal. *Journal of Applied Psychology, 66,* 127–148.

Gordon, R., Rozelle, R., & Baxter, J. (1988). The effect of applicant age, job level, and accountability on the evaluation of job applicants. *Organizational Behavior and Human Decision Processes, 41,* 20–33.

Harris, L., & Associates, Inc. for N.C.O.A. (1975). *The myth and reality of aging in America.* Washington, DC: N.C.O.A.

Havighurst, R. (1973). Social roles, work, leisure, and education. In C. Eisdorfer & M. P. Lawton (Eds.), *The psychology of adult development and aging* (pp. 598–618). Washington, DC: APA Task Force on Aging.

Kasschau, P. L. (1976). Perceived age discrimination in a sample of aerospace employees. *Gerontologist, 16,* 166–173.

Landy, F., & Farr, J. (1980). Performance rating. *Psychological Bulletin, 87,* 72–107.

Lee, J., & Clemons, T. (1985). Factors affecting employment decisions about older workers. *Journal of Applied Psychology, 70,* 785–788.

McCauley, W. (1977). Perceived age discrimination in hiring: Demographic and economic correlates. *Industrial Gerontology, 4,* 21–28.

Organization for Economic Cooperation and Development Social Affairs Division. (1967). *Employment of older workers IV: Promoting the placement of older workers.* Paris: Author.

Parnes, H., & Meyer, J. (1972). Withdrawal from the labor force by middle-aged men. In G. Shatto (Ed.), *Employment of the middle-aged* (pp. 63–86). Springfield, IL: Charles C. Thomas.

Rand, R., & Wexley, K. (1975). A demonstration of the Byrnes similarity hypothesis in simulated employment interviews. *Psychological Reports, 36,* 535–544.

Rosen, B., & Jerdee, T. (1976). The nature of job-related age stereotypes. *Journal of Applied Psychology, 61,* 180–183.

Schwab, D., & Heneman, H. (1978). Age stereotyping in performance appraisal. *Journal of Applied Psychology, 63,* 573–578.

Sheppard, H. (1971). *New perspectives on older workers.* Kalamazoo, MI: Upjohn Institute for Employment Research.

Sherif, C. (1976). *Orientation in social psychology.* New York: Harper & Row.

Smith, J. (1967). Age and re-employment: A regional study of external mobility. *Occupational Psychology, 41,* 239–243.

CHAPTER TEN

Use of Complex Thought and Resolving Intragroup Conflicts: A Means to Conscious Adult Development in the Workplace

Jan D. Sinnott
Towson State University

Adult life involves participation in groups that are larger than the individual. Thinking and complex problem solving occur taking into account products of several minds, not of one mind alone. The several minds may belong to a group called the family, or to the two partners in a couple, or to a work group, the focus of this chapter. In every case, being part of a thinking group—larger than the self—creates cognitive and procedural dangers and challenges both for the group and for the thinking individual in the group. The process of change is predictable, although specific outcomes are not.

This chapter is a discussion of "*conscious* adult development," "*complex thought*," and "resolving *intragroup conflicts*." The basic argument is that intragroup conflicts and complex thought stimulate each other to bring about (if all goes well) adult development and group development. The "conscious" part—inclusion of that word—is a sneaky way to suggest that we can use this process on purpose to further our own growth, even if the intragroup conflict is accidentally inflicted upon us. This chapter is a theoretical synthesis and a description of case history and phenomenological data, with a focus on the workplace. Although the process would lead to development of the *organization along with* the development of the worker, organizational development patterns are not discussed in great detail here.

This chapter consists of five sections. The first describes the characteristics and challenges of intragroup conflicts in terms of postformal thought, and in general systems theory, chaos theory, and new biology terms. The second describes the seemingly "natural" laws governing the development of groups over time, predictable sequences that could lead to such intragroup conflicts and ways out of those conflicts. The third discusses the positive and negative ways such conflicts could impact on cognitive development. The fourth suggests how we (as individuals or groups) can make conscious developmental use of our almost inevitable intragroup conflict experiences. The fifth speculates about effects on an organization or group if most members consciously choose to use intragroup conflict as a means for adult development.

CHALLENGES OF INTRAGROUP CONFLICTS

In spite of Riegel's (1975) rather compelling argument that conflict is a necessary stimulus to growth, I know of very few persons who welcome it in real life. We say, as couples' therapists, that partners who recognize and work with their conflicts as a couple usually feel closer to one another as they resolve the situation (e.g., Efron, Lukens, & Lukens, 1990; Paul & Paul, 1983), yet few of us, including myself, want to have one of those nice, intimacy-enhancing experiences with the most important persons in our lives. A teen-ager begins to have fights with every other member of the family—a prelude and rationale for necessary "breaking away"— and no one says "OK great, here's the conflict that is part of personal and family development!" It's too frustrating and it hurts too much. And in larger groups, I remember no shouts of joy among Democrats when the Vietnam antiwar movement first challenged traditional party politics, nor among movement activists when we "won" but solidified that victory by being absorbed again into the larger political organizations. There was too much fear of disaster and too many bruised egos. There was no special joy at IBM when it was challenged by Apple Computers, even if everyone agreed it was "for the best."

It is terrifying to realize that one's "success" comes at the price of being irrelevant and superseded by new forms, but this occurs when a child becomes an adult or an employee's ideas are attended to and improved upon. To be aware that to be a "success" is to be a seed that is destroyed as it produces new fruit, later after we are gone, creates the philosophical and mystical dilemmas that have troubled and challenged humans (e.g., Campbell, 1988; Farrell & Rosenberg, 1981; Frankl, 1963; Gandhi, 1951; Gould, 1978; Hugo, 1938; Maslow, 1968). Intragroup conflict offers challenges to personal safety and to the existence of the group and inflicts personal pain on all involved. Yet without it, groups do not change (e.g., Land, 1973; Mahoney, 1991; Peters & Waterman, 1982).

It may help us to get a fresh perspective on the intragroup conflict picture by looking for a moment at some new science models, and how they represent intragroup conflict. In the past few years, new paradigms have emerged in physics, biology, math, and cognitive science, new paradigms that overall are more synthetic or holistic; that remove at least a part of the subject/object separation while retaining an experimental model; that focus more effectively on process and change over time; that deal simultaneously with many variables or factors; that include effects of the "spiritual" (by some definition); and that show the tremendous potential of the action of one element or individual. Consequently, they are harder for most people to understand and tend to be overlooked, although they could be more powerful models than those we usually employ.

New Physics Models

New physics ideas (e.g., Sinnott, 1981, 1984; Wolf, 1981) have made a tremendous impact on science, technology, and philosophy. New physics concepts are difficult and describe the less familiar "big picture" reality. (Newtonian physics concepts, although limited, describe small-scale local reality.) In times of change, or when one is trying to bring about change, the breadth of the big picture is needed in research or application questions because small-scale descriptions have proved inadequate. However, new physics ideas seem somewhat alien to us because they do not concur with our Western shared cultural myths about reality (Campbell, 1988). Until we are motivated by desperation, curiosity, or cognitive shifts to explore multiple views of reality, we are wise to avoid the challenge of new physics ideas.

In earlier work, I described new physics ideas related to developmental psychology, change, teaching, and cognition (e.g., Sinnott, 1981, 1984, 1986, 1989a, 1989b, 1989c, 1989d). Table 10.1 summarizes shifts in world views from Newtonian to new physics ideas. Notice that the shifts have huge implications for psychological reality. The nature of existence (in psychological terms, identity), time (life-span development), causality (personal action, power, ability) all shift. As an example, Table 10.2 (Sinnott, 1984) describes these two world views (new and old physics) in terms of one behavioral area, interpersonal relations.

One conclusion drawn from the new physics is that sometimes multiple contradictory views of truth are all "true" simultaneously, although they appear contradictory at first. Reality is, therefore, the view of truth to which we make a "passionate commitment" (Perry, 1975; Polanyi, 1971). Ideally, this commitment is done in awareness, with consciousness. We know that no one view of reality is, in Bronowski's (1974)

TABLE 10.1
Old Physics/New Physics Concepts

Old	New
Space is Euclidean.	Space is non-Euclidean, except in small regions.
Time and space are absolute.	Time and space are relative and better conceptualized as the space/time interval.
Space is uniform in nature.	Space is composed of lesser and greater resistances.
Events are located topologically on a flat surface.	Events are located topologically on the surface of a sphere.
Undisturbed movement is on a straight line.	Undisturbed movement is on a geodesic, i.e., by the laziest route.
Events are continuous.	Events are discontinuous.
No region of events exists which cannot be known.	Unknowable regions of events exist.
Observed events are stable.	Observed events are in motion, which must be taken into account in the observation.
Formation of scientific postulates proceeds from everyday activity through generalizations based on common sense, to abstractions.	Formation of scientific postulates also includes a stage characterized by resolution of contradictions inherent in the abstractions.
Causality is deterministic.	Causality is probabilistic except in limited space/time cases.
Cause is antecedent to and contiguous with effect.	Cause is antecedent and contiguous to event only in limiting cases. When events are grouped about a center, that center constitutes a cause.
Egocentrism is replaced by decentration during development of scientific methods.	Egocentrism and decentration are followed by taking the ego into account in all calculations.
Concepts in natural laws conform to verbal conventions.	Concepts in natural laws may appear contradictory in terms of verbal conventions.
Universe is uniform.	Universe is non-uniform—either because it is continually expanding or because it is continually being created and negated.

Note: From Sinnott (1984)

words, the "God's eye view"; they are all limited by one's chosen vantage point, history, or measuring tool. This argues that anything is known only within a region of tolerance, of error, but not absolutely. If we *share* a vantage point—and only then—we share a reality. To create another personal or social reality (within limits), we need to change vantage points as individuals or groups. For example, in the physical world, from a small-scale local space vantage point, parallel lines never converge; change vantage points to universal space and parallel lines always converge. Vantage point over time, and trajectory already established, also determine the event.

TABLE 10.2
Applications: Interpersonal Relations

Relativistic

Our relations are logical within a set of "givens" that we choose to utilize.
They are based on both our past relations to each other and our relations to other significant persons.
Relating means knowing "where you are coming from" and interacting on that level.
Relating is never knowing "YOU" completely, because in knowing you I am necessarily subjectively "creating" you.
Relations are always "in process"; cannot be described as stable until they end.

Formalistic

There is only one way to structure our relationship to reflect reality.
Our relationship exists "out there" in reality.
Our relationship involves only us, now.
The relationship has just one "reality" — no need to match levels to understand.
We can know the essence of each other.
Role is more important than process.

Note: From Sinnott (1984)

The impact of a simple and profound idea like that of new physics can be monumental, in the world of cognition, especially for cognition between two or more social learners. We could be speaking of behavior in the office, the factory, the boardroom; classroom behavior; therapists confronting a changing person; development programs in third-world countries; mid-life development of a couple; or interpersonal relations studies. From a new physics viewpoint and in interpersonal cognition, different incompatible truths are not necessarily to be narrowed to one correct truth; they may each have their own correct logic. From a new physics viewpoint, learning the truths of others can teach us greater flexibility and give us more tools for working with reality, and interpersonal cognition demands we learn others' truths. From a new physics viewpoint, the line between two knowers may be a vague one because several truths are valid. So dialogue is necessary among knowers. Awareness of the new physics idea that "truth" is partly a choice of vantage points around which we build our reality lets the worker, the supervisor, the organizational expert, or the classroom teacher, Peace Corps volunteer, negotiator, student of aging, or therapist begin to recognize in others the power to construct and experience—and be responsible for—their intellectual lives. Accepting shifts in reality, bridging, and dialoging between two "truths" is likely to lead to more permanent, useful, adaptive mutual learning that is not sabotaged by a rigid world view during times of change.

New Biology Models

Proponents of the new biology (e.g., Augros & Stanciu, 1987; Maturana & Varela, 1988; McLean, 1988) go to the original data on which evolutionary theory was formed and add the new experimental data of modern medicine and biology to attempt to answer new and difficult biological questions. In doing so, they come to conclusions that stand evolutionary theory on its head. Their basic argument is that, rather than modeling aggression or conflict, biological systems model synergy or cooperation. Species do not fight for the same niche in an environment; they evolve to fit a free space so that they can *prevent* conflict with another species. Intrapersonally, "higher" more evolutionarily recent brain centers (like the cortex and prefrontal cortex) do not so much *control* instinct or "lower" centers, but instead provide clever ways to *help* both lower centers reach their goals, leading to a sense of community and mutual goal setting between the organism and those around it. The human immune system in this model is more than an army that attacks invaders; it is a sense of wholeness, of mind, body, and emotional well-being. In the new biology, opposing parts or individuals seem meant to mate and appreciate each other, not fight.

How is this like intragroup development in the workplace? For one thing, although biological entities are clearly individuals, they are also part of a larger whole, just as a cognitive event or a person is part of a context or group. In this theory, the whole does not subsume us or make us unimportant; rather, it desperately needs our specialness to reach its own goals. The context or species needs us. The part or individual provides the means; the whole provides a large part of the motivation and meaning. Empty evolutionary niches go quickly out of ecological balance if they have lost touch with their meaning. Immune systems having missing elements turn on the very body that sustains them. Over and over, this seems to be the biological message: each part is important; each part is related; each part *becomes* through relationship, in context, and only in context.

What does this theory suggest for workplace intragroup conflict and cognitive development? Meacham and Emont (1989) noted that most problem solving is teamwork, not individual work. Johnson and Johnson (1975) and collaborators demonstrated the value of cooperative learning and group work. Kohn (1987) listed the detrimental effects of competition in any setting. The suggestion offered by the new biology seems to be to maximize individual cognitive growth by capitalizing on belonging to a larger team and working together.

In terms of the new biology, we might reinterpret conflict among elements in a group and see if it helps to think of the situation as other than a zero-sum game. The new biology suggests that species want to cooperate, and can, if they "see" the possibilities. The new biology suggests ties need to be maintained among members of a group and information needs to flow. With this view, we see that the secretiveness and rugged individualism we have been taught to glorify leads to an "adolescent" sort of group unnecessarily prone to conflicts. From triune brain theory, we learn the danger (within our cognitive systems) of poor informational links among the instinct, emotion, thought, and imagination areas of our still-evolving brains. We can speculate, then, that we act in a dangerous way when we do whatever "sets off" semi-automatic protective or aggressive responses in others, and, conversely, that we have our own interpersonal instinctive responses that feel very right at the time but that are "dumb" evolutionary holdovers. Recognizing them for what they are, we can learn to make them work for the group by ritualizing their instinctive response. In this way, our loners can become our specialists in quiet thought, and our aggressive competitors can become lawyers or soldiers, ritualizing conflict.

Chaos Theory in Mathematics

Chaos theory is a new mathematical model used to describe phenomena as different as weather, the structure of coastlines, brainwave patterns, normal or abnormal heartbeat patterns, and the behavior of the mentally ill (Alper, 1989; Cavanaugh, 1989; Cavanaugh & McGuire, in press; Crutchfield, Farmer, Packard, & Shaw, 1986; Gleick, 1987; Pool, 1989; Sinnott, in press). Chaos theory answers questions about the orderly and flexible nature of apparent disorder by describing dynamic complex systems with nonlinear equations. One striking feature of chaotic systems is the way in which a tiny perturbation can lead to complete reordering of the entire pattern of the system (termed *the butterfly effect*). Another is the way a seemingly random set of events, after many iterations, can coalesce around a point in an apparently orderly way so as to give the impression of a dominant feature of some sort analogous to a dominant personality trait being present (termed *strange attractors*). Think of chaos as organized disorder (as opposed to sheer randomness, or *dis*organized disorder). Without some chaotic flexibility, some orderly readiness to fluctuate built into the system, a system (especially one like the heart or the brain) is too rigid to adapt and live. For example, a rigid heartbeat pattern (no chaos) cannot effectively correct for a small perturbing error, so a heart attack occurs; a rigid brainwave pattern cannot respond to an intellectual challenge, so poor performance results. Chaotic disorder is *non*random and is a kind of potential to correct errors. Chaos is an order enfolded into apparent disorder, the pattern in the hologram, akin to the "implicate order" described by Prigogene and Stengers (1984). However, it makes even a very minor event powerful enough to create major effects. Chaos theory gives a rationale for synchronous effects because it demonstrates entrainment in which one system locks onto the mode and pattern of another nearby system so even the minor event in one system can move other systems too.

What might such a theory imply in general? First, it suggests that there is more than one sort of disorder. Useful (chaotic) disorder provides fresh options and room to maneuver to correct for past errors. Second, it suggests the immense importance of each element in the system for the final outcome to the system. As computer models demonstrate, the perturbation caused by the butterfly's wing can alter the weather pattern! Third, it suggests the importance of openness to innovation to provide natural sorts of corrective devices for complex events or groups.

What does this model suggest for theories about intragroup conflict in the workplace? How are these two models linked? First, if there are two types of disorder—useful and useless—in systems, we as managers, therapists, or problem solvers must learn to foster creative disorder or a larger problem space to foster cognitive development. This will lead to greater adaptive flexibility for the workers. Second, chaos theory points to the potentially tremendous importance of each person's contribution during the information exchange process of the work team. One individual can totally alter everyday interpersonal cognitive meaning or dynamics, the way one shift in wind can alter a complete weather pattern. In the rapidly changing interpersonal cognitive situation, one agent can have real and far-reaching power to influence change and cognitive meaning for all. These are just two similarities between the models.

New Cognitive Science Models

One new key area now developing within cognitive science is called postformal thought (Commons, Richards, & Armon, 1984; Commons, Sinnott, Richards, & Armon, 1989; Sinnott, 1989a, 1989b, 1989c, 1989d, in preparation-b; Sinnott & Cavanaugh, 1991). It includes cognitive epistemology (or the knowing of reality) and life-span development. This cognitive development is theorized to be accompanied by increases in social-cognitive experience and skills, perhaps caused by interpersonal experience. Postformal Piagetian thought is one theory describing this development (Sinnott, 1984). Such cognitive approaches go beyond traditional information-processing approaches. Postformal thought is a complex way of solving problems, which develops with social experience, usually in mature adulthood. It allows a person to solve problems even in situations where many conflicted belief systems and priorities overlap. In postformal thought (Sinnott's version of the model), the solver faces multiple conflicting ideas about what is true, ideas often contributed by members of a group. He or she realizes that it is not possible to get outside the mind to find out which "truth" is "TRUE," but that a solution must be found to the problem anyhow. He or she then realizes that the truth system he or she chooses as true will become true, especially in relation to other people, as she/he lives it to a conclusion, within the limits of other active knowers in the system.

The main characteristics of these relativistic postformal cognitive operations (Sinnott, 1984) are: self-reference, and the ordering of formal operations. *Self-reference* is a general term for the ideas inherent in the new physics (e.g., Wolf, 1981) and alluded to by Hofstadter (1979) using the terms *self-referential games, jumping out of the system,* and *strange loops.* The essential notions are that we can never be completely free of the built-in limits of our system of knowing and that we come to know that this very fact is true. This means that we take into account, in all our decisions about truth, the fact that all knowledge has a subjective choice component and therefore is, of necessity, incomplete. So, any logic we use is self-referential logic. Yet we must act, and do so by making a lower level decision about the higher level rules of the game (nature of truth), then play the game by those rules. Sooner or later, we come to *realize* that this is what we are doing. We then can consciously use self-referential thought.

The second characteristic of postformal operations is the ordering of Piagetian formal operations. The higher level postformal system of self-referential truth decisions gives order to lower level formal truth systems and logic systems, one of which is somewhat subjectively chosen and imposed on data.

Now this is the logic of the new physics (relativity theory and quantum mechanics) (Sinnott, 1981). New physics is the next step beyond Newtonian physics and is built on the logic of self-reference. It is reasonable that the development of logical processes themselves would follow that same progression to increasing complexity.

A new type of cognitive coordination forced by everyday and social cognitive task demands occurs at the postformal level. Another kind of coordination of perspectives also seems to happen, on an emotional level, over developmental time (Labouvie-Vief, 1987). This coordination parallels the cognitive one and probably is in a circular interaction with it. It is expected that postformal thought will be adaptive in a social situation with emotional and social components (Sinnott, 1984) because it is hypothesized to ease communication, to reduce information overload, and to permit greater flexibility and creativity of thought. The postformal thinker knows he or she is helping to create the eventual truth of a social interaction by being a participant in it and choosing to hold a certain view of it.

What would intragroup conflict in the workplace look like in each of these models? In Sinnott's postformal thought terms, the intragroup conflict is an occasion for members of the group, and the group itself, to develop more complex patterns of thought, emotion, and interaction.

This happens in bonded or somewhat independent, cohesive work groups every day. However, to study the interactions in their "cleanest" form—to see the patterns—one needs to observe very isolated groups. Results can then be extended to less-isolated group process. Let me illustrate this by a brief analysis of a very isolated group of survivors of an airline disaster. The cognitive level of a group should depend on the collective level of its participants. Levels of participants should tend to converge over time. Individual members of the group were expected to interact at several predominant levels of cognitive development. Individuals would be expected to create their own "social reality" as a group evolves.

The dialogues and interpersonal behaviors reported by Read (1974) centered on the experiences of a group of 45 Uruguyan air travelers who crashed in the peaks of the Andes in winter and were officially given up for dead. Ten weeks later, 2 of the survivors walked out of the mountains and found help for the 14 others still alive. The analysis presented here focuses on the state of the group at the time of the crash and 1 month later, as expressed in the dialogues and in the reports of the interpersonal behaviors of the 19 who survived for an entire 1-month period.

According to preliminary analyses, the survivors formed three basic types of groups on the day of the crash. These groups were identified as family clusters, friend clusters, or isolates. Except for the few families or friends, relationships were very superficial and infrequent. In the first few moments after the crash, virtually every survivor seemed to be interpreting on a concrete preoperational level, creating a hysterical, demanding social situation with rapidly escalating immature conflicts. Soon those who generally related at a concrete operational, formal operational, or postformal level were able to engage in a dialogue with others until a temporary concrete operational level milieu was reached. As a result, some degree of interpersonal calm was restored.

Those who generally related at concrete or formal operational levels at the time of the crash based their understanding on role hierarchies that might well have been valid for the precrash social system but were invalid for dealing with severities on the snow-covered peaks of the Andes. Persons most frequently relating at preoperational level generally interpreted the behaviors of everyone in the group at the same level. Concrete operational level persons often "talked down" to preoperational persons, meeting them at the lower cognitive level until the latter exhibited (or feigned) more complex understanding of the interpersonal event.

One month later, the group appeared to have restructured its society. An ordered, logical social system appeared, one at extreme variance with the ordered, logical, highly valued social system of the group's previous experience in civilization. Individuals had frequent and intense interactions with one another during the preceding month. One tightly clustered subgroup characterized by a flexible postformal level approach had appeared. Members of this group could respond on any level, depending both on the circumstances of the moment and on the level of the person with whom they were communicating. These individuals were either leaders or were extremely well liked by all, in spite of their earlier status as strangers. Many persons had reacted to intense interactions by raising their dominant social-cognitive level several steps, some achieving a postformal level. The most effective leaders were those who appeared to use their postformal level skills to coordinate the system of roles from the precrash society with the disparate system of roles in the postcrash survivor society.

A second subgroup typically responded on a preoperational level, although they might temporarily feign a higher level when socially coerced. While past friendships, skills, or philosophical/ethical systems kept the complex thinkers interacting with the preoperationals, the latter were perceived as an infantile burden. The first group frequently interacted harmoniously within itself. Members of the second seldom did because their interactions, based on structures of social relations embedded in needs, were less mutually satisfying. Cross-group interaction took place when members of the first subgroup were flexible enough to interact at the second's lower level. However, this demanded extra effort on the part of the higher level persons and, therefore, was seldom attempted. The members of the higher level subgroup, therefore, experienced more stimuli for restructuring than did the members of the lower level subgroup.

If we substitute "air disaster survivors" with "members of an organization or a work team," we see the same kinds of processes occur. The good manager is usually the postformal, Level 5 thinker!

From general systems theory, we can learn that groups, like individuals, strive to keep living, to maintain some boundaries, and to set part of their own courses over time. In the next section, I describe some regularities (based on systems theory) governing development of groups over time, predictable sequences that could lead to intragroup (and intergroup!) conflicts.

PREDICTABLE GROUP DEVELOPMENT
AND CONFLICT

General systems theory (Ford, 1987; Heylighen, Rosseel, & Demeyere, 1990; Lumsden & Wilson, 1981; Miller, 1978) can be a metaphor to help us organize ideas about change in social systems and in social roles over time. We can draw implications about the interactions of multiple changing groups over time as well as implications about the interactions of changing individuals and changing groups over time.

Table 10.3 (adapted from Sinnott, 1989a) displays patterns of change in physical open systems and living systems plus their analogues in the two-person groups (couple), family, society or organization, and social role (gender roles). Table 10.4 is a summary of the system characteristics that influence change in living systems. Table 10.5 includes rules of system change. Imagine a situation where two systems—societies or organizations, for example—come up against each other and try to influence each other (i.e., intrude on each other's boundaries). If the first system is not too rigid and too ordered, the influence and energy of the second will have an impact on and alter the first. The reciprocal will also be true. However, if the first system is rigid, the second will not be able to influence it. Now, if the energy of the second becomes stronger still, and it cannot influence the first subtly, violent influence might result in a complete shattering of the first. Instead of gradual change, complete change occurs. Defenses sometimes, then, become problems in their own right and destroy rather than protect. The gentler dynamic—mutual influence of semiordered systems—occurs during political dialogues or organizational evolution. The second more catastrophic dynamic—destruction of an old overordered system—occurs during revolutions or takeovers. Some other examples of the dynamics of change over time in a number of very different systems are in Table 10.3. Table 10.3 describes, in Column 1, six steps that typically occur over time in any living system. Examples of their presence are given for physical systems (Column 2), couple or dyad systems (Column 3), family systems (Column 4), social/organizational systems (Column 5), and gender role systems (Column 6) to show how common and widespread evidence is for such dynamics over time.

What goes on when intragroup conflict occurs? We can suppose that there is a challenge to the status of things as they are either, because of normal dynamics at one time or because of normal dynamics of change over time. To illustrate, let us look at the evolution of any new culture. At first, a group or culture more or less integrates all individuals or factions under its banner: for example, the colonies were reasonably willing to be part of a new republic after the American Revolution ended;

TABLE 10.3

Patterns of Living System Change Over Time in Six Types of Systems

Living System	Physical System	Couple System	Family System	Social or Organizational System	Sex Roles System
1. Symbiosis undifferentiated	High entropy, low order	Honeymoon period, finding roles in the marriage	Parent-infant relationship	New nascent culture indwelling in old forms/work group	No role yet defined
2. Differentiation	Increasing boundary creation; increasing structure	Power struggle	Parent-adolescent relationship	Emergence of new culture/work group	Developing masculinity or femininity
3. Temporary homeostasis	Balanced, flexible; half-ordered, with moderate boundaries to permit assimilation of new information	Stability	Temporary agreement about rights/duties of parent vs. adolescent	New culture/work group is now an active force or organizational component	Person is defined as either masculine or feminine-permanent label
4. Dynamic homeostasis	Balanced, flexible; half-ordered, with moderate boundaries to permit assimilation of new information	Commitment to the paradox of the other	Long-term changing, open interaction with adult child-parent as peers	Forms and structures are complexified and blended; some members lament the passing of old culture/organization	Androgyny and transcendence of roles
5. Reproduction/ synthesis		Cocreation of the relationship and the world	Grandparenthood	Nascent subcultures begin to rise and revitalize old society/organization	Transcendence of roles
6. Decay/Death	Rigid boundaries, no information flow; any one perturbation can lead to disaster and final entropy	Divorce, widowhood	Breaking of family ties leads to end of relationships, estrangement	Old system/organization too rigid for new demands on it-becomes terminal	Idiosyncratic fragments of old role remain and are religiously adhered to

Note: From Sinnott (1989a)

TABLE 10.4
System Characteristics That Influence Change

The system must permit more information to enter . . . flexibility, but under bounded control.
Systems resist disorder.
Change means temporary increase in disorder.
Systems monitor and control the amount of disorder.
Surviving systems contain the seed of their own change, are programmed to get to the next
  highest level of order (e.g., puberty is inherent in an infant).
Surviving systems balance potentials and activated processes.
Surviving systems fit may contexts.
Surviving systems are programmed to interfere with each other.
Nonsurviving systems have the same parts as surviving systems, but different processes.

Note: From Sinnott (1989a)

once upon a time, psychologists within the new American Psychological Association (APA) were reasonably satisfied to belong to that new professional group. These were "their people," members of each could say (symbiosis). As time passed, differentiation in the colonies or psychologists took place, and, in a Piagetian sense, societal structures could not accommodate to the new set of differences they began to know: The colonies (states) evolved differing philosophies about citizenship and boundaries; APA members formed divisions and clinicians differed from researchers on the priorities of the professional organization. Sometimes one "side" forced the other side to be quiet and a temporary homeostasis occurred. But differentiation ultimately continued and the noise level grew louder.

Now at this point are found both danger and opportunity. Either (a) the group can go on to a more complex dynamic homeostasis where all sides evolve a means of mutual respect and ongoing more complex dia-

TABLE 10.5
Rules of System Change

All systems change, except those near death, so change is a sign of life, even if the specific
  content of the change is pathological.
Patterns of change are predictable in the long run, based on the state of the system, the
  state of adjacent systems, and principles of emergence. Patterns of change are predictable in the short run (i.e., locally) based on analyses of contiguous, and often merely
  reliable time-slice artifacts with no real relation to what is happening.
Change in any one system will influence other nearby systems. Whether this leads to useful or maladaptive changes in those other systems depends upon their states.
Boundary rigidity in the face of information or energy flow means death; being completely unbounded means dissolution of the system. Systems strive for continuity.
Interaction with a new system that is powerful can efficiently and effectively reorient a
  system whose relations with earlier powerful systems (e.g., parents, family) were distorted.

Note: From Sinnott (1989a)

logue; or (b) the friction splits the group into multiple, splintered groups; or (c) the original group, although maintaining its wholeness, gives birth to a new group. It seems that American culture resolved its conflict (ultimately, after a bloody civil war) by creating a dynamic homeostasis; the APA has (so far) fragmented into the American Psychological Association and the American Psychological Society. The more rigid a group is, the less likely it can survive the challenge of change. The recent IBM/Apple detente illustrates the goal of flexibility being served by one rigid organization allying with one breakaway organization. A similar pattern of growth can be seen in both individual and group development over time when an individual who is very identified with a group begins to differentiate and challenge the group (and visa versa). The outcome here, too, is either greater complexity of both units (still joined), or two fragmented units, or the death of one unit to be replaced by the other. It is my assumption that none of this development over time can take place without the growth of cognitive complexity to process the changes in persons or organizations.

It is also my assumption that when there is a difference in cognitive complexity, it may be among subgroups in a group or units in a workforce; between member and group; or between original group/team and young group/team about to be "born." In any of these three cases, a mismatch in complexity can be the spur to growth of either unit. For example, in an organization composed of "haves" (e.g., entrenched managers, unions) and "have nots" (e.g., new workers or new work groups) (two subgroups), the "haves" seeking stability and equilibrium, as mid-life systems do, often conflict with "have nots" who counsel "breaking away," as adolescents do. As another example, an "adolescent" society rejects factions seeking "law and order," whereas a "middle-aged" society welcomes their input. (So, we have been the people our parents warned us about and are becoming those who control them.) The main principle is that mismatch of developmental stages is a potential stimulus for conflict and growth of the group, or even within a person.

POSITIVE AND NEGATIVE EFFECTS
OF INTRAGROUP CONFLICT

There can be both positive and negative developmental results for the person or group from participating in intragroup conflicts. This is a truism that can be observed in families and workplaces any day of the week. What is less often observed is *conscious* participation in intragroup conflict with the intent to learn or grow from it.

We recall the old saying about greatness and begin to realize that its analog is true for intragroup conflict: some are born great, some achieve greatness, some have greatness thrust upon them; some are born in conflict with others in their group, some achieve intragroup conflict, some have conflict thrust upon them by others in their group. A person may have a seemingly mindless predisposition to be in conflict or to create conflict with others, whether due to lack of "skilled" behaviors, to biology, or to other causes. Certain members of President Bush's staff seem to fall in this category, as do the "difficult" children in dysfunctional families who draw attention away from real problems and onto themselves. Having a "born to fight" member who "starts fires" in the organization at every opportunity may lead to development of the person or group by accident, but generally leads to destructive ends. The energy of others is spent containing this group member or defending against him or her rather than doing the real work of the group. Some, however, are not born in conflict, but have intragroup conflict thrust upon them, against their wills. For example, I once applied for a job not knowing that the other main contender for the slot was very closely connected to a supervisor in the organization who was a member of the interview group. I soon was impressed by the rather wild and incoherent fight that broke out almost immediately within the interviewing group! I withdrew from that competition, honoring the principle that "she who fights, then runs away, lives to fight another day." It was not a bad move, but neither I nor the group seemed to develop from this particular conflict experience.

There is a third possibility expressed in the old saying: "those who *achieve* greatness." Its analog, "those who achieve conflict" sounds undesirable at first until it is recast as: those who willingly experience inevitable intragroup conflict in order to learn. Neither Bush's staff member, nor the APA, nor the job-hunting author, nor the colonies could effectively wish away the conflicts in which they got embroiled, but they could—with eyes wide open—observe their thoughts and feelings and reactions, try various interventions, and perhaps modify their schemes of things. The groups could do the same. The next conflict experience might be better and more skilled due to the learning.

Master therapists, creative managers, mystics, and wise persons have always counselled others to live consciously, experience the present moment, embrace cognitive and emotional reality. One of my favorite metaphors for this state of willing awareness is that of the warrior of whom Don Juan speaks in Carlos Castaneda's books (Castaneda, 1971). The warrior goes through life with death on his (*sic*) back, death as his teacher, but does not fear, letting fear be replaced by a state of heightened readiness and awareness. Consider the metaphors of the oriental martial arts where one welcomes the blow that makes contact, because it can be a gift of awareness about one's vulnerabilities. In Western legends too—for example, the Quest for the Holy Grail—a seeker purposely takes on the challenge of facing tests, sometimes alone against physical forces, sometimes as a member of a culture who is in conflict with his or her own society (e.g., Thomas More, Joan of Arc). The Eastern growth traditions suggest one go up the mountain (be alone) to first learn, but then return down the mountain (back into society) to continue the learning experience (Tart, 1986). In psychotherapy, one even can consciously explore alternative conflict resolutions through guided imagery (Shorr, 1983). In the crucible of the intragroup conflict, one can refine one's motives, skills, goals, values, and strength of purpose. Conscious understanding of one's life experiences of conflict is, therefore, very different from surviving conflicts or picking fights. It is truly *achieving* a special kind of conflict experiences.

On a cognitive level, carrying Piaget's ideas, those of postformal thought, and those of new biology's autopoeisis further, one would need to be able to see or know multiple realities in order to keep one's balance in the rapidly shifting system of an intragroup conflict and to develop within that conflict. Less-than-useful things happen without that cognitive balancing skill. Without the postformal thinking component, one of us always has to be "wrong" and no one understands anyone else's perspective. Without it, a synthesis cannot occur, although one position can dominate another. Without it, relationships seem to calcify and become rituals lacking diversity and flexibility. Without it, it is impossible for members of the group to change. Without it, intragroup conflict leads to a breaking apart of the group.

The co-created reality of postformal knowing—once we see the world in those terms—gives us a chance to welcome the inevitable conflict and freely play with the options of creating some different relationship. We are given a new power with this complex thinking tool—the power to see that we have some control over conflict. Knowing that we are not simply victims of external circumstances, however horrible they may be, is very liberating. Being in a conflict—and changing it to an intragroup opportunity—may provide the first opportunity a person, an organization, or a nation has to see that he, she, or it can think of a situation in fresh ways and make it into a new situation that works. This is the polar opposite of one combatant simply capitulating to another in the group.

HOW CAN WE MAKE USE OF INTRAGROUP CONFLICT?

This section and the final section of this chapter are attempts to apply the models of intragroup conflict so that conflict can promote individual and organizational development. Previously, I argued that intragroup conflict can be used for the purpose of (among other things) challenging ourselves (as team members) to grow, testing the adaptivity of our current concepts, getting information about "simmering" interpersonal conflicts, and aiding in the birth of our own and others' next developmental stages. These are all ways to make use of these conflicts. They are used by America's best-run companies (Peters & Waterman, 1982).

The following are methods for getting more comfortable with these conflicts and for using them to induce development. They also seem to induce postformal thought (see Table 10.6). The methods are discussed more fully elsewhere (Sinnot, in preparation-b). Although the table makes reference to the "person" in the group, the same principles would apply to the organization, work group, nation within the multiorganization conglomerate, the company, the family of nations, respectively.

EFFECTS ON SOCIETY:
WHAT IF WE DO USE CONFLICTS TO GROW?

One can speculate that the work group or organization itself (or any interpersonal group) would also develop along with its members if its members consciously used their intragroup conflicts to learn (Harman & Hormann, 1990). Table 10.7 shows several changes that could be expected in such a case. (This topic is addressed further in Sinnott, in preparation-a.) To see these results in action, we need only take a moment to see the results of observing our own conflicts in our own offices.

TABLE 10.6
Methods for Transforming Intragroup Conflict Experience
Into Personal Developmental Experiences

Purposely attempt to shift realities to some other reality about the problem.
Consciously look forward to conflicts in the group.
Consciously expect intragroup conflict (at some level of intensity) as a routine experience.
Consciously see ourselves as "all in this together."
Posit that "no one is to blame for this problem."
Assume that others act in the best way they know how (but that not all their actions need be tolerated even if they mean well).
Consciously face facts about the conflict, but don't assume that others see the same "facts."
Create a story around the conflict . . . and let the story resolve itself at a higher level.
Try to argue the position of an opponent in the conflict (convincingly!).
Enlarge the "problem space" by redefining the problem or its parameters.
Consciously shift the metatheory the group uses to frame the problem.
Generate many "crazy" solutions to the conflict.
Shift from focus on a concrete solution to focus on finding a good *process*.

TABLE 10.7
Some Effects on Society/Organization/Family of Nations (on the Group)
if Members Consciously Use Intragroup Conflicts to Grow

Energy formerly used to hold polarized positions can be available to go toward goal or to observe the learning process.

Members will be less "touchy" or reactive since they are not in a state of high (and angry) tension.

Group solutions will be more numerous and more adaptive.

The group will get stronger.

"Bullies" can be contained without the situation escalating. Social change will be possible with less pain and destruction.

There will be fewer group crises and more gradual changes.

Group focus will shift to "good process," rather than specific content solutions to problems.

The "politics of paradox" will be used (e.g., we will learn to defeat our "enemies" by becoming a resource to fill their needs).

We will create much more realistic solutions to cross cultural problems.

The "group" identity will expand to be a global one.

Group depression/despair/anguish will be replaced by rejuvenated group hope.

Members will cooperate better.

The "chaotic" transition will be revealed as orderly and purposeful.

Members will feel less split between their emotions and their cognition, and will feel more valued.

"Winning" by dominating will be replaced by "winning" by mutual empowerment.

Opponents will honor each other.

ACKNOWLEDGMENTS

This chapter was presented as a Plenary Address at the Sixth Adult Development Symposium, Suffolk University, Boston, MA, July 1991. I acknowledge support from the Faculty Development Fund at Towson State University, from the Center for Study of Adult Development and Aging and its staff at Towson State University, and from Psychology Department staff who offered technical support.

REFERENCES

Alper, J. (1989). The chaotic brain: New models of behavior. *Psychology Today, 23,* 21.

Augros, R., & Stanciu, G. (1987). *The new biology.* Boston: New Science Library.

Bronowski, J. (1974). *The ascent of man.* Boston: Little, Brown.

Campbell, J. (1988). *The power of myth.* New York: Doubleday.

Castaneda, C. (1971). *A separate reality.* New York: Pocket Books.

Cavanaugh, J. (1989). *Utility of concepts in chaos theory for psychological theory and research.* Paper presented at the fourth Adult Development Conference at Harvard University, Cambridge, MA.

Cavanaugh, J., & McGuire, L. (in press). The chaos of lifespan learning. In J. D. Sinnott (Ed.), *Interdisciplinary handbook of adult lifespan learning.* Westport, CT: Greenwood.

Commons, M. L., Richards, F. A., & Armon, C. (Eds.). (1984). *Beyond formal operations.* New York: Praeger.

Commons, M. L., Sinnott, J.D., Richards, F. A., & Armon, C. (Eds.). (1989). *Adult development II: Comparisons and applications of adolescent and adult developmental models.* New York: Praeger.

Crutchfield, J. P., Farmer, J. D., Packard, N. H., & Shaw, R. S. (1986). Chaos. *Scientific American, 255,* 46–57.

Efron, J. S., Lukens, M. D., & Lukens, R. J. (1990). *Language, structure and change.* New York: Norton.

Farrell, M. P., & Rosenberg, S.D. (1981). *Men at midlife.* Boston: Auburn House.

Ford, D. (1987). *Humans as self-constructing living systems.* Hillsdale, NJ: Lawrence Erlbaum Associates.

Frankl, V. (1963). *Man's search for meaning.* New York: Washington Square Press.

Gandhi, M. K. (1951). *Satyagraha.* Ahmedabad: Navajivan.

Gleick, J. (1987). *Chaos: Making a new science.* New York: Penguin Books.

Gould, R. (1978). *Transformation.* New York: Simon & Schuster.

Harman, W., & Hormann, J. (1990). *Creative work.* Indianapolis, IN: Knowledge Systems, Inc.

Heylighen, F., Rosseel, E., & Demeyere, F. (Eds.). (1990). *Self steering and cognition in complex systems.* New York: Gordon & Breach Science Publishers.

Hofstadter, D. R. (1979). *Godel, Escher and Bach: An eternal golden braid.* New York: Basic Books.

Hugo, V. (1938). *Les miserables* [The unfortunate ones] (L. Wraxall, Trans.). New York: Heritage Press.

Johnson, D., & Johnson, R. (1975). *Learning together and alone.* Englewood Cliffs, NJ: Prentice-Hall.

Kohn, A. (1987). *No contest.* Boston: Houghton Mifflin.

Labouvie-Vief, G. (1987). *Speaking about feelings: Symbolization and self regulation through the lifespan.* Paper presented at the third Beyond Formal Operations Symposium at Harvard, Cambridge, MA.

Land, G. T. (1973). *Grow or die.* New York: Random House.

Lumsden, C. J., & Wilson, E. O. (1981). *Genes, mind, and culture: A coevolutionary process.* Cambridge, MA: Harvard University Press.

Mahoney, M. J. (1991). *Human change processes.* New York: Basic Books.

Maslow, A. H. (1968). *Toward a psychology of being.* New York: Van Nostrand Reinhold.

Maturana, H., & Varela, F. (1988). *The tree of knowledge.* Boston: New Science Library.

McLean, P. (1988). *Evolutionary biology.* Paper presented at the Gerontology Research Center, National Institute on Aging, NIH, Baltimore, MD.

Meacham, J., & Emont, N. C. (1989). The interpersonal basis of everyday problem solving. In J.D. Sinnott (Ed.), *Everyday problem solving* (pp. 7–23). New York: Praeger.

Miller, J. (1978). *Living systems.* New York: McGraw Hill.

Paul, J., & Paul, M. (1983). *Do I have to give up me to be loved by you?* Minneapolis, MN: Compcare.

Perry, W. G. (1975). *Forms of intellectual and ethical development in the college years: A scheme.* New York: Holt, Rinehart & Winston.

Peters, T. J., & Waterman, R. H. (1982). *In search of excellence: Lessons from America's best run companies.* New York: Harper & Row.

Polanyi, M. (1971). *Personal knowledge.* Chicago: University of Chicago Press.

Pool, R. (1989). Is it healthy to be chaotic? *Science, 243,* 604–607.

Prigogene, I., & Stengers, I. (1984). *Order out of chaos.* New York: Bantam.

Read, P. P. (1974). *Alive: The story of the Andes survivors.* New York: Lippincott.

Riegel, K. (1975). Adult life crises: A dialectical interpretation of development. In N. Datan & L. Ginsberg (Eds.), *Lifespan developmental psychology: Normative life crises* (pp. 99–129). New York: Academic Press.

Shorr, J. E. (1983). *Psychotherapy through imagery* (2nd ed.). New York: Thieme-Stratton Inc.

Sinnott, J. D. (1981). The theory of relativity: A metatheory for development? *Human Development, 24,* 293–311.

Sinnott, J. D. (1984). Postformal reasoning: The relativistic stage. In M. Commons, F. Richards, & C. Armon (Eds.), *Beyond formal operations* (pp. 288–315). New York: Praeger.

Sinnott, J. D. (1986). *Sex roles and aging: Theory and research from a systems perspective.* New York: Karger.

Sinnott, J. D. (1989a). Changing the known, knowing the changing. In D. Kramer & M. Bopp (Eds.), *Transformation in clinical and developmental psychology* (pp. 51–69). New York: Springer.

Sinnott, J. D. (Ed.). (1989b). *Everyday problem solving: Theory and application.* New York: Praeger.

Sinnott, J. D. (1989c). General systems theory: A rationale for the study of everyday memory. In L. Poon, D. Rubin, & B. Wilson (Eds.), *Everyday cognition in adulthood and old age* (pp. 59–70). New Rochelle, NY: Cambridge University Press.

Sinnott, J. D. (1989d). Lifespan relativistic postformal thought. In M. Commons, J. Sinnott, F. Richards, & C. Armon (Eds.), *Beyond formal operations I* (Vol. 1, pp. 239–278). New York: Praeger.

Sinnott, J. D. (Ed.). (in press). *Interdisciplinary handbook of adult lifespan learning.* Westport, CT: Greenwood.

Sinnott, J. D. (in preparation-a). *Affects of conscious intragroup development on development of society: Growing mature societies.*

Sinnott, J. D. (in preparation-b). *The development and application of postformal thought in adulthood: Learning to create our lives with others.*

Sinnott, J. D., & Cavanaugh, J. (Eds.). (1991). *Bridging paradigms: Positive development in adulthood and cognitive aging.* New York: Praeger.

Tart, C. (1986). *Waking up.* Boston: New Science Library.

Wolf, F. A. (1981). *Taking the quantum leap.* New York: Harper & Row.

PART THREE

DEVELOPMENT OF ORGANIZATIONAL CULTURE IN THE WORKPLACE

CHAPTER ELEVEN

Learning Organizations:
Settings for Developing Adults

Linda E. Morris
Ernst & Young, New York

Popularized by Peter Senge (1990a) in *The Fifth Discipline*, the term *learning organization* is currently under extensive discussion in training and development and in management circles. Beck (1989) provided an apt working definition of a learning organization as "one which facilitates learning and personal development of all its employees whilst continuously transforming itself" (p. 23). This concept of "an organization that learns" has sparked much interest and energy around which individuals and organizations are coalescing. Thus, this chapter relates information on the sources and content of current theory, research, and practice related to this term as well as a discussion of its implications for the workplace, especially for professional services firms.

Interest is mounting. Recent articles by Willis (1991) in the *Human Resource Development Quarterly*, Argyris (1991) in the *Harvard Business Review*, and Senge (1991) in *Training and Development* are a few among many that have addressed learning organizations. Further, this concept has been explored theoretically from an economic point of view by Harman and Hormann (1990) in *Creative Work: The Constructive Role of Business in a Transforming Society*, and from a management perspective by Savage (1990) in *Fifth Generation Management*.

Learning organizations have been a key discussion topic among management and organizational leaders and consultants. They have been the main topic of several conferences and the focal point of a number of collaborative efforts. For example, Michael Ray of Stanford University

179

discussed the concept in his courses and has led a computer conference on the topic within the World Business Academy. George Pór (Pór & Harrington, 1992a) presented an overview of his related work at a December 1991 conference, entitled *Learning Expedition: Collective Intelligence*, sponsored by the International Center for Organization Design (ICOD). In June 1991, Gus Jaccaci and Eric Vogt facilitated a discussion of learning organizations as a form of social architecture. At a subsequent session, the Collaboration in Social Architecture formed. Including Jaccaci and Pór among its leaders, it has linked together many practitioners who are conducting research and acting on this idea. Other collaborative efforts include the Learning Organizations Network of the American Society of Training and Development (ASTD).

What is happening here? Is this idea fad or fancy for managers, consultants, and trainers? Is there anything new? What is a learning organization anyhow? What does an organization "know"? How does it "learn"? Does a learning organization differ from other organizations? Does it provide new ways to gather, build, and distribute information and knowledge? Are there ideas and systems inherent in this notion that are valuable for businesses and other societal organizations? What, if any, are the implications for human resource development? These are some of the questions that arose for Bob St. Cyr of Digital Equipment Corporation, and Katharine Weldon, Mary Byrd, and myself from Ernst & Young, as we decided to explore the concept.

Thus, in early 1991, we conducted a computer-assisted search of the literature, pulling all available references to learning organizations and organizational learning from four databases. We located 25 citations in PsycInfo; 62 in Eric; 16 in ABI Inform; and 12 in Dissertation Abstracts (115 references in total). Reading some of these articles produced an annotated bibliography of 24 articles for initial reading. We also delved into books, attended conferences, and began exploring the concept with colleagues. Our purpose was to describe learning organizations by unearthing the definitions people had developed and the characteristics they had ascribed to learning organizations. We also explored implications for our own and our organizations' actions. This chapter includes some of the findings from that research as well as observations and insights from reflections and dialogue.

UNDERLYING QUESTION
AND CHAPTER ORGANIZATION

Underlying my thoughts, and a potentially useful question for the reader is: How does the concept of a learning organization—its purpose, values, vision, strategies, and structure—relate to the notion of and research on adult development? Other researchers and practitioners whose views are expressed in this volume are helping to fill out our still incomplete picture of how adults develop across the life span. Currently, most organizational structures, processes, and procedures do not take into account the transitions and transformations of adulthood that impact feelings, motivation, thought, and behavior in intellectual, emotional, social, and moral domains. By incorporating what is known about adult development into the purpose, vision, and values of learning organizations, we may develop organizations that consciously recognize human beings' passages as well as encourage and assist people through them. Thus, leaders in the workplace can intentionally provide a setting and a focus that will honor individual development and thereby enhance organizational development.

Against this backdrop, the remainder of the chapter is divided into four additional sections. In this first section, I note the growing interest in the topic and indicate the extent of the research performed. Some sources of the interest in learning organizations are noted in the section on reasons to act. Definitions, themes, and metaphors drawn from reading and discussion are highlighted in the third section. In the fourth section, I synthesize findings and raise issues related to creating a learning organization in a professional services firm and in the workplace more generally. In the conclusion, I raise issues for future research and exploration.

REASONS TO ACT

Critical questions in reviewing the literature were: Why would an organization need or want to be a learning organization? Where are the benefits? What value do people and organizations find in the concept? As Argyris (1991), Beck (1989), Kiechel (1990), and Senge (1990a) pointed out, management interest in learning organizations stems from a deep-seated conviction that businesses need to reorganize to retain a competitive position in the global marketplace. From this perspective, the interest in learning organizations is driven by the same environmental factors focusing attention on Total Quality Management or Business Process Reengineering and other recent initiatives aimed at revamping products and services. These factors include: the continuing shift from the industrial age to the knowledge age and the concomitant emphasis on intellectual capital as a source of wealth; the increasing complexity in all parts of life and business; globalization; an increasingly diverse workforce; and heightened attention to quality and client satisfaction. These factors affect both individuals and organizations.

For example, in an international professional services firm such as Ernst & Young, individuals early in their careers are expected to master their technical discipline (i.e., audit, tax, actuarial services), acquire expertise in an industry (i.e., electronics, health care, insurance), and employ interpersonal and leadership skills to manage work and to serve clients. Moreover, the prevailing client-centered approach requires the professional services worker to focus on identifying the client's problems and to bring to bear the firm's capability to help the client—no matter what the service need is or where in the world the capability to provide it resides. Thus, somewhat strikingly, the individual managing the client relationship can be viewed as a node through which the collective knowledge and wisdom of the firm's 70,000 plus practitioners reach the client's operations.

The firm, on the other hand, is challenged to study, codify, and disseminate information and knowledge that affects its diverse clients, the problems those clients face and, most significantly, the resources available to serve clients. Additionally, it is challenged not only to exchange existing information among its members, but also to generate and document new knowledge, for example, on environmental factors affecting clients and the implications of these, on whole new methodologies developed to provide services to clients, on experiences in one situation that might be applied to another, and on insights or creative ideas that break new ground for clients, practitioners, or the firm.

Therefore, to be able to perform work, the firm must continually build the performance capability of both the individual and the organization. As Saint Onge (1992) aptly pointed out, performance and performance capability can be viewed as two separate but integrated dimensions that are ideally in balance. Organizations may put more weight on one side than on the other. However, if an imbalance occurs, an organization may end up either reaching performance limits with little ability to expand, or having unused capacity. (See Fig. 11.1 for a visualization of this concept.)

Thus, learning organizations may be viewed more generally as an organizational response to environmental conditions, an approach to developing needed performance capability. Indeed, business leaders such as Ray Stata (1989), president and chairman of Analog Devices, are beginning to believe that "the rate at which individuals and organizations learn may be the only sustainable competitive advantage, especially in knowledge-intensive industries" (p. 74). Adopting the philosophy and practices of a learning organization may benefit organizations by increasing individuals' and organizations' knowledge and skills, thereby fueling current and future performance.

As Wiig (1990) explained, knowledge is more than information (e.g., facts or data organized to describe a particular situation); rather, "knowledge consists of truth and beliefs, perspectives and concepts, judgement and expectations, methodologies and know how" (p. 1).

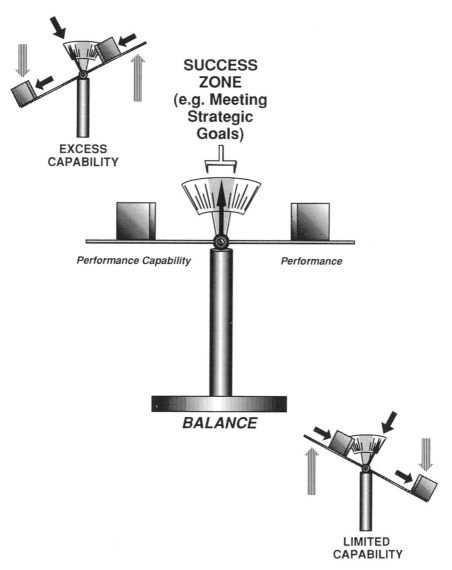

FIG. 11.1. Based on comments by Hubert Saint Onge (1992). Micromentor Corporate Learning Conference, 1992. Cambridge, Mass., January 8–10, 1992.

Specifically, he noted that many chief executive officers view knowledge as more important than financial resources, market position, technology, or any other asset. Knowledge is the main resource used in performing work in an organization. The organization's traditions, culture, technology, operations, systems, and procedures are all based on knowledge and expertise. To provide quality service to their clients and to grow, companies must do more than just help employees maintain and/or increase abilities to provide specific products or services. They must update products and services, change systems, structures, and capacities, and most importantly communicate these changes to employees so that they can link client problems to solutions that the organizations can provide.

Thus, there are needs for organizations, as well as for individuals, to elicit, organize, store, codify, build, generate, and transmit knowledge. These needs will increase with the rapidity of change and the increasing complexity of our interdependent global society. The benefits and value of the learning organization seem clear and substantial from the perspectives of providing enhanced client service and increased revenue. Moreover, the concept is a logical and comprehensive extension of the Total Quality movement.

However, the chord that all this strikes seems far beyond the reaches of a business strategy. At first glance, it seems to provide a basis for organizational acceptance of the sense of being overwhelmed that many workers, especially those in the knowledge industries, feel today. For example, many of us recognize that we cannot learn all that we need to do our jobs as well as we might like because what we need to know increases daily. A move to the culture of a learning organization may help us alleviate these feelings or at least signal to us that our employers grasp the situation.

The movement also seems both parallel to and connected with our increased understanding that adults develop over the life span. That is, there is the growing recognition that adults not only acquire more information over time, but that their capacity to act also changes. Indeed, if we as adults undertake the developmental journeys described by other authors in this volume, the learning organization may be critical to adulthood. Perhaps, for example, an entity that supports and enhances continuous growth learning and development for individuals is the only type of organization in which a self-actualizing individual will be happy. Perhaps the movement of the baby boom generation through organizational ranks and its arrival at mid-life are connected to this interest in learning organizations.

At a societal level, other forces may also converge to make this idea significant for us. For example, Harman and Hormann (1990) suggested that when it no longer makes sense for an economically successful society to have economic production and consumption as its central focus, learning and development can become the society's central project. They argued that our society has reached this point and that employment's real purpose is self-development (e.g., fundamentally we work to create and only incidentally to eat). Learning organizations are, thereby, important because they provide meaning to work and reflect the beginnings of a fundamental restructuring of the purpose of business and of society.

Indeed, upon reflection, the concept of a learning organization is so attractive because it affords us the potential to address problems affecting us in all the contexts in which we act, for example, as individuals, in teams, in organizations, and in communities of interests, professions, and nations (see Fig. 11.2). Moreover, although the concept has broad implications for all sectors of society, it seems particularly pertinent to the workplace and to its leaders because leaders are poised between societal and environmental factors that drive change and the people who must carry out changes. Thus, workplace leaders are positioned to develop an organizational form that meets business and organizational ends through addressing individual and societal development. Critical for that purpose will be the acceptance of a broad definition of and a commitment to learning organizations that includes a focus on individual and organizational learning and development as organizational ends, as well as means to build and distribute knowledge.

DEFINITIONS, METAPHORS, AND CHARACTERISTICS

Definitions

Given the relative newness of this concept, it is not surprising that a single, comprehensive, and agreed upon definition does not exist in the literature or among my colleagues. Each definition presented a slightly different nuance on a learning organization, company, expedition, or culture. For example, Senge (1990a) described learning organizations as:

> Organizations where people continually expand their capacity to create the results they truly desire, where new and expansive patterns of thinking are nurtured, where collective aspiration is set free, and where people are continually learning how to learn together. (p. 1)

There were, however, a number of complementary definitions. In addition, an examination of the current practices of organizations identified as, or aspiring to become, learning organizations revealed some

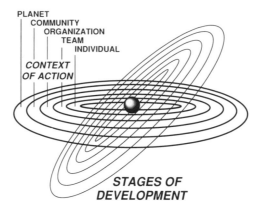

PLANET
COMMUNITY
ORGANIZATION
TEAM
INDIVIDUAL

CONTEXT
OF ACTION

STAGES OF
DEVELOPMENT

FIG. 11.2.

emerging metaphors and organizational characteristics associated with the concept. These extend the concept of the learner learning from that of an individual learning in an individual setting to that of individuals and organizations or communities learning within a planetary learning culture.

For example, Huczynski and Boddy (1979) described learning organizations as places "which set out to maximize the attainment of the individual members' learning goals through formal structures" (p. 273). Pór (1991) spoke of a corporate learning expedition as "a community that learns, not only a community of learners, but a self-organizing, collective intelligence aware of itself" (p. 1). Jaccaci (1989) presented a comprehensive view of a learning culture that includes many different learning communities:

> One where collaborative creativity in all contexts, relationships, and experiences is a basic purpose of the culture. It is a culture where the measure of success is the combined wisdom of groups and synergy, leadership, and service of the organization as a whole. Up to now, individuals have done the learning, but in a learning culture with multiple interactions among learning groups, the whole culture learns in a self-aware, self-reflective, and creative way. The groups become cells in the body of an organization, which itself becomes a new learning individual in the emergent global culture. (p. 50)

As a group, these definitions link the concepts of personal and organizational development. They suggest that organizations create a balance where both an individual's and an organization's development needs are addressed—a belief others (e.g., Schein, 1978) have shared. The definitions also encompass the idea of organizational learning. Acebo and

Watkins (1988) defined this as a *process* that enables organizations to change in response to new demands from the environment. Thus, through organizational learning, the organization learns.

What is different, then, about the concept of learning organizations? The difference that has emerged appears to be the combination of the ideas of a collective intelligence, of organizational learning, and of intentional, planned, personal, and organizational transformation. For example, organizational learning may be viewed as a means for organizational success; embedded in the idea of learning organizations is the concept of using collective intelligence and organizational learning to change personal and organizational outcomes. This powerful convergence of the notions of collective intelligence, organizational learning, and transformation provides a directional framework for personal and collective action.

Metaphors

Two of the most useful vehicles I have found for trying to understand the idea of a learning organization have been metaphors. The first, generated in a meeting at Ernst & Young's National Professional Development Group, is illustrated in Fig. 11.3. Specifically, our learning designers

FIG. 11.3. The Enterprise is peopled by an interdependent self-sustaining community supported by a complex and integrated technology.

viewed the learning organization as a "learning enterprise." Like the starship, it ventures into the unknown. Its voyagers are a community of interdependent, self-sustaining people able to handle present and future tasks.

The second, described in Table 11.1, is that of the "learning expedition." According to its designer George Pór, "knowledge can be defined as information organized for action" (Pór & Harrington, 1992b, p. 14). The learning expedition is a way for groups of people to organize knowledge. Each expedition creates a new context for unfolding the individual and collective genius as well as for developing new products and processes for sharing the learning with its future stakeholders. As an expedition continues, the explorers continue to define three key interlocking and evolving sets of systems, that is, the cognitive, social, and technological architecture required to support learning.

In an interesting manner, both of these metaphors provide a framework or context for individuals and organizations to consider movement to other places (e.g., goal attainment). They also provide a way to explore ideas visually. Metaphors and other such tools as Jaccaci's (1989) Metamatrix may be especially helpful in defining the key terms and specifications of learning organizations and in helping organizations create them.

Characteristics

Although no one organization has as yet fully incorporated all aspects of a learning organization, several companies or units of companies have been identified as having characteristics of learning organizations or as being committed to high performance and the development of their employees (Beck, 1989; Kiechel, 1990; Pedler, 1988; Senge, 1991; Vogt, 1991; Willis, 1991). Characteristics for learning organizations shared by these organizations have included:

- Individual learning/development is linked with organizational learning/development in an explicit and/or structured way.
- Learning is work and knowledge is product.
- There is a focus on innovation, creativity, and adaptability.
- Teams of all types are a part of the learning/working process.
- Networking—personal and aided by technology—is important to learning and to accomplishing work.
- The idea of the conscious evolution of self and organization prevails.
- Systems thinking—as expressed, for example, in the concepts of deutero-learning and substantive learning—is fundamental.
- Values and value creating are important drivers.

TABLE 11.1
What is a Learning Expedition?

A learning expedition is a gathering of mind and spirit focused on developing a collective body of knowledge, awareness, and wisdom; a means for supporting the purposes and objectives of the larger community. The expedition participants venture into uncharted territory ("what we know we don't know") as well as unexplored territory ("what we don't know we don't know"); they do not return unchanged. Barriers are broken, new genius is discovered, and the back home reality will never look quite the same.

While a learning expedition is marked by milestones or events, known as "base camps," the real work of the expedition is done between the meetings. Base camps primarily serve as the opportunities for celebrating and sharing learnings and successes.

A learning expedition is supported by an integrated set of social, knowledge, and technical architectures. The social architecture is that of a network of self-managed teams performing a variety of interrelated and essential functions.

Scouting Parties are special focus learning teams chartered by the expedition to investigate particular questions or issues of interest to the whole learning community. They are led by a committed champion and resourced by guides familiar with the trails leading to the frontier.

Action Teams represent the individual organizations participating in the expedition, and are accountable for maximizing the value of the expedition to the organization.

The **Stakeholder's Council** is a steering committee comprising members of each larger community served by the expedition. The council works with and coaches the design team, and vice versa.

The **Design Team's** responsibility is to craft an energizing context and empowering infrastructure to maximize the expedition's synergy, leverage, and generativity.

The **Support Team** includes dedicated professionals whose services include logistical support, group dialogue facilitation, video and multimedia support, and electronic networking.

The key element to the development of a collective intelligence is the **Weavers Team**. With the help of the support team, the weavers access, synthesize, and maintain the knowledge base of the learning community. Weavers need to be skilled in identifying underlying and emerging patters of energy and meaning in the community; they also serve to model that kind of listening for the rest of the community.

The learning expedition is ultimately responsible for creating both the process and the product known as the knowledge architecture for the community. The knowledge architecture produces and maintains the pool of shared knowledge and collective intelligence, organized for easy access by any community member, anytime, anywhere.

Learning expeditions can be used within organizations, as a collaborative venture among organizations, or within an industry or region.

Within an organization, a learning expedition can

- Help dissolve barriers between levels and between functions; build collaborative bridges to stakeholders.
- Serve both as a model and a way to accelerate the organization's evolution into a conscious, generative learning phase.
- Invent means to build organizational change capabilities.
- Impregnate the traditional organizational forms and practices with possibilities for unleashing its highest human potential.
- Prototype a social architecture of the learning organization.

(Continued)

189

TABLE 11.1
(Continued)

Between organizations a learning expedition can

- Spearhead the evolution of organizational learning alliances.
- Provide extraordinary economies of scale and scope for improving the work of large-scale system change.
- Provide a crow bar for breaking out of the box of current best thinking.

Within an industry or region a learning expedition can

- Lead to the formation of value-adding networks for improving the industry's responsiveness to challenges it's facing as a whole.
- Be the conduit for fostering collaboration between business, education, government, and citizen associations, on high-stakes issues that impact the future of the region.

Source: Pór and Harrington (1992a).

Given the dynamic business and social environment, the current level of experimentation, and the variety of perspectives on the purpose and shape of the learning organization, today's workplace leaders have a variety of definitions, metaphors, and directions to choose from as they design the future's learning organizations. We can most probably expect a rich variety of shapes.

Indeed, if we take as a premise that individual and societal development are appropriate and perhaps necessary ends for organizations, the idea of a learning organization becomes not only comprehensive, but also incredibly complex. As Fig. 11.2 indicates, individuals not only act in a number of different contexts, but also move through a number of different stages of development. Simultaneously, the teams, organizations, and communities we are in also develop over time. The dynamics of these interactions seem to prohibit easy solutions or uniform rules to uncover or create learning organizations. There are no prescriptions.

At the same time, however, this complexity calls for us to take a comprehensive view—to shape and build learning organizations within a learning culture. Not only to prosper but to thrive in the 21st century, we will need constantly to build and develop new knowledge and skills; we can expect to focus on continually learning new things, rather than on only remembering or sharing existing information.

ORGANIZING PRINCIPLES

The pressures of today's business environment and the malaise and unhappiness of the workforce, coupled with our desires as developing adults to work in environments that support and encourage growth, are likely to increase the pressure to create learning organizations, that is, organizations that consciously and intentionally develop their members while transforming themselves. Envisioning and implementing the type of change required to transform today's institutions into such entities require a clarity of purpose and a commitment to certain organizing principles around which a community can coalesce and upon which designers can build a foundation for an evolving design.

To some extent, the purpose and principles differ with the organization's role in society, the activities it performs or services it provides, its location, and even the industry in which it is located. From a somewhat different perspective, however, much of what has been articulated in this chapter implies that tomorrow's organizations may more clearly focus on the development of its members than do those of today. Given this, I posit three central principles for organizational designers to consider as key organizing principles of learning entities:

- Learning organizations are transformative.
- Learning organizations are collaborative and integrative.
- Learning organizations are supported by appropriate technologies.

Learning Organizations are Transformative

The dialogue around learning organizations contains the seeds of transformative change. Such a shift is fundamental. To make this shift involves readdressing the basic purpose, values, and vision of an organization and of work itself. People are discussing organizations moving to a different place, to a place that is constantly moving. The learning organization concept encompasses personal and organizational strategies to deal with constant change. Thus, its proponents posit a constantly changing organization whose members consciously and intentionally take charge of personal and organizational learning and direction.

When such deep changes occur, people do not only perform different tasks, but also speak differently, assume different roles, and see themselves in different relationships with one another. For example, in the future, educational institutions may be referred to as learning systems or communities; curricula may be discussed as planned learning activities; measurement may be regarded as feedback; teachers may be considered guides; and topics may be replaced with questions as the primary focus of study. In a learning organization, we might find that personal and organizational emphasis shifts from knowing to learning; from objectives to outcomes; from testing to goal attainment; from information dissemination and recall to pattern recognition and action; and from evaluating to "valuating." Thus, the organization and everyone in it would consider learning a primary, expected task and this would be reflected in organizational culture, language, structures, and values.

Many have suggested that the roles of manager and worker will change, for example, to those of teacher and learner or leader and colleague (e.g., Wisdom & Denton, 1991). More specifically, Bradford (1992) suggested the following as a beginning list of ideas to address in order to reshape such roles.

How can one re-define the role of the manager to that of leader? Including:

- How to support self-driven learning design for self, others, and the organization.
- How to create an information-rich environment that enable autonomous learning.
- How to gain a $3 + 3 = 9$ synergy in the workplace.
- How to challenge and oppose colleagues using trust and integrity.
- How to avoid one-upmanship.
- How to tolerate confusion and chaos in the work experience.
- How to keep knowing from destroying learning.
- How to give power away to be enhanced by it.

How can one re-define the role of the worker to that of member or colleague? Including:

- How to develop people's internal autonomy.
- How to recruit advocates for participant creativity.
- How people can take ownership and responsibility for their own learning and actions.
- How to compete cooperatively.
- How to accept chaos and certainty as part of the work experience.
- How to cordially invite the strange.

The responses to these questions and issues will differ depending on specific organizational contexts. However, the questions raised suggest that within a learning community people will, at the same time, assume more responsibilities for self and others and have more connectivity of purpose and action than is present in many of today's organizations. Michael (personal communication, January 1992) posited that how we address these questions will be a significant challenge to individuals and organizations who choose this path. He pointed out that being a learner requires acknowledging that one is vulnerable, an acknowledgment exceedingly difficult to make. Indeed, from our youth, most of us have been led to believe that it is what we know that is important and that knowledge brings stability and status.

Learning Organizations are Collaborative and Integrative

Two of the most beneficial challenges and aspects of learning organizations are collaboration and integration. The idea of learning, thinking, and working with others is central to the emphasis on team learning and action, collective intelligence, communities of learners, and learning systems. The power and synergy achieved by linking with one another is an incredible lure to individuals and organizations. Rudd (1992), for example, presented an analogy of a learning organization as an organization where members move together like a flock of geese rather than in divergent directions like a stampeding herd of buffalo. Achieving concentrated and focused action might provide us with a better opportunity not only to reach individual and organizational ends, but to address the critical problems facing our communities and society. The emphasis on collaboration seems a welcome recognition of the limits and limitlessness of a human being's capacity. With the shift from knowing to learning, the transition from individual to collaborative action seems a daunting task. How can it be achieved?

Savage (1992) suggested a focus on integrative processes, which he defined as putting people and processes in touch with one another around whole challenges. This notion encompasses the idea, for example, of an individual's being responsible for managing a specific project or client relationship and having access to the resources of the entire organization across discipline and geographical lines. It also seems to include the practice of establishing cross-functional teams to shorten product cycle time and to enhance quality. Individuals' focusing on or managing whole challenges has been associated with mastery of competency (Dreyfus & Dreyfus, 1984). Thus, the use of integrative processes meets a basic need of individuals as well as one of customers and of organizations. Integrative processes could also involve personnel in multiple locations, or even those beyond the boundaries of a single organization. Savage (1992) viewed the organization's challenges related to integrative processes to be: to overcome organizational fragmentation; to develop a new approach to accountability; to learn to focus and coordinate multiple task-focused teams; and to capture the team learning.

Learning Organizations are Supported
by Appropriate Technologies

Key to creating a learning organization is using technologies appropriate to support such an organization. Such technologies are broad-based and include the arts and sciences of learning, discovery, and communication as well as information technology and computer science. For example, more organizations may follow the lead of a number of companies that have recently established the centers of creative thinking and learning (Merritt, 1992). Organizations might help people learn how to develop systems thinking and mental models (Senge, 1990b). They might also help employees learn how to identify tacit knowledge and make it explicit (Nonaka, 1991). We can also expect widespread use of global communications networks that connect those with the problem or challenge with those who can help them address problems and challenges. Successful learning organizations will use technology to elicit, code, and store knowledge and to create knowledge. Of special interest is the blend of technologies now being used to design technology to support individual and group thinking and problem-solving activities. Vital to the technology platform of the learning organizations are research findings and new practices related to neurosciences, adult development, and psychology. Equally vital are advances in computer software and hardware that will help people act as teams despite geographic and discipline differences.

CONCLUSION AND ISSUES
FOR FUTURE EXPLORATION

This chapter presented an opportunity to share the findings of a collaborative exploration into the concept of a learning organization. In it, I described the process followed, noted the importance of the concept to the workplace and to those interested in adult development, reported definitions, metaphors and characteristics, and presented some organizing principles that seem to underlie its application. Not attempted were a description of the ideal learning organization or prescription for implementation. These are issues that specific organizations and the individuals in them will address. Also not attempted, and a subject for future study, are the questions of measurement and accountability in learning organizations. For example, how do we value individual and organizational knowledge as assets? What are the array of measurement techniques used to measure performance capability and its growth?

Throughout the chapter, I suggested that the concepts of adult development and of learning organizations are intertwined. For example, the organization is the setting for development; the workplace is a context in which it occurs. Environmental factors such as increasing complexity, globalization, and rapid change affect us all individually. They also affect us as we operate in teams, in organizations, in communities, or in nations. As members of teams, groups, and organizations, we are both leader and led; affected by the environment, we also shape it.

In the chapter's introduction, I raised the issue of how the concept of a learning organization relates to the notion of and research on adult development. Later, I posited that a learning organization is an organization that intentionally transforms its members and itself. Additionally, a learning organization acts as a collective intelligence in a collaborative way, puts into place integrative processes, and is supported by appropriate technologies.

Questions remain about how the concept of learning organizations can inform that of adult development and how what we have learned in adult development can be used to create effective learning organizations. Interesting also are questions that arise from the interaction of these two concepts. Questions include, for example: What can organizations learn about eliciting, coding, storing, and disseminating knowledge from studying adult development (cognitive, social, and emotional)? What might be the consequences to individuals if organizations intentionally supported their development? What might happen to organizational goals and culture if adult development is included as a primary organizational end?

These are broad questions. The current interest in learning organizations presents an opportunity for practitioners and researchers to explore them. Moreover, many organizations are currently seeking ways to create the kind of work environments that foster continuous improvement and learning. Results of inquiry and exploration may find waiting ears both in those theorizing about the contextual aspects (here, the workplace) of adult development and in those creating the context of future organizations.

ACKNOWLEDGMENT

One of the emerging premises of the concept of learning organizations is that knowledge and intelligence are possessed not only by individuals but also by teams and organizations. A second is that, if individual and team competition are replaced by collaboration and alliance, the team or organization will have a greater store of knowledge to use as a basis for interpretation and decision making. Collaboration certainly has been the modus operandi for the generation of this chapter. I would especially like to acknowledge Tony Adams, Allyn Bradford, Gus Jaccaci, and

Michael Snyder for visions of a "break-the-mold" learning system that they shared at a Collaboration in Social Architecture exchange (January 6–9, 1992). Eric Vogt and the participants at MicroMentor's Corporate Learning Conference 1992 (January 8–10, 1992) also helped shape the work. The thoughts of Suzanne Merritt (Polaroid), Hubert St. Onge (Canadian Imperial Bank of Commerce), Nicholas Rudd (Young and Rubicam), and Charles Savage (Digital Equipment Corporation), helped me address workplace applications. I would also like to acknowledge those individuals such as Jim Botkin, Gus Jaccaci, George Pór, Peter Senge, and Eric Vogt who have taken action to create collaborative vehicles to increase and expand our knowledge of learning organizations.

REFERENCES

Acebo, S. C., & Watkins, K. (1988). Community college faculty development: Designing a learning organization. *New Directions for Continuing Education, 38,* 49–61.

Argyris, C. (1991). Teaching smart people how to learn. *Harvard Business Review, 69*(3), 99–109.

Beck, M. (1989). Learning organizations—How to create them. *Industrial & Commercial Training, 21*(3), 21–28.

Bradford, A. (1992, January). Comments, Collaboration in Social Architecture exchange, Cambridge, MA.

Dreyfus, H., & Dreyfus, S. (1984). Putting computers in their proper places: Analysis versus intuition in the classroom. *Teachers College Record, 85*(4), 578–601.

Harman, W., & Hormann, J. (1990). *Creative work: The constructive role of business in a transforming society.* Indianapolis, IN: An Institute of Noetic Sciences Publication, Knowledge Systems, Inc.

Huczynski, A., & Boddy, D. (1979). The learning organization: An approach to management education and development. *Studies in Higher Education, 4*(2), 211–222.

Jaccaci, A. (1989). The social architecture of a learning culture. *Training & Development Journal, 43*(11), 49–51.

Kiechel, W., III (1990). The organization that learns. *Fortune, 121*(6), 133–136.

Merritt, S. (1992, January). *Creativity and the learning organization.* Paper presented at the Micromentor Learning Conference, Cambridge, MA.

Nonaka, I. (1991). The knowledge-creating company. *Harvard Business Review, 69*(6), 96–104.

Pedler, M. (1988). Applying self-development in organisations. *Industrial & Commercial Training, 20*(2), 19–22.

Pór, G. (1991, June). *What is a corporate learning expedition?* Paper presented at the Collaborative in Social Architecture, Cambridge, MA.

Pór, G., & Harrington, K. (1992a). *What is a learning expedition?* Report of December 1991 conference, Learning Expedition and Collective Intelligence, International Center for Organizational Design, Colorado Springs, CO.

Pór, G., & Harrington, K. (1992b). *Where do we go from here?* Report of December 1991 conference, Learning Expedition and Collective Intelligence, International Center for Organizational Design, Colorado Springs, CO.

Rudd, N. (1992, January). *Learning to serve, modeling tomorrow's business today.* Paper presented at the Micromentor Learning Conference, Cambridge, MA.

Saint Onge, H. (1992, January). *Creating a developmental learning culture at CIBC.* Paper presented at the Micromentor Learning Conference, Cambridge, MA.

Savage, C. (1990). *Fifth generation management.* Maynard, MA: Digital Press, Digital Equipment Corporation.

Savage, C. (1992, January), *Discovering core competencies.* Paper presented at the Micromentor Learning Conference, Cambridge, MA.

Schein, E. (1978). *Career dynamics-matching individual and organizational needs.* Reading, MA: Addison Welsey.

Senge, P. (1990a). *The fifth discipline.* New York: Doubleday.

Senge, P. (1990b). The leader's new work: Building learning organizations. *Sloan Management Review, 32*(1), 7–23.

Senge, P. (1991). The learning organization made plain. *Training & Development Journal, 45*(10), 37–44.

Stata, R. (1989). Organizational learning—The key to management innovation. *Sloan Management Review, 30*(3), 63–74.

Vogt, E. (1991, May). *Building learning organizations.* Paper presented at the American Society for Training and Development, Financial Services conference, San Francisco.

Wiig, K. M.(1990, November). *The company as a learning organization.* Adapted from a presentation to idmi *Technology Transfer,* Lugano, Switzerland.

Willis, V. J. (1991). The new learning organization: Should there be a chief learning officer in the house? *Human Resource Development Quarterly, 2*(2), 181–187.

Wisdom, B. L., & Denton, K. D. (1991). Manager as teacher. *Training & Development Journal, 45*(12), 54–58.

CHAPTER TWELVE

Atmosphere and Stage Development in the Workplace

Michael L. Commons
Harvard Medical School

Sharon R. Krause
Gregory A. Fayer
Harvard Divinity School

Maryellen Meaney
Harvard University

This chapter presents a method for characterizing the relationship between individuals and their workplace environment with respect to individual moral development. We hypothesize that this is a dynamic, two-way relationship and that connections exist between individual development and the stage of development embodied in the workplace environment. We construe development in terms of the stage of response that people give to moral dilemmas. Using a scoring scheme derived from the General Stage Model (Commons & Richards, 1984a, 1984b), we score individual responses to moral dilemmas and compare the stage of individual responses to the stage of response embodied in organizational decision making, both formal and informal. We are particularly interested in identifying the contingencies by which this relationship is governed and the reinforcement mechanisms (Skinner, 1938) through which they are enforced. This chapter describes a nonarbitrary and highly precise method for investigating and characterizing these relations.

Institutional atmosphere refers to the dynamic relationship between an institution and those individuals who comprise it. Atmosphere includes the contingencies that affect individual behavior within an organization and the methods by which contingencies are set. We define a *contingency* as a relationship between events (i.e., behaviors or responses) and outcomes. Consequences that increase the likelihood of the event that they follow are termed *reinforcers*. Consequences that decrease the likelihood of the event that they follow are termed *punishers*. What the environment contributes to behavior, we suggest, can be described in terms of contingent relations among events. We also maintain that the reasoning of individual members within any workplace has significant bearing upon organizational atmosphere. As reasoning develops in complexity, individuals are increasingly capable of understanding the perspectives of others, and of evaluating and integrating competing perspectives. These skills are integrated into the formal and informal policymaking and policy enforcement structures of the organization. The explicit statements of perceived organizational contingencies are referred to as *verbalized causal rules* or contingencies (Commons, Kantrowitz, Buhlman, Ellis, & Grotzer, in preparation). The implicit perceptions of causality are the *perceived causal rules* or contingencies.

In order to characterize atmosphere at the level of organizational macrostructure, we believe that it is necessary to examine the individual contingencies embodied in atmosphere, which constitute the organizational microstructure (Goffman, 1967). Microstructure and macrostructure are inseparable. Atmosphere is, therefore, a characterization of the sum of individual contingencies operative within an organization and as Kohlberg (1985) emphasized, their justifications. Atmosphere, therefore, refers to the manner in which the institution and individuals either constrain or motivate the development of individuals and the development of the organization.

Background

Because human experience unfolds almost exclusively in fields of activity that are interpersonal, social forces both act upon persons and provide the conceptual frameworks through which people understand the world and themselves. For example, Damon and Hart (1988) characterized self-understanding as basically a social process. This notion is not idiosyncratic, but stands in a strong theoretical tradition. As Mead (1934) and other theorists of the self (e.g., Kohlberg, Hart, & Wertsch, 1987) emphasized, understanding one's self is a social communicative act. Similarly, Durkheim's contention (cited in Thompson, 1985) that social processes fundamentally characterize the individual has found a significant following in theorists who contend that "each kind of community is a thought world . . . penetrating the minds of its members, defining their experience, and setting the poles of their moral understanding" (Douglas, 1986, p. 128). As Foucault (1979) said, "the individual is carefully fabricated" (p. 217) in this interactive system of social structures.

Characterizing the interaction between individuals and their culture, however, has been a central problem. The problem is to account for the large variety of individual and cultural differences, while still providing a coherent framework that can be applied to many groups and individuals. Explanatory models have typically fallen into one of two camps; namely, positivistic versus process theories. Positivistic interpretations, in the tradition of British and U.S. analytic philosophy, offer reductionistic models of social processes and their impact on individuals. Such approaches attempt to find a single factor or group of factors to which learning can be reduced. The social world, in this view, is governed by fixed structures that exert a unidirectional force upon individuals. Because the locus of power is seated primarily within environmental factors, little attention is given to the ways in which individuals work a reciprocal influence upon social structures.

In contrast, process models (e.g., Barth, 1966; Moore, 1975) have rejected the notion of a strictly deterministic social world. Instead, they have offered generative models for interpreting the often unpredictable ways in which atmosphere and individuals reciprocally affect one another. Social systems are seen as grounded in the interpersonal interactions of concrete individuals, rather than in necessary, abstract social categories. Barth's (1966) model of transaction characterized this interaction as "the compounded effects which multiple independent actors, each seeking to pursue the transactional optimal course of behavior, have on each other" (p. 11), and social systems as "the gross frequentive patterns of behavior which will tend to emerge in such situations" (p. 11).

Such models contrast sharply with positivistic ones in that the former have located the foundations of social systems in the interactions of concrete individuals and in the shifting contingencies through which individuals impact one another. Social categories, in this view, emerge from particular sets of transactions rather than governing such transactions externally. Process theories have also assumed that change within social systems is both continuous and necessary. Change is construed as a natural feature of social systems with a twofold character. On the one hand, change arises as society responds to the actions of individuals. On the other hand, individuals change as they interact with others and with social institutions. The two sorts of change influence one another. These models, however, provide few resources for understanding the precise nature of this relationship at the microstructural level of individual development.

Positivistic theories tend to reduce complex interactions between society and individuals to a deterministic model. Process theories often lack sufficiently clear explication of the microstructural mechanisms that govern this interaction. Both positivistic and process models of social processes remain incomplete so long as they lack the conceptual resources to justify particular nonarbitrary links between the complexity of responses by individuals and the complexity of the atmosphere in which they function. Also, they must account for the real and unpredictable developmental variance observable among individuals at the same time.

The General Stage Model (GSM) when combined with contingency analysis provides just such resources. The GSM orders both individual and organizational processes in a nonarbitrary sequence. This sequence both affects and is affected by the contingencies in atmosphere. Further, the model describes formal processes through which individuals and atmosphere interact whether in the workplace, the family, or the state. The GSM also allows for a precise, microstructural analysis of these processes as they impact individual behavior. Moreover, the GSM accounts for a wide variety of individual behaviors and for the creativity and dynamism of organizational behavior as a continuous collective process. At the same time, it provides means for interpreting this relation in a nonreductionistic, nonarbitrary way.

General Stage Model

The GSM is a universal stage system that classifies development in terms of the task-required hierarchical organization of response. Commons and Richards (1984a) suggested that developmental theory should address two conceptually different but related issues: (a) the hierarchical complexity of the task to be solved; and (b) the psychology, sociology, and anthropology of how such task performance develops.

Scoring by stage is related to the first issue because the GSM uses the hierarchical complexity of tasks as the basis for the definition of stage. An action is at a given *stage* when it successfully completes a task of a given hierarchical order of complexity. *Hierarchical complexity* refers to the number of recursions that the coordinating actions must perform on a set of primary elements. Actions at a *higher order of hierarchical complexity*: (a) are defined in terms of the actions at the next lower order of hierarchical complexity, (b) organize and transform the lower order actions, (c) produce organizations of lower order actions that are new and not arbitrary, and (d) cannot be accomplished by these lower order actions alone.

The discussion of atmosphere and its contingencies relates to the second issue. The two are interrelated insofar as reinforcement contingencies determine stage of response. The GSM provides a means for identifying how contingencies are set and transferred within organizations. Therefore, it gives a measure of the sensitivity of individuals to the reinforcement contingencies that shape social systems and individual development. To counter the possible objection of arbitrariness in the definition of stages, the GSM stages are grounded in the hierarchical-complexity stage criteria of mathematical models (Coombs, Dawes, & Tversky, 1970) and information science (Commons & Richards, 1984a, 1984b; Lindsay & Norman, 1977; Rodriguez, 1989). The GSM also posits that individuals perceive the world through conceptual frameworks. These frameworks embody the individual's cultural, educational, religious, political, and social background (as well as many other factors). Such a framework is referred to as one's perspective. Perspectives differ in terms of hierarchical complexity. As the hierarchical complexity of an individual's response to task demands increases (i.e., as stage of development goes up), the individual is increasingly able to take many such perspectives into account (Commons & Rodriguez, 1990; Rodriguez, 1989).

In adult development, and consequently in professional-level workplace interactions, three developmental stages predominate: formal operational (GMS Stage 4b, Kohlberg Stage 3/4), systematic (GSM Stage 5a, Kohlberg Stage 4), and metasystematic (GSM Stage 5b, Kohlberg Stages 5 and 6). Following are GSM descriptions of these stages.

Formal Operational Stage 4b.   Stage 4b responses identify and isolate relations in complex sets of variables as well as label interactions of events abstractly in a linear fashion. For example, in discourse at this stage, the verbalized perceived causal rules are empirical statements of causality and analytic if–then propositions. Such formal-operational statements have the formal structure of an order relationship, "A > B," where A and B are both abstract-stage propositions (GSM Stage 4a). In forming justifications, the logical arguments at this stage usually have the form, "A → B." That is, the relationship between A and B is made explicit through a causal statement with evidence, a logical statement or by some other clear coordination (e.g., of equivalence, proportionality) of at least two propositions or abstract-stage elements. Logical arguments are used to convince people of the soundness of a deduction from premises. Causal arguments are used to convince people of an empirical relationship between events and outcomes. For an empirical example, "A—If you hope to get a good academic job, then B—you must publish a good deal." Authority in the form of local norms, rules, and regulations is given pre-eminence, whereas particular individuals or situations play only a minor role. Reasons and justifications relate to expected behavior based on these bureaucratic rules or norms.

Systematic Stage 5a.   A Stage 5a response is characterized by systematizing formal-operational relations into a network. Here, the products of the formal stage actions—coordinated abstract-stage propositions—

become the elements to be coordinated. The product of the more hierarchically complex Stage 5a statement is the coordination of the relations constructed by formal operational actions into a system. A suitable systematic-stage action coordinates two or more relations, for example, System$_1$: "A → C and A → B." This system could be "If you have a large number of publications, some teaching experience, a coherent research program then you might get a good academic job." This constitutes a single, unified system, which the subject takes to be comprehensive. For example, social interactions are seen as integrated systems of relationships. Yet the importance of the individuals is determined with respect to their relation to and/or role in the system. Norms, laws, rights, duties, rules, and regulations form a logically coherent system; reasoning centers around how action would impact one's individual role and status within the system and the functioning of the institution.

Metasystematic Stage 5b.

A Stage 5b statement coordinates and transforms two or more systems according to a principle that is external to both systems. Such metasystematic principles take precedence over the concerns of any particular system. The concern is never to preserve a system or institution for its own sake. Rather, the needs and interests of a number of systems are taken into account without regard to the particular system or institution within which one finds oneself. Systems are compared and contrasted in terms of their properties. The focus is on the similarities and differences in each system's form as well as constituent causal relations and persons within it. At Stage 5b, perspective-taking skills are well developed. A wide range of perspectives can be taken into account and coordinated in a nonarbitrary manner. For example, a metasystematic Stage 5b statement might have the form, "A merit system, [S$_1$]—in which having a large number of publications, some teaching experience, a coherent research program lead to a good academic job"—can be transformed into a discriminatory system, if "minority students are unable to work with faculty who have grants." The discriminatory system [S$_2$] entails that "Students who work with faculty who do not have grants have a lower likelihood of publishing and forming a coherent research program than students who work with funded faculty"; and "Minorities are less likely than nonminorities to have an equal opportunity to work with faculty who have grants." By adding these last two formal operational conditions, the system of merit [S$_1$] is transformed into a discriminatory system [S$_2$], written as $T_1(S_1) → (S_2)$. In system [S$_2$] past discrimination influences one of the merit criteria. Likewise, a merit system is transformed into a merit system with politics if active support from an influential person is required, $T_2(S_1) → (S_3)$. Taking all these transformations together, one can build a supersystem of these systems.

Because the purpose of this chapter is to illustrate a method and argument, only samples of data from a few subjects are presented here. The method characterizes the relationship between individuals and their workplace environments. The characterization consists of identifying some of the contingencies involved and scoring the stage of justification of those contingencies.

METHOD

Subjects

Twenty-eight subjects from the Harvard University community were interviewed. The subjects included students, faculty members, and administrators. All subjects were working, teaching, or studying in the field of ethics. Four subjects were women, and two were African-American.

Procedure

The study applies the GSM to an interview consisting of a series of open-ended questions and two dilemmas. The format is similar to those used by Armon (1984a, 1984b) in the Good Life Interview and by Perry (1970). The first section of the interview centers around the following questions: (a) What is a good university? (b) What is a good government? and (c) What is a good government for a university? The second section consists of a dilemma involving a conflict between students and administration on the issue of free speech and is followed by the standard Heinz Dilemma (Colby & Kohlberg, 1987; Kohlberg, 1969, 1984). Subjects were probed for responses in the domains of justice, epistemology, attachment, and the good. Interviews were conducted in person and recorded on audiotape for later transcription.

Applying the GSM

The General Stage Scoring System (GSSS), derived from the GSM, is used to determine the stage of subjects' responses to a given task demand. In GSSS, stage of behavior is regarded as a function of the hierarchical complexity of the actions required to solve a task. In distinction to other content-based scoring systems, GSSS scoring involves an analysis of the microstructure of subject responses, as embodied in specific statements. In applying GSSS, the stage score of responses is usually equivalent (Commons & Grotzer, 1990) to scores determined through other procedures

(Armon, 1984a, 1984b; Colby & Kohlberg, 1987; Perry, 1970, 1981). Fewer statements, however, require "guess-scoring" or are designated unscorable. A further advantage of GSSS is that, theoretically, any statement is scorable. Scoring can, therefore, be applied across a range of tasks and is not limited to standardized dilemmas.

Two types of scoring are used to determine stage: (a) signal-detection scoring and (b) dialectical scoring. Signal-detection scoring determines the stage of the basic elements that individuals coordinate in a given statement, or response. The stages of these responses are constrained by the atmosphere in which the individual is operating as well as by how good the individuals involved are in forming such coordinations. For example, an attorney may construct higher stage statements in addressing a judge's inquiry on legal principles, but not when speaking with her child at home. Lower stage responses, which are appropriate to the conversation with her young child, would be punished in the courtroom. Such lower stage arguments would fail to address the questions of legal principle. Yet, the atmosphere of the court requires attorneys to address legal principles. The punishments might include the judge's admonishing the attorney to address the question and ultimately finding against her client. Higher stage responses, which are appropriate when addressing a judge, may not be reinforced by her child. The attorney might prefer that her child respond positively to a high-stage argument. The child may also prefer to do so. Because her child would have a low proclivity for coordinating the elements in the attorney's higher stage response, her behavior would not be affected by the attorney's response in the way the attorney planned. The lack of the desired behavior would be a lack of reinforcement for addressing the child at too high a stage.

The hierarchical organization of stage, according to the GSM, entails that implicit in every response is a series of increasingly complex coordinations. The lowest order of complexity begins with the primary elements of the subjects' explanations (for these subjects, abstract Stage 4a or beginning-formal operations) and proceeds to the order of complexity signified by the assigned stage of response. Individual responses, however, tend to address those stages that the atmosphere rewards. Although the presence of lower stage elements is always implicit in higher stage statements, they are seldom made explicit. The task of signal-detection scoring, then, is to identify all of these basic, lower stage primary elements that are successfully used and assign stage scores to each of them. The highest is usually deemed the stage of the response.

Once the lower stage primary elements within a response are identified and staged, dialectical scoring can begin. Dialectical scoring determines the point of transition between stages of the coordinations of primary elements within a given statement.

In scoring interviews, the scores that are assigned apply to subject responses to particular task demands. Stage scores, then, should not be interpreted as indicators of fixed structures internal to the subject. As performance varies in response to reinforcement, subjects will construct statements at different stages.

ILLUSTRATIVE EXAMPLES

In the following examples, GSSS is applied to sample subject responses from the interview previously described in order to demonstrate how the GSM can be used to characterize the relationship between individuals and organizational atmosphere in the workplace. The examples are applications of the theory presented in this chapter. Additionally, they suggest an association between the stage of individual responses and the stage of organizational atmosphere. Example 1 is taken from a parallel study conducted at the Medical School at Universidad Autonóma de Baja California in Mexicali, México in 1989 by Galaz-Fontes called the "The Ethical Doctor" (as cited in Meaney, 1990; Galaz-Fontes, Pacheco-Sanchez, & Commons, 1989). Like snapshots, these examples "freeze" subject responses at a particular point in the performance of a task. This allows for closer scrutiny of the organization of the response, although it does not do justice to the dynamism of the typical subject performance in responding across a variety of tasks.

Example 1 (Stage 4b)

Subject: *The main office, the office of the dean, has a door by which all of the faculty enters, and beside the door there is a little window, and it says, "Students are attended here." I think that is significant. That way of dealing with students is telling them, "You are outside, you are a student. Your right is to knock on the window and tell us what your problem is and we will solve it for you. And don't get too close, you might be contagious." What has happened within the Medical School is that there is a lot of noninterest of the faculty in terms of the school. They are just interested in giving their classes, fulfilling the minimum requirements, but are not interested in discussing things more deeply. . . . [There is] no enthusiasm for the institution. People just stay there and keep working. Like, for example, the recently approved new curriculum. It was centrally done. They invited professors to participate but they did not participate in the discussion. So, for example, it is like a passive attitude. "This is the new curriculum, what do you think?" But they [the administration] did not want to really know. . . . A lot of professors are interested in improving things but more on a personal level than in terms of the program, or in terms of the institution.*

Here, authority is construed in terms of linear chains of causality where the administration makes decisions without input from other sources. No participatory network is present. Logically justified bureaucratic solutions by the administrators in this atmosphere are characteristic of formal-operational Stage 4b. Decisions such as curriculum development are "centrally done." The evidence for the linear contingencies is illustrated next. Because central authority dominates so thoroughly, invitations to participate in the decision-making processes go unheeded. There was a history of the administration appearing to ask questions of the faculty, but punishing or at least not reinforcing responses to those questions. As a result of these contingencies, professors "are interested in improving things . . . more on a personal level than in terms of the program or in terms of the institution." Individual interests are not integrated with the systematic interests of a larger whole.

Even the personal problems of students are solved by appeal to this logical chain of authority indicative of Stage 4b. This may be contrasted with a higher stage dialogical process in which the students themselves take part. Rather demeaning contingencies control student–administration interaction. The respondent states that "the office of the dean, has a door by which all of the faculty enters, and beside the door there is a little window, and it says, 'Students are attended here.' " The verbalizations of faculty who enter the door are responded to at least verbally, but the verbalizations of students who enter the door are not. Students are responded to only if they go to the little window. The administration places students into a different category, not even afforded a door but "a little window." Faculty may enjoy the appearance of interaction, but students are "attended to." The linear logic of Stage 4b is, If faculty, use the door; if student, use the little window.

Example 2 (Stage 5a Transition to Stage 5b)

Subject: *If the university says this to the student [that students should always lend their support to university goals], why would this be bad, you were saying? Why should we? The question is what is the argument for all rallying behind anyone within an institution. It denies the sense of social responsibility if we're always to rally around institutions; it makes us not critics, but ralliers, followers, enthusiasts. For what? For the university, that abstraction? Why should I rally around it . . . ? I'll rally around it insofar as it represents things that I think important. And one of the things that I think important is the students saying this would be, that it would stimulate independent and critical thought, and doesn't try to rally around a notion except in the notion in those who want to rally around this flag and without threatening those who don't in some official way.*

The university's injunction to students to rally around the institution typifies a Stage 5a "conventional" response in which a single, closed system predominates. The administrative contingencies identify individuals strictly in terms of their place in the system rather than just within a hierarchy. They also make clear that deviations may be punished or not reinforced. These reinforcement contingencies are described as "threatening those who don't [support the university goals] in some official way." These contingencies place a ceiling on individual development, which the subject identifies by saying "it makes us not critics, but ralliers, followers, enthusiasts."

The subject, however, sees beyond the single system of the institution. This places the response at a transitional step between Systematic Stage 5a and Metasystematic Stage 5b. The subject identifies an alternative system. This alternative system is characterized by "independent and critical thought" where individuals are not defined strictly in terms of their position within a single system. The subject has not articulated relationships between the system of critics and system of ralliers. In the system of critics, various critiques of the current system are discussed and in the system of ralliers enthusiastic support of the present system is given. The subject's behavior can be seen as a struggle against the Stage 5a expectations of his workplace atmosphere. At the metasystematic stage, the critiques and the rallying would all be part of a supersystem of appraisal and evaluation from multiple perspectives.

Example 3 (Stage 5b)

> Interviewer: *What is a good government for the university?*
> Subject: *I don't think of a university as having a government. It's more like a company. It's not like a state. In this case it's a business . . .*
> Interviewer: *How should it run itself then? As a business?*
> Subject: *As a modern business which would be pretty much participatory, and people that work in the business, etc., etc. I mean a business today has lots of stakeholders, and serves a lot of people so . . . like in the lumbering business you have to consider your employees, your clients, your suppliers, the ecology of the land you work on, etc., etc., etc. The communities you work in, all these sort of things. These are all stakeholders in the organization as well as your stockholders. The problem with businesses in this country is we have a rather myopic view, in the sense that businesses are too beholden to their stockholders, and they're too much involved in their quarterly profits. Take companies, countries which do most of their equity raising through, uh banks, like Japan, they take a much longer term*

*perspective because their banks . . . you know, they have lifetime employees
and banks with a long-term perspective, they serve their community in
a different kind of way. And there's a balance of constituencies here. . . .*
Interviewer: *What do you think would be a bad way to run the University?*
Subject: *Bureaucracy is your biggest problem.*
Interviewer: *Why is that bad?*
Subject: *Well it stifles creativity.*

In this example, the subject describes a metasystematic ideal for the
workplace. The subject also identifies ways in which his own university
workplace falls short of this ideal by remaining entrenched in systematic
stage action. The subject compares a Japanese model of business management to the U.S. model and implicitly equates this with the university.
A key feature of the metasystematic, Stage 5b, business is that it is participatory in the sense that it considers the interests of employees, clients,
suppliers, the environment, and the stockholders. The setting of contingencies takes place in such a manner that all the constituencies are
represented. The subject considers each of these groups as systems in
themselves and sees the company as a synthesis of these systems. Doing
so involves being able to see things in terms of "a long-term perspective." The reinforcement associated with these contingencies is considered from the perspectives of all the participants, not just one or two,
which is metasystematic Stage 5b perspective-taking. The possible reper-
cussions or side effects from various actions are also considered. For example, gross harm to relatively disadvantaged persons is seen as
demoralizing. The government requires that companies not pollute because the citizens have no direct control over company policy in the area.
Such a perspective, the subject suggests, will not arise in the absence of
"a balance of constituencies." With such a balance, there might be some
cooperative contingencies within the community as well as competitive
ones outside of the community. To the extent that the subject calls for
respect for the universal persons, the "stakeholders" in and around the
institution, and an integration of their perspectives, the subject is making metasystematic Stage 5b responses consistent with what Kohlberg
termed "postconventional" reasoning.

In contrast, the university workplace in which the subject actually exists is characterized by the "myopic" view of an institution that cannot
see beyond the limits of a single system. In his case, the single dominant
system is that determined by the stockholders. The subject describes his
workplace, then, as entrenched in some systematic stage acts such as maximizing short-term profits for the managers and stockholders. He sees the
"bureaucracy," typical of Stage 4b and Stage 5a, as directly impacting
upon individual creativity. This observation is consistent with what Kohlberg labeled "conventional" stages.

DISCUSSION

Social forces impact individuals in different combinations and with varying degrees of intensity. Because the variables are numerous and frequently unperceived, the character of this interaction between atmosphere and individual is often obscure. Nevertheless, we would argue that reinforcement contingencies are the immediate controlling relationships for both individual and organizational behavior. In their work on education, for example, Commons and Hallinan (1989) demonstrated that reinforcement helps people form strategies and representations that include both the implicit perceived causal rules and the explicit verbalized rules. Reinforcement also leads them to select the more successful strategies and causes them to continue actively solving the problems. By reinforcing more (vs. less) developed strategies during students' progression to formal operations, a teacher can reinforce students' more complex reasoning (Commons, Handel, Richard, & Grotzer, in preparation; Richard, Unger, & Commons, 1988).

Commons, Grotzer, and Davidson (1991) recently demonstrated this in a study of a large number of young students from mixed socioeconomic backgrounds. All students were asked to solve a series of adult-stage problems requiring them to detect causes. One group of students received no feedback about their performance, a second group received feedback alone, and a third group received both feedback and points for correct answers. They were told that their team could accumulate these points to win a prize. A fourth, control group of students took only the pretest and posttest without undergoing the problem-solving task series. Only students in the reinforcement (i.e., in this case, points leading to possible prizes) group improved their proficiency in detecting causal relations from the pretest to the posttest. Students who received no feedback and those who received feedback without reinforcement did not demonstrate this stage development. These students did not learn any more than the control students. The study implies that, even when academic achievement does not motivate some students, all students' reasoning can develop when success receives the appropriate reinforcers.

We suspect that the hierarchical complexity of the contingencies that constitute a particular workplace atmosphere affects the patterns of individual choice making within that organization. As the hierarchical complexity of an individual's response to task demands increases (i.e., as stage of development goes up), the individual is increasingly able to take the perspectives of others into account (Commons & Rodriguez, 1990; Rodriguez, 1989). Successful decision making in the workplace demands proficiency in taking a variety of perspectives into account, particularly the perspectives of those individuals whom one's decision may affect. In situations involving conflicting viewpoints, individuals need to understand both the perspectives of other people and the frameworks that shape those perspectives. The better one's perspective-taking skills, the better one's managing skills (see Weathersby, this volume). When the perspective of an individual or group is excluded from the decision-making process, unresolved tensions often dominate the workplace and may hinder productivity.

Organizations in which decision making is grounded in lower stage perspective-taking may perpetuate an atmosphere in which individuals' higher stages of perspective-taking are not reinforced. These individuals are likely to demonstrate interest only in how decisions affect themselves. Consequently, organizational decision making that excludes the perspectives of constituent groups may ultimately produce constituent decision makers who exclude the perspective (and interests) of the organization. At the higher stages of perspective-taking, by contrast, organizations reinforce individual behavior that takes the perspectives of others into account. This may include other members of the organization, the organization itself, and even individuals and groups that lie beyond its boundaries.

Development and Propagation of Atmosphere

So although individuals are constrained by the stage of atmosphere, at the same time the stage of individual response continually reproduces and may revise the stage of atmosphere. This interactive relationship requires the effective transfer of information regarding the operative contingencies in any given situation. The transference of cultural information (Boyd & Richerson, 1982, 1985; Cavalli-Sforza & Feldman, 1981; Cavalli-Sforza, Feldman, Chen, & Dornbusch, 1982) carried by contingencies can be described analogously as *infection by memes*. A *meme* is a unit of sociocultural information. It is defined by a single individual dichotomous choice (Dawkins, 1989). Memes are released from the atmosphere and carried by particular sets of operative contingencies. Atmosphere constitutes the source of memes insofar as it specifies contingencies. In detecting a set of contingencies that apply in a particular situation, an individual is thereby infected with the meme carried by those contingencies. In executing a behavior that is controlled by that set of contingencies, the individual is further infected. Thus, there are degrees of infection by memes. Moreover, because any contingency selects behavior, it can represent one or more memes.

The infecting meme can be identified in the subject's resulting behavior. Because new behaviors set new contingencies, memes are continually being transferred. All effective educating, training, and communicating results in a transmission of memes. If such infection did not exist, individual choices would be random or unperformed. The identification and tracking of memes brings precision to the task of describing social conditioning so that it becomes possible to trace the evolution of behaviors. Moreover, because memes may be characterized in terms of stage, they aid in identifying stage development of individuals within interactive frameworks such as the workplace.

The atmosphere of the workplace is sustained and transferred through communication networks. These networks distribute information about the contingencies that affect individuals (e.g., individual advancement) within the organization. The complexity of the reasoning used to justify these contingencies embodies the stage of atmosphere of the workplace. The detection of contingencies by individuals occurs primarily during acquisition or reacquisition of the stage reinforced by the atmosphere. Contingencies tend to go undetected once the individual and the atmosphere are functioning at the same stage. Contingencies are clearly revealed only when the individual is struggling against the atmosphere from the point of view of another stage or when the individual is excluded from power.

Reciprocal Effect of Stage and Atmosphere

It is our contention that the stage of the behavior that sets contingencies has a reciprocal effect on the atmosphere of an organization. For example, when U.S. policymakers have to raise millions of dollars to be elected, the power of the individual relative to the power of the dollar is small. In such circumstances, incumbents—because of access to large amounts of funds—have a great advantage over challengers. Such incumbents set the rules or contingencies for how elections are to be conducted.

Likewise, within the workplace of the university, the transmission of knowledge and values is controlled by a network of contingencies that begins with the persons who pay for the university and with the structure of the channels through which funds are allocated to universities and then distributed within them. The stage of the justifications given for accreditation and for form of governance partly determines the stage of the institutional atmosphere. This includes a ceiling on the stage of development of the institution's top decision makers. The transmission of knowledge and values to students within the university can be traced through a series of steps: (a) through the contingencies that describe how the top decision makers are chosen and how a ceiling is set on the developmental complexity of their behavior; (b) through the contingencies that describe how money is distributed to the various sections of the university, how staff are chosen in those areas, and how power is distributed within them; and (c) the contingencies that establish the rules (both implicit and explicit) themselves that govern how future contingencies develop. We believe that similar processes govern the transmission of knowledge and values as well as influence the developmental stage of individuals within any workplace.

In most universities, the control of funds is inaccessible to students, such that students can only influence decision making by attending or not attending school. Faculty members, on the other hand, represent long-lasting human capital who use and, indirectly, produce funds. Their power is derived from the fact that they exercise some control over these resources as well as influence the perceived value of the university experience. *Power*, from our viewpoint, is the behavioral control of contingencies that distribute reinforcement and reinforcement opportunity. To say that Person A "has power over" Person B in a given situation is, then, to say that Person A controls more reinforcing outcomes and punishers with respect to Person B's behavior than the reverse. If Person B behaves inappropriately according to Person A, reinforcement may be withdrawn from B by A. The implicit or explicit rule that A follows is contained within the network of contingencies operative within the organization. The sum total of such rules and the rules by which they are set constitutes the atmosphere.

In their empirical study of moral development in worker owned companies, Higgins and Gordon (1985) found that the organizational structure of a workplace (i.e., atmosphere) may facilitate the sociomoral development of its members. Similarly, in an exploratory study of atmosphere and moral development in the academic setting, researchers (Johnstone et al., 1991) found that the atmosphere of the university may constrain the developmental complexity with which its members respond to ethical dilemmas. For example, one subject in that study reported that the perceived compromise of values by administrators "very much tells the students that, well, this is all very interesting, but what really counts is big bucks, and what really counts is. . . . And kids get the message, and kids will go over exactly where they see the reward of the society as being exemplified." Similar processes set contingencies for faculty members, staff, and administrators as well. In fact, the study revealed that the reasoning of most ethics professors fails to achieve the highest developmental stage. Johnstone et al. explained this finding by arguing that the institutional atmosphere of the university fails to reward more complex reasoning that may challenge its norms.

There are multiple layers of contingencies for individual responses within such complex organizations as the modern workplace. The hierarchical structure of stages of development, as given by the GSM, suggests that lower stage tasks and responses must be adequately integrated into the contingencies that constitute atmosphere in order for higher stage responses to develop. By the same token, some tasks do not require higher stage solutions yet are necessary for the functioning of the institution. Contingencies and stage of response will be perceived differently by individuals functioning at different stages within the same workplace. Yet, stage assignments can be made for the overall network of contingencies and responses that constitute the atmosphere of the organization. We believe that the reinforcement contingencies set by organizational activity play a vital role in the development of individuals within the workplace. We believe that the organizational atmosphere largely controls the reinforcement contingencies impacting upon individuals within a particular workplace. The setting of contingencies is the exercise of *power*. The atmosphere can either assist in the developmental process of individuals and the organization or impede it. Using the GSM, we can characterize this interaction with a high degree of precision.

CONCLUSIONS

The preliminary results of this research indicate that workplace atmosphere typically places a ceiling on individual moral development rather than encouraging development to the highest stages. The ceiling identified in the samples from the Mexicali Medical School study were at the formal stage. In the samples from the Harvard study, transitional reasoning between Stage 5a and Stage 5b predominated, at least in the social domains investigated. We suspect that, in less politically charged arenas, many reason at the fully metasystematic Stage 5b. This suggests that behavior beyond the systematic stage is reinforced in some domains and not in others. For instance, in the university, one's postconventional (metasystematic) thinking in one's research might be reinforced, but not one's postconventional thinking with regard to policy decisions involving the university itself. This theme was clearly brought out in many of the interviews.

At the metasystematic stage, individuals in the workplace are not simply defined in terms of their position or status within the organization. Individuals are considered in terms of a wide range of perspectives, all of which may be taken into account in the decision-making process. Metasystematic responses typically challenge the existing norms and policies of a workplace by integrating perspectives that fall outside of the organizational bureaucracy. For this reason, organizations tend not to reinforce responses at the metasystematic stage (see Rulon, this volume). We contend, however, that the failure of systematic stage reasoning to integrate a range of workplace perspectives is contrary to organizational interests. An organization that reinforces higher stage responses to moral dilemmas, thereby, increases the perspective-taking abilities of its members. The better the perspective-taking skills of individuals within an organization, the more likely they will be to integrate the organization's perspectives into their own decisions. In practical terms, this may be called *loyalty* or *allegiance*. The company or business that reinforces higher stage responses, thereby, fosters allegiance to its own causes and interests.

This study has provided a framework for research on the interaction between workplace atmosphere and the development of individuals within it. The applications of this model extend far beyond the workplace. This model may be applied to forms of social interaction as various as families, religious groups, street gangs, and governments. We believe that contemporary challenges in all of these spheres increasingly call for post-conventional responses on the part of both individuals and organizations. The GSM provides a model for understanding the developmental processes through which these challenges may be met.

REFERENCES

Armon, C. (1984a). Ideals of the good life and moral judgment: Ethical reasoning across the life span. In M. L. Commons, F. A. Richards, & C. Armon (Eds.), *Beyond formal operations: Vol. 1. Late adolescent and adult cognitive development* (pp. 357–380). New York: Praeger.

Armon, C. (1984b). *Ideals of the good life: A cross-sectional/longitudinal study of evaluative reasoning in children and adults.* Unpublished doctoral dissertation, Harvard Graduate School of Education, Cambridge, MA.

Barth, F. (1966). *Models of social organization.* Royal Anthropological Institute Occasional Paper, No. 23.

Boyd, R., & Richerson, P. J. (1982). Cultural transmission and the evolution of cooperative behavior. *Human Ecology Forum, 10,* 325–351.

Boyd, R., & Richerson, P. J. (1985). *Culture and the evolutionary process.* Chicago: University of Chicago Press.

Cavalli-Sforza, L. L., & Feldman, M. W. (1981). *Cultural transmission and evolution: A quantitative approach.* Princeton, NJ: Princeton University Press.

Cavalli-Sforza, L. L., Feldman, M. W., Chen, K. H., & Dornbusch, S. M. (1982). Theory and observation in cultural transmission. *Science, 218,* 19–27.

Colby, A., & Kohlberg, L. (1987). *The measurement of moral judgement: Vol. 1. Theoretical foundations and research validation.* New York: Cambridge University Press.

Commons, M. L., & Grotzer, T. A. (1990). The relationship between Piagetian and Kohlbergian stage: An examination of the "necessary but not sufficient relationship." *Adult development: Models and methods in the study of adolescent and adult thought* (Vol. 2, pp. 205–231). New York: Praeger.

Commons, M. L., Grotzer, T. A., & Davidson, M. N. (1991). *The necessity of reinforcing problem solutions for transition to formal operations: An examination of Piaget's equilibration theory of stage change.* Manuscript submitted for publication.

Commons, M. L., & Hallinan, P. W. with Fong, W., & McCarthy, K. (1989). Intelligent pattern recognition: Hierarchical organization of concepts and hierarchies. In M. L. Commons, R. J. Herrnstein, S. M. Kosslyn, & D. B. Mumford (Eds.), *Quantitative analyses of behavior: Vol. 9, Computational and clinical approaches to pattern recognition and concept formation* (pp. 128–153). Hillsdale, NJ: Lawrence Erlbaum Associates.

Commons, M. L., Handel, A. N., Richard, D. C., & Grotzer, T. A. (in preparation). *The development of strategies during the transition to formal operations.*

Commons, M. L., Kantrowitz, S., Buhlman, R. A., Ellis, J., & Grotzer, T. A. (in preparation). *Perceiving development: Immediate formal operational detection of a causal relation embedded in contemporaneous non-causal relations.*

Commons, M. L., & Richards, F. A. (1984a). A general model of stage theory. In M. L. Commons, F. A. Richards, & C. Armon (Eds.), *Beyond formal operations: Vol. 1. Late adolescent and adult cognitive development* (pp. 120–140). New York: Praeger.

Commons, M. L., & Richards, F. A. (1984b). Applying the general stage model. In M. L. Commons, F. A. Richards, & C. Armon (Eds.), *Beyond formal operations: Vol. 1. Late adolescent and adult cognitive development* (pp. 141–157). New York: Praeger.

Commons, M. L., & Rodriguez, J. A. (1990). "Equal access" without "establishing" religion: The necessity for assessing social perspective-taking skills and institutional atmosphere. *Developmental Review, 10,* 323–340.

Coombs, C. H., Dawes, R. M., & Tversky, A. (1970). *Mathematical psychology: An elementary introduction.* Englewood Cliffs, NJ: Prentice-Hall.

Damon, W., & Hart, D. (1988). *Self-understanding in childhood and adolescence.* Cambridge, England: Cambridge University Press.

Dawkins, R. (1989). *The selfish gene.* New York: Oxford University Press.

Douglas, M. (1986). *How institutions think.* Syracuse, NY: Syracuse University Press.

Foucault, M. (1979). *Discipline and punish: The birth of the prison* (A. Sheridan, Trans.). New York: Vintage Books.

Galaz-Fontes, J. F., Pacheco-Sanchez, M. E., & Commons, M. L. (1989). *La experiencia universitaria y el desarrollo moral* [University experience and moral development]. Paper presented at the I Foro Estatal "Desarrollo social y productivo de Baja California," Mexicali, Baja California.

Goffman, E. (1967). *Interaction ritual.* Garden City, NY: Anchor Books.

Higgins, A., & Gordon, F. (1985). Work climate and socio-moral development in two worker-owned companies. In M. W. Berkowitz & F. Oser (Eds.), *Moral education: Theory and application* (pp. 241–268). Hillsdale, NJ: Lawrence Erlbaum Associates.

Johnstone, J., Straughn, J. B., Meaney, M., Krause, S. R., Fayer, G. A., & Commons, M. L. (1991, July). *Ethics within a university: A scoring application of the general stage model.* Paper presented at the Sixth Adult Development Symposium, Boston, MA.

Kohlberg, L. (1969). Stage and sequence: The cognitive-developmental approach to socialization. In D. A. Goslin (Ed.), *Handbook of socialization theory and research* (pp. 347–480). Chicago: Rand McNally.

Kohlberg, L. (1984). *Essays on moral development: Vol. 2. The psychology of moral development: The nature and validity of moral stages.* San Francisco: Harper & Row.

Kohlberg, L. (1985). The just community approach to moral education in theory and practice. In M. Berkowitz & F. Ozer (Eds.), *Moral education: Theory and application* (pp. 27–87). Hillsdale, NJ: Lawrence Erlbaum Associates.

Kohlberg, L., Hart, D., & Wertsch, J. (1987). The developmental social self theories of James Mark Baldwin, George Herbert Mead and Lev Seminovich Vygotsky. In L. Kohlberg (Ed.), *Child psychology and childhood education* (pp. 223–258). New York: Longman.

Lindsay, P. H., & Norman, D. A. (1977). *Human information processing: An introduction to psychology* (2nd ed.). New York: Academic Press.

Mead, G. H. (1934). *Mind, self and society.* Chicago: University of Chicago Press.

Meaney, M. (1990). *Social change: The Universidad Autonoma de Baja California.* Unpublished manuscript, Program in Psychiatry and the Law, Department of Psychiatry, Harvard Medical School, Massachusetts Mental Health Center, Boston.

Moore, S. F. (1975). Epilogue: Uncertainties in situations, indeterminacies in culture. In S. F. Moore & B. Myerhoff (Eds.), *Symbol and politics in communal ideology.* Ithaca, NY: Cornell University Press.

Perry, W. G. (1970). *Forms of intellectual and ethical development in the college years: A scheme.* New York: Holt, Rinehart & Winston.

Perry, W. G. (1981). Cognitive and ethical growth: The making of meaning. In A. Chickering (Ed.), *The modern American college* (pp. 76–116). San Francisco: Jossey-Bass.

Richard, D. C., Unger, C. M., & Commons, M. L. (1988, April). *Strategies as knowledge: Subjects' methods of determining causality during the shift from concrete to formal operations.* Paper presented at the Eastern Psychological Association annual meeting, Buffalo, NY.

Rodriguez, J. A. (1989). *Exploring the notion of higher stages of social perspective taking.* Unpublished qualifying paper, Harvard Graduate School of Education, Cambridge, MA.

Skinner, B. F. (1938). *The behavior of organisms: An experimental analysis.* New York: Appleton.

Thompson, K. (1985). *Readings from Emile Durkheim.* New York: Tavistock.

PART FOUR

DIRECTIONS FOR FUTURE RESEARCH

Some Open Research Problems on Development in the Workplace: Theory and Methodology

Jack Demick
Patrice M. Miller
Suffolk University

Based on the previous contributions in this volume, this chapter describes a number of open research problems in the area of development in the workplace. Pursuit of these problems has the potential to: (a) move the exploratory nature of the chapters presented herein toward solidifying the synergistic relationship between the subfields of (adult) developmental and organizational psychology; (b) uncover areas of study that may ultimately contribute to more general theory development and, thus, to a more integrated view of the science of psychology; and (c) suggest practical applications to optimize human functioning in the workplace environments of our daily lives (cf. Arthur, Hall, & Lawrence, 1989; Montross & Shinkman, 1992; Murphy & Saal, 1990).

We have chosen to present these open research problems in the context of a discussion of a recent elaboration and extension of Heinz Werner's (1957a) organismic-developmental approach (e.g., Demick & Wapner, 1988a; Wapner, 1987; Wapner & Demick, 1990). We have done so for several reasons. First, from early on, this approach has been strongly concerned with the integration of developmental and other (here, organizational) subfields of psychology. In Werner's (1957b) own words:

> The field of developmental psychology, as it is conceived here, transcends the boundaries within which the concept of development is frequently applied: development is here apprehended as a concept not merely applicable to delimited areas such as child growth or comparative behavior of

animals, but as a concept that proposes a certain manner of viewing behavior in its manifold manifestations. Such a developmental approach to behavior rests on one basic assumption, namely, that wherever there is life there is growth and development, that is, formation in terms of systematic, orderly sequence. The basic assumption, then, entails the view that developmental conceptualization is applicable to the various areas of life science, and is potentially useful in interrelating the many fields of psychology. (p. 125)

That the ultimate goal of integration may be possible gains support, for example, from our more recent attempts to delineate some relations between developmental and environmental psychology (Demick & Wapner, 1990; Wapner & Demick, 1991a) and between developmental and clinical psychology (Demick, in preparation-a; Wapner, 1991).

Second, although Werner's and our work constitute general developmental approaches, they both have close, perhaps somewhat hidden, linkages to organizational psychology. For instance, Werner's work was heavily influenced by that of Kurt Lewin (1935, 1948, 1951). Lewin's field theory—which acknowledged the dynamic interplay between the person and his or her environment with foci on, for example, action research, systems change, and work design—has recently been recognized as constituting the first seeds for the contemporary subfield of organizational psychology (Weisbord, 1991). Thus, it is not surprising that some of these same themes were echoed in Werner's writings. In a related manner, the elaborated approach has provided a general theoretical framework on person–environment relationships for the relatively new subfield of environmental psychology (Gifford, 1987). Originally conceived of as the study of the effects of the physical environment on behavior (cf. Proshansky, Ittelson, & Rivlin, 1976), this subfield has more recently broadened to include the examination of larger scale human activities (e.g., working, learning, traveling, urban living) as they affect and are affected by (physical, interpersonal, and sociocultural) aspects of the environment. Thus, this volume bridges not only developmental and organizational psychology but the related area of environmental psychology as well.

Third and most importantly, by extending the person–environment theme to include consideration of the everyday life functioning of individuals in all of its complexity, the elaborated approach (e.g., Wapner & Demick, 1990) has already demonstrated powerful heuristic potential for integrating diverse literatures as well as for framing a wide range of empirical inquiry (reviewed later). Likewise here, the approach should be of value in conceptualizing open research problems and/or in identifying gaps heretofore unexplored in the general area of development in the workplace.

Thus, in order to provide some background for the proposed research, there follows: (a) a brief historical sketch of the Wernerian approach and its various elaborations, and (b) a description of some issues raised by our recent extension of the approach relevant for open research problems on development in the workplace. Hopefully, this material will stimulate other investigators to conduct research in this important problem area from their own perspective or from variations of that described here.

WERNERIAN THEORY

Werner's (1926, 1940) original comparative developmental psychology was later recast as the organismic–developmental approach (Werner, 1957a; Werner & Kaplan, 1963). In his now classic work, *Comparative Psychology of Mental Development* (1957a), Werner described two interrelated positions: the *organismic* and the *developmental*. Stated most simply, the organismic position maintained that we should not study psychological processes in isolation, but rather as they occur within the whole (thinking, feeling, valuing, acting) organism. For example, rather than studying solitary cognitive processes as if they existed in a vacuum, a more useful empirical question might be "Under what conditions does affect compromise cognition and vice-versa?" In a sense, Werner was with these ideas one of the forerunners of contemporary holistic, systems, and/or biopsychosocial approaches.

The developmental position inherent within the approach maintained that, rather than pertaining to mere increases in size, development involves changes in structure that may be defined according to the orthogenetic principle: "Whenever development occurs, it proceeds from a state of relative lack of differentiation to a state of increasing differentiation and hierarchic integration" (Werner & Kaplan, 1956, p. 866). With Kaplan (1966, 1967), Werner systematized this principle and described it as a heuristic law, that is, as one that directs inquiry but is not subject to empirical test. In line with this, Werner also delineated four sets of polarities (global–articulated; syncretic–discrete; labile–stable; rigid–flexible), each of which characterized development, ranging from less advanced to more advanced functioning. His approach was also comparative in that these developmental notions were considered equally applicable to ontogenesis (development of the individual), pathogenesis (e.g., development of psycho- and neuropathology), ethnogenesis (development of a culture), phylogenesis (development of a species), and to various states of the normal adult (e.g., fatigue–rested; drug intoxicated–sober).

Werner (1957a) characterized the organismic–developmental approach as one treating all psychological events as developmental processes. In line with this, the approach spawned numerous articles and two larger programs of research: one, with Wapner, on *cognitive (perceptual) development*; and another, with Kaplan, on *conceptual (symbolic) development*. Wapner and Werner's (1957) sensory-tonic theory of perception combined a general analysis of systems and subsystems in holistic (organismic) terms with the characterization of principles underlying perception and other cognitive processes in formal, structural (developmental) terms (cf. Wapner, Cirillo, & Baker, 1969). Werner and Kaplan's (1963) work on symbol formation argued that inner (organismic) ties between symbols and referents are never lost; throughout life (developmental), we perceive words as expressive forms that evoke the same bodily and emotional reactions as their referents.

Following Werner's death in 1964, Wapner (Wapner, Kaplan, & Cohen, 1973) and Kaplan (Kaplan, Wapner, & Cohen, 1976) began to apply the approach to problems of environmental psychology. At least partly precipitated by societal events (i.e., the Vietnam War and psychologists' accompanying commitment to problems that could be studied not only in the laboratory but also in the real world), the application was a natural one, given the approach's longstanding concern with the organism (person), the environment, and their interrelations. Kaplan (1983a, 1983b; Cirillo & Kaplan, 1983) went on to integrate Wernerian concepts with those of Burke (1945, 1972) through an approach that he labeled *genetic–dramatism*. In this approach, the dramatistic aspect focused on the means that individuals use to accomplish their ends, whereas the genetic, or developmental, aspect highlighted individuals' desire to move toward perfectionism. Wapner (Wapner, Ciottone, Hornstein, McNeil, & Pacheco, 1983) identified and analyzed what he termed *critical person-in-environment transitions* from the organismic–developmental approach.

Since this time, the organismic–developmental approach to the study of person-in-environment transitions has been further elaborated (e.g., Wapner & Demick, 1991a, 1991b). Specifically, we have attempted to delineate the regressive changes and/or the progressive development of the person-in-environment system following a transition, or critical perturbation to any part of the system at any level of organization. As we see it, a perturbation might be initiated at any level of the person (physical/biological, intrapersonal, sociocultural), of the environment (physical, interpersonal, sociocultural), or of both. Table 13.1 provides a diagram of the person-in-environment system with sites and examples of possible perturbations.

In addition to theory development, we have also conducted numerous empirical studies on various aspects of these transitions. Specifically, some of the transitions studied thus far include: the child's transition to nursery school (e.g., Ciottone, Demick, Pacheco, Quirk, & Wapner, 1980); the adolescent's transition to college (e.g., Lauderback, Demick,

TABLE 13.1
Sites and Examples of Perturbations to Person-in-Environment System
That May Initiate Critical Transitions

Person (x Environment)	Environment (x Person)
Biological/Physical	*Physical*
Age	Objects
Pregnancy	Disaster
Disability	Relocation
Illness	Urban change
Psychological/Intrapersonal	*Interpersonal*
Body experience	Peers
Self-experience	Family
	Neighbors
	Co-workers
Sociocultural	*Sociocultural*
Role	Educational
Ethnicity	Legal
Gender	Political
	Religious

& Wapner, 1987); the physician's transition through residency training (Frey, Demick, & Bibace, 1980); the young adult's transition to parenthood (Demick & Wapner, 1991) with emphasis on adoptive parenthood (Demick, in preparation-b; Demick & Wapner, 1988b); the patient's transition "into" and "out of" the psychiatric setting (Demick, 1985; Demick & Wapner, 1980); adults' experience and action following the transition to mandatory automobile safety belt legislation (Demick et al., in press); the older adult's transition to retirement (e.g., Wapner, Demick, & Damrad, 1988); and the elderly individual's transition into the nursing home (Wapner, Demick, & Redondo, 1990). As is evident, this body of empirical work covers the life span from infancy/early childhood through old age. Accordingly, based on Werner's orginial proposition that all psychological events may be treated as developmental processes, such a focus has afforded us the opportunity to begin to develop a comprehensive theory of life transitions as well as a more general approach to person-in-environment functioning across the life span.

Although this sketch of the Wernerian approach and its more recent extensions are admittedly sketchy (cf. Crain, 1992, and Wapner, 1987, for more complete treatments), it sets the stage for subsequent discussion. That is, the following questions now arise: In what ways do our most recent extension of the Wernerian approach suggest ways to frame empirical inquiry on development in the workplace? From this holistic, developmental perspective, which areas of human functioning in the workplace have already been charted and which are yet to be explored?

Toward addressing these questions, we now present several theoretical and/or methodological issues that have figured prominently in our approach for some time. The theoretical considerations are stated in the form of underlying assumptions that guide our research; examples of the ways in which they pertain to functioning in the workplace are also provided. The methodological issues are framed in terms of contemporary controversies within the field. Although some of these assumptions and issues have already been incorporated into the work of the other authors in this volume, these researchers by no means share, and possibly even reject, our overall perspective. Nonetheless, we present them to: (a) discuss similarities and differences among all the approaches to development in the workplace expressed herein; and (b) highlight areas of omission that become clearer against the backdrop of a holistic, developmental approach to real life (here, workplace) functioning in all of its complexity.

THEORETICAL CONSIDERATIONS

Unit of Analysis

We assume that the unit to be analyzed is the person-in-environment system with mutually defining aspects of both person and of environment. Stated as such, our approach has integrative value built into its conceptualization because "context" is part and parcel of every analysis. Applied to the workplace, the person and his or her work environment would be seen as interdependent, requiring each other and the whole configuration for their meaning. Thus, for example, an individual's difficulties in the workplace would be conceptualized as a function of the complex interrelationships between the person (e.g., motivation, perception, wishes) and the environment (e.g., physical features, co-workers, organizational culture).

Although all the authors in this volume focused on the specific context of the workplace, there is some variation with respect to their unit of analysis. For example, constructivist–developmental theories in general—as exemplified here by the majority of authors including Miller and West (chapter 1), Armon (chapter 2), Rulon (chapter 3), Cleave-Hogg and Muzzin (chapter 4), and Weathersby (chapter 5)—consider the individual as unit of analysis, seeing developmental stages inherent within the person with each stage representing a qualitatively distinct frame of reference for understanding the world. Further, most relevant to our own focus on the person-in-environment system as unit of analysis is Weathersby's (chapter 5) work on Sri Lankan managers. Although her formal unit of analysis is the individual (focus on ego development), she nonetheless also considers the broader sociocultural context toward determining the ways in which experience and action at the sociocultural level impact experience and action at the individual level.

In contrast to this focus on the individual, Barnes-Farrell (chapter 9) chose the (supervisor–subordinate) dyad as her unit of analysis, highlighting the notion of "person–environment fit" (i.e., optimal workplace functioning when characteristics of the person such as worker's age match characteristics of the environment such as supervisor's age). Further, although both Sinnott (chapter 10) and Commons et al. (chapter 12) begin from a constructivist–developmental framework, they have expanded their approaches to consider even larger units of analysis, namely, the workplace group or environment more generally.

Specifically, Sinnott has integrated constructivist–developmental theory with some newer theories from biology, cognitive science, mathematics, and physics toward understanding intragroup conflict. As she states, "Thinking and complex problem solving occur taking into account products of several minds, not of one mind alone" (p. 155); this is in tune with more recent work within developmental psychology that has highlighted the role of social relationships in cognitive development (e.g., Rogoff, 1990; Vygotsky, 1978) and, hence, the need to expand the unit of analysis to more than the individual alone. In an equally broad manner, Commons et al. utilized measures of individual moral development, but with an eye toward discerning the developmental stage of the workplace environment as a whole (cf. Morris, chapter 11).

In summary, the units of analysis (individual, dyad, group, organization) in all of these chapters represent viable approaches to the problem at hand. Given the array of approaches that might be taken, we feel that researchers would do well to consider the theoretical implications of their chosen unit of analysis. Future empirical studies may also have the potential to shed light on which of these units is most appropriate for the study of development in the workplace.

Aspects of Persons and of Environments: Holism

In line with our organismic orientation, we assume that the person is comprised of mutually defining *physical/biological* (e.g., worker's age, health), *intrapersonal/psychological* (e.g., self-esteem derived partly from work), and *sociocultural* (e.g., role as worker) aspects. Analogously, the environment is comprised of mutually defining *physical* (e.g., job location, office temperature), *interpersonal* (e.g., co-workers), and *sociocultural* (e.g., office/company rules, customs) aspects.

Related to this is our assumption that processes or functions may be characterized in terms of levels of integration (Feibelman, 1954; Herrick, 1949; Novikoff, 1945a, 1945b; Schneirla, 1949; Wapner & Demick, 1990). That is, *biological* functioning (e.g., breathing), *psychological* functioning (e.g., thinking), and *sociocultural* functioning (e.g., living by a code of ethics) are hierarchically organized so that sociocultural functioning requires both psychological and biological functioning and psychological functioning requires biological functioning. We further assume that the person-in-environment system (with its constituent aspects of person and of environment) functions as a holistic entity so that a disturbance within or among aspects or levels affects other parts and the totality.

In the main, the chapters presented here span all aspects of the person and of the environment. Within the person, for example, Barnes-Farrell (chapter 9) deals with the physical/biological aspect (e.g., worker's age), the constructive–developmentalists (e.g., Miller & West, chapter 1; Armon, chapter 2; Rulon, chapter 3; Cleave-Hogg & Muzzin, chapter 4; Weathersby, chapter 5; Sinnott, chapter 10; Commons et al., chapter 12) with the intrapersonal/psychological aspect, and Golberg (chapter 6), Mangione (chapter 7), and Bachiochi (chapter 8) with the sociocultural aspect (or role of the psychotherapist, artist, worker/leisurite respectively). Within the environment, Barnes-Farrell (chapter 9) also treats the interpersonal aspect (i.e., supervisor–subordinate relations), whereas Armon (chapter 2) and Weathersby (chapter 5) address the sociocultural aspect (e.g., Armon through conceptions of good work and Weathersby through comparison of Sri Lankan and American managers).

The only aspect of our conceptualization that has not been treated here is the physical aspect of the environment. Further, although the chapters primarily address one or another aspect of person or of environment, they do not characteristically concern themselves with holistic relations among these aspects (e.g., the ways in which conceptions of good work impact self-esteem, etc.). Thus, we are of the opinion that an increased understanding of development in the workplace may be obtained from future research that attempts to fill in the gaps (e.g., are there developmental differences in the ways that individuals cope with the physical aspects of their workplace environments such as poor lighting and/or temperature?) and to consider relations among aspects and levels. As an example of the latter, Tenglund and Demick (in preparation) are currently in the process of constructing a scale that assesses physical, interpersonal, and sociocultural aspects of stress in the workplace. Tenglund and Demick are interested in determining, for example, the ways in which dissatisfaction with one aspect of the workplace environment impacts other aspects of—as well as overall satisfaction with—self and environment. Consideration of such holistic questions has the potential to advance conceptualization not only in the area of development in the workplace, but also for developmental and organizational psychology more generally.

Multiple Worlds

Extending our holistic conceptualization even further, we assume that people live in different, yet related experiential worlds (Schutz, 1971) or spheres of activity such as the multiple worlds of family, work, school, recreation, community, and so on. Further, consonant with Koffka (1935), we distinguish between physical (geographic) and experienced (behavioral) worlds. Relations between or among these worlds may be described with respect to a given individual's involvement in one or more person-in-environment systems; these relations may also be characterized in structural, developmental terms (see later).

Bachiochi's work (chapter 8) comes closest to these ideas. Specifically, he is concerned with the relationship between one's roles as worker and as leisurite. Although his current analyses appear mechanistically oriented, his work might be further developed to include consideration of structural relationships between one's worlds of work and of recreation. We strongly feel that such research is needed because individuals' ability to integrate, or not to integrate, their work and other worlds is arguably a problem that captures the heart of our everday life experience.

As an example of the ways in which the negotiation of the relationship between one's work and other worlds may impact adaptation, see Hornstein and Wapner (1984, 1985) and Wapner, Demick, and Damrad (1988). Utilizing our approach, it has been demonstrated that the structure of an individual's life prior to retirement (defined in terms of the formal relationship among experiential worlds) can be used to predict that individual's adaptation following retirement. That is, subjects with greater integration between their work and other (e.g., family, friends, community, recreation) worlds in the pre-retirement phase of their life exhibited more successful adaptation to retirement than subjects whose pre-retirement worlds were structurally isolated.

Transactions With Objects: Experience and Action

We assume that one's experience with physical, interpersonal, and sociocultural objects occurs in terms of cognition (knowing), affect (feeling), valuation (prioritizing), and action (behavior). In line with our orientation, these processes are also assumed to function in a holistic manner. Further, to handle aspects of the complexity of the relationship between experience and action, we have employed Turvey's (1977) musical instrument metaphor in which "tuning" corresponds to the category of general factors preparing an individual for action/nonaction and "activating" corresponds to specific precursors that trigger/initiate/activate a concrete behavior (see Demick et al., in press, for application of this theory to the action/nonaction of automobile seat belt usage).

These assumptions have import for the chapters presented herein. First, although researchers from within the constructive-developmental approach (e.g., Miller & West, chapter 1; Armon, chapter 2; Rulon, chapter 3; Cleave-Hogg & Muzzin, chapter 4; Weathersby, chapter 5; and, to a lesser extent, Sinnott, chapter 10, and Commons et al., chapter 12) have highlighted the role of cognition in behavior and experience, there is clearly the need to go beyond this toward examining more specific ways in which cognitive–developmental status impacts affective, valuative, and behavioral functioning. That is, because much of this research has supported Piaget's (1967) and Kohlberg's (1969) original theories and/or extensions of these theories, advances in both conceptualization and empirical inquiry might be obtained in future research that considers the holistic nature of person-in-environment functioning not only between and among levels, but within a given (e.g., psychological) level itself. Second, although the way(s) in which experience becomes translated into action is dealt with primarily by Rulon (chapter 3), future research might also profit from increased focus on this issue.

Constructivism

We assume a constructivist view of knowledge. That is, the organism (individual) constructs objects of perception and thought and, thereby, actively contributes to the cognitive process. Thus, we reject all "copy" theories of perception and instead posit that reality is relative to the organism's construction or interpretation (cf. Lavine, 1950a, 1950b). In the larger scheme, this leads us to a strong acknowledgment of perspectivism: There is no objective inquiry or knowledge because one's underlying theory, at least in part, determines one's problem and method (see later).

Although the constructive–developmentalists represented in this volume certainly share our view of the nature of knowledge, we are most struck in this regard by the work of Miller and West (chapter 1). In attempting to discern the underlying world views of individuals in various occupational groups, these authors are consonant with, for example, Groat (1982; Groat & Canter, 1979), who demonstrated that one's occupational status (architects vs. nonarchitects) has the potential to affect one's interpretation of the meaning (communication, purpose) of the environment. Miller and West's work suggests that individuals in different occupations have differing underlying world views. A question that remains unanswered, however, is whether one's world view determines one's occupational aspirations, whether one's actual occupation determines one's world view, or both. Particularly for future research on development in the workplace, questions such as this have implications for both theory (e.g., developmental changes in world view and hence the constructivist nature of knowledge) and practice (e.g., the matching of individuals to appropriate occupations).

Development and Self-World Relationships

Our view of development transcends the boundaries within which the concept of development is ordinarily applied. For most psychologists, development is limited to ontogenesis. In contrast, we assume (as stated previously) that "wherever there is life, there is growth and systematic orderly sequence" (Werner, 1957b, p. 125). Thus, we are concerned with examining both processes of formation (e.g., development of one's social network in the workplace) and of dissolution (e.g., developmental changes in experience and action following job termination) as individuals negotiate maximally optimal relationships with their environments.

Components (person, environment), relations among components (e.g., means–ends), and part-processes (e.g., cognition, affect) are assumed developmentally orderable in terms of the orthogenetic principle (Kaplan, 1966, 1967; Werner & Kaplan, 1956). This principle defines development with respect to the degree of organization attained by a system. The more differentiated and hierarchically integrated a system is in terms of its parts and of its means and ends, the more highly developed it is considered to be. Further, we assume that optimal development involves a differentiated and hierarchically integrated person-in-environment system characterized by the individual's freedom, self-mastery, and flexibility (cf. Wapner, 1987; Wapner & Demick, 1990, 1991a).

In line with these notions, we have described four self-world relationships ranging from lesser to more advanced developmental status. These relationships—which have already been applied to the acculturation of the Puerto Rican migrant to the United States (e.g., Pacheco, Lucca, & Wapner, 1985) and to the family systems of those practicing open versus closed (communication vs. no communication between biological and adoptive parents) adoption (Demick & Wapner, 1988b)—are as follows:

1. lack of differentiation between person and environment characterized by the person's passive accommodation to the environment (e.g., after receiving a written warning, a worker consciously or

unconsciously denies that there is a problem with his or her performance);

2. person differentiated yet isolated from environment characterized
   by the person's disengagement (e.g., after receiving a written warning, a worker continues in his or her job, but disengages from co-
   workers and the organization);

3. person differentiated from yet in conflict with environment characterized by the person's nonconstructive ventilation (e.g., after
   receiving a written warning, a worker argues with anyone willing
   to listen that the warning was unjust, etc.); and

4. person differentiated from and integrated with environment characterized by the person's constructive assertion (e.g., after receiving
   a written warning, a worker approaches his or her supervisor for
   discussion of the ways that he or she might improve his or her performance).

These ideas appear relevant to the general area of development in the
workplace. That is, given our broad view of development, future investigators might opt to examine the developing worker, the developing
work group(s), or even the developing organization. This suggestion
resonates with our previous discussion of unit of analysis. However, because development is here seen as a mode of analysis rather than a content area, one could likewise examine the structural relationships between
one's work and home worlds, between one's expectations and actuali-
ties of a job, and so on. Further, our discussion of developmentally ordered self-world relationships suggests that another profitable study might
involve assessing changes in individuals' experience and action (including coping styles) over the course of adaptation to a general occupation
and/or to a specific job. A broader definition of development such as
the one offered by our approach opens up numerous empirical studies
concerning development in the workplace.

Teleological Directedness and Planning

In line with our developmental orientation, we assume that transactions
are not simply random and chaotic, but rather teleologically directed,
that is, oriented toward both short-term (e.g., getting through the work
week) and long-term (e.g., obtaining a promotion) goals. Thus, following from this teleological or goal-directed character of the person-in-
environment system, we are also concerned with dynamic (means–ends)
analyses as evidenced, for example, by our focus on the concept of planning (plotting or preparing symbolically for a future course of action).

Further, for us, the ultimate telos of development is a differentiated and integrated person-in-environment system characterized by flexibility, freedom, and self-mastery.

Once the notion of planning entered into our conceptualization, it has figured importantly in problem formulation and method (cf. Apter, 1976; Wapner, 1987; Wapner & Demick, 1990, 1991a; Wofsey, Rierdan, & Wapner, 1979). Of all the chapters in this volume, only that of Bachiochi (chapter 8) addresses the general issue of career planning. From our approach, this general omission highlights an area for future research because the cognitive activity of planning has extreme relevance for functioning not only within the workplace, but also within all contexts in which individuals transact. For example, in line with our recent volume on cognitive style (Wapner & Demick, 1991c; cf. Demick, 1991), are there individual differences in the use of planning both generally and across the stages of career development?

Further, although none of the authors share our specific telos for development, the constructive–developmentalists, who constitute the prime voice in this volume, would instead posit the attainment of postformal operational thinking as the telos of adult development. In this context, it should be noted that other researchers (e.g., Langer et al., 1990; cf. Goldberg, chapter 6) adhere to nonsequential models of adult development. Thus, future theory and research into development in the workplace needs to reconcile and/or integrate these different points of view (e.g., Do some theorists reject the notion of sequential development simply because of its rarity or because they do not view such thought as hierarchically more complex? Is postformal thinking more likely to occur in the workplace than in other contexts?). These and other questions have the potential to advance theory and application in both the fields of (adult) developmental and organizational psychology.

METHODOLOGICAL ISSUES

Natural Versus Human Science Approaches

Contemporary psychologists are engaged in an ongoing controversy over whether the field should adhere to a "natural science" (characterized by controlled experimentation and quantitative analysis, after Wundt, 1912) or a "human science" (characterized by phenomenological methods and qualitative analysis, after Giorgi, 1975) perspective. Although some might argue that a paradigm shift (cf. Kuhn, 1962) is well underway, our approach would advocate that both models have a place in psychological science. For us, choice of method depends in part on the level of integration to which the research question is addressed. For example, if we were interested primarily in describing and understanding (e.g., the sociocultural role of "worker"), we might opt—as Mangione (chapter 7) has—to employ the phenomenological method. Alternatively, if we were interested in predicting (e.g., satisfaction as a worker), we might instead choose an experimental/quasi-experimental method (cf. Bachiochi, chapter 8; Barnes-Farrell, chapter 9). Within the experimental method, we would also argue for the necessary complementarity of cross-sectional (e.g., Cleve-Hogg & Muzzin, chapter 4) and longitudinal (e.g., Armon, chapter 2) designs to understand developmental change (cf. Wapner, 1987).

As descendants of Werner, it is not surprising that we are strong proponents of methodological eclecticism. Werner himself was equally amenable to both natural and human science methods. For instance, he employed strict experimental methods in his work with colleagues (most notably Wapner), while at the same time writing enthusiastically about the phenomenological research of Muchow and von Uexkull (cf. Wapner, 1985). He would most certainly agree with Wapner's (1987, p. 1439) more recent statement that "A rule that must appropriately hold for social scientist and practitioner alike is that the method must not dictate the nature of the problem; we must remain problem oriented and be creative in developing new methods to fit the requirements of the particular research problem to be solved (Maslow, 1946)." Thus, we think that, in the true Wernerian sense, the profitable nature of employing a range of methods is clearly demonstrated by the papers in this volume.

Basic Versus Applied Research

As with the last issue, we feel that the distinction between basic (knowledge generating) and applied (immediate problem solving) research is an artificial one. For us, theory and praxis are flip sides of the same coin. Beginning with some of Werner's (e.g., Strauss & Werner, 1942; Werner & Strauss, 1941) earliest work, namely, cognitive dysfunction in brain-injured children, this focus has consistently figured prominently in the approach. For example, our (Tenglund & Demick, in preparation) current research on physical, interpersonal, and sociocultural aspects of stress in the workplace attempts to gather data in support of theoretical ideas (e.g., holistic nature of person-in-environment system; broader conceptualization of environment) as well as to generate implications for practice (e.g., development of both an assessment technique and programs to reduce stress in the workplace).

This conjoint focus on theory and practice is evident in many of the papers in this volume. Perhaps the best example is the work of Cleave-Hogg and Muzzin (chapter 4), who conduct developmental assessments of pharmacy and medical students towards designing specific criteria for admission selection policies and curriculum change. A second, clear example of theory translated into practice is provided by Rulon (chapter 3). Even those chapters with a prime theoretical focus (e.g., Sinnott, chapter 10; Morris, chapter 11) have strong implications ultimately for practice. Thus, future research on development in the workplace would do well to maintain this balance between the goals of both basic and applied research.

Theory Versus Empiricism

Although some psychologists take a strong stand on the relative import of the construction of theory versus the generation of data, our holistic, developmental approach again argues that each should be welcomed within psychological science. In line with our previously discussed belief in perspectivism and, hence, the lack of an objective reality, we are clearly convinced of the powerful interrelationships among problem, theory, and method in psychology: One's theory, at least in part, determines what one studies and how one studies it. Specifically, we see the interrelationship between theory construction and data generation as powerfully synergistic: Theories shape research problems and empirical data suggest and/or refine theories. Thus, although some of the chapters in this volume take primarily a theoretical (e.g., Sinnott, chapter 10; Morris, chapter 11) and others primarily an empirical (e.g., Bachiochi, chapter 8; Barnes-Farrell, chapter 9) bent, both foci are important. For example, some of Sinnott's (chapter 10) future work will most probably consist of generating data to test her general, integrative theory of intragroup conflict, which is applicable to any context not just to the workplace. Following additional investigations, Barnes-Farrell (chapter 9) will perhaps be in a position to propose an integrated, contextual theory of older adults in the workplace. Through a combination of both practices, we will come one step closer to bridging theory and research in both (adult) developmental and organizational theory.

SUMMARY

Toward integrating the chapters in this volume, we have attempted to uncover some similarities and differences among the authors' theoretical orientations and our own with a focus on delineating possible directions for future research in the area of development in the workplace. Specifically, from our elaborated approach, we have focused our suggestions on consideration of such issues as: unit of analysis, the holistic and systemic nature of human functioning, broader conceptualizations of both the person and the environment, a broader conceptualization of development and its purpose, the need for methodological eclecticism, and the complementarity of basic and applied research as well as of theory construction and data gathering. Although the chapters presented herein are themselves illustrative of the exploratory stages of a possible marriage between (adult) developmental and organizational psychology, we hope that they will, nonetheless, encourage other researchers, either from their own perspective or from variations of that described here, to conduct research in the important area of development in the workplace.

Further, the integration of subfields in psychology—as exemplified by our holistic, developmental approach and, more generally, by this volume—has the potential to aid in the conceptualization of problems that are more in line with the complex character of everyday life. In turn, this may help psychology see itself and be seen by others as the differentiated and integrated, unified science of behavior and experience.

REFERENCES

Apter, D. (1976). *Modes of coping with conflict in the presently inhabited environment as a function of variation in plans to move to a new environment.* Unpublished master's thesis, Clark University, Worcester, MA.

Arthur, M. B., Hall, D. T., & Lawrence, B. S. (Eds.). (1989). *Handbook of career theory.* New York: Cambridge University Press.

Burke, K. W. (1945). *A grammar of motives.* New York: Prentice-Hall.

Burke, K. W. (1972). *Dramatism and development.* Worcester, MA: Clark University Press.

Ciottone, R., Demick, J., Pacheco, A., Quirk, M., & Wapner, S. (1980, November). *Children's transition from home to nursery school: The integration of two cultures.* Paper presented at the American Association of Psychiatric Services for Children annual meeting, New Orleans, LA.

Cirillo, L., & Kaplan, B. (1983). Figurative action from the perspective of genetic-dramatism. In S. Wapner & B. Kaplan (Eds.), *Toward a holistic developmental psychology* (pp. 235–252). Hillsdale, NJ: Lawrence Erlbaum Associates.

Crain, W. (1992). *Theories of development: Concepts and applications* (3rd ed.). Englewood Cliffs, NJ: Prentice-Hall.

Demick, J. (1985, March). *Transition "into" and "out of" the psychiatric setting: Implications for policy and procedure.* Paper presented at the Eastern Psychological Association annual meeting, Boston, MA.

Demick, J. (1991). Organismic factors in field dependence-independence: Gender, personality, psychopathology. In S. Wapner & J. Demick (Eds.), *Field dependence-independence: Cognitive style across the life span* (pp. 209–243). Hillsdale, NJ: Lawrence Erlbaum Associates.

Demick, J. (in preparation-a). *Adult life transitions: Implications for a clinical-developmental psychology.*

Demick, J. (in preparation-b). *Adaptation of marital couples to open versus closed adoption.*

Demick, J., & Wapner, S. (1980). Effects of environmental relocation on members of a psychiatric therapeutic community. *Journal of Abnormal Psychology, 89,* 444–452.

Demick, J., & Wapner, S. (1988a). Children-in-environments: Physical, interpersonal, and sociocultural aspects. *Children's Environments Quarterly, 5*(3), 54–62.

Demick, J., & Wapner, S. (1988b). Open and closed adoption: A developmental conceptualization. *Family Process, 27,* 229–249.

Demick, J., & Wapner, S. (1990). Role of psychological science in promoting environmental quality: Introduction. *American Psychologist, 45*(5), 631–632.

Demick, J., & Wapner, S. (1991). Transition to parenthood: Developmental changes in experience and action. In T. Yamamoto & S. Wapner (Eds.), *A developmental psychology of life transitions* (pp. 243–265). Tokyo: Kyodo Shuppan.

Demick, J., Inoue, W., Wapner, S., Ishii, S., Minami, H., Nishiyama, S., & Yamamoto, T. (in press). Cultural differences in impact of governmental legislation: Automobile safety usage. *Journal of Cross-Cultural Psychology.*

Feibelman, J. K. (1954). Theory of integrative levels. *British Journal of Philosophy of Science, 5,* 59–66.

Frey, J., Demick, J., & Bibace, R. (1980). Variations in physicians' feelings of control in a family practice residency. *Journal of Medical Education, 56,* 50–56.

Gifford, R. (1987). *Environmental psychology: Principles and practice.* Boston, MA: Allyn & Bacon.

Giorgi, A. (1975). Convergence and divergence in qualitative and quantitative methods in psychology. In A. Giorgi, W. F. Fischer, & R. von Eckartsberg (Eds.), *Duquesne studies in phenomenological psychology* (Vol. 2, pp. 72–79). Pittsburgh, PA: Duquesne University Press.

Groat, L. (1982). Meaning in post-modern architecture: An examination using the multiple sorting task. *Journal of Environmental Psychology, 2,* 3–22.

Groat, L., & Canter, D. (1979). Does post-modernism communicate? *Progressive Architecture, 12,* 84–87.

Herrick, C. J. (1949). A biological survey of integrative levels. In R. W. Seelars, V. J. McGill, & M. Farber (Eds.), *Philosophy for the future* (pp. 222–242). New York: Macmillan.

Hornstein, G. A., & Wapner, S. (1984). The experience of the retiree's social network during the transition to retirement. In C. M. Aanstoos (Ed.), *Exploring the lived world in readings in phenomenological psychology* (pp. 119–136). Carrollton, GA: West Georgia College Press.

Hornstein, G. A., & Wapner, S. (1985). Modes of experiencing and adapting to retirement. *International Journal on Aging and Human Development, 21*(4), 291–315.

Kaplan, B. (1966). The comparative developmental approach and its application to symbolization and language in psychopathology. In S. Arieti (Ed.), *American handbook of psychiatry* (Vol. 3, pp. 659–688). New York: Basic Books.

Kaplan, B. (1967). Meditations on genesis. *Human Development, 10,* 65–87.

Kaplan, B. (1983a). Genetic-dramatism: Old wine in new bottles. In S. Wapner & B. Kaplan (Eds.), *Toward a holistic developmental psychology* (pp. 53–74). Hillsdale, NJ: Lawrence Erlbaum Associates.

Kaplan, B. (1983b). Reflections on culture and personality from the perspective of genetic dramatism. In S. Wapner & B. Kaplan (Eds.), *Toward a holistic developmental psychology* (pp. 95–109). Hillsdale, NJ: Lawrence Erlbaum Associates.

Kaplan, B., Wapner, S., & Cohen, S. B. (1976). Exploratory applications of the organismic-developmental approach to transactions of men-in-environments. In S. Wapner, S. B. Cohen, & B. Kaplan (Eds.), *Experiencing the environment* (pp. 207–233). New York: Plenum.

Koffka, K. (1935). *Principles of Gestalt psychology.* New York: Harcourt Brace.

Kohlberg, L. (1969). Stage and sequence: The cognitive-developmental approach to socialization. In D. A. Goslin (Ed.), *Handbook of socialization theory and research* (pp. 347–408). Chicago: Rand McNally.

Kuhn, T. S. (1962). *The structure of scientific revolutions.* Chicago: University of Chicago Press.

Langer, E. J., Chanowitz, B., Palmerino, M., Jacobs, S., Rhodes, M., & Thayer, P. (1990). Nonsequential development and aging. In C. N. Alexander & E. J. Langer (Eds.), *Higher stages of human development* (pp. 114–136). New York: Oxford University Press.

Lauderback, A., Demick, J., & Wapner, S. (1987, April). *Planning and coping with conflict: Transfer versus nontransfer college students.* Paper presented at the Eastern Psychological Association annual meeting, Arlington, VA.

Lavine, T. Z. (1950a). Knowledge as interpretation: An historical survey. *Philosophy and Phenomenological Research, 10,* 526–540.

Lavine, T. Z. (1950b). Knowledge as interpretation: An historical survey. *Philosophy and Phenomenological Research, 11,* 88–103.

Lewin, K. (1935). *Dynamic theory of personality.* New York: McGraw-Hill.

Lewin, K. (1948). *Resolving social conflicts: Selected papers on group dynamics.* New York: Harper & Row.

Lewin, K. (1951). *Field theory in social science: Selected theoretical papers.* New York: Harper & Row.

Maslow, A. H. (1946). Problem-centering versus means-centering in science. *Philosophy of Science, 13,* 326–341.

Montross, D. H., & Shinkman, C. J. (Eds.). (1992). *Career development: Theory and practice.* Springfield, IL: Charles C. Thomas.

Murphy, K. R., & Saal, F. E. (Eds.). (1990). *Psychology in organizations: Integrating science and practice.* Hillsdale, NJ: Lawrence Erlbaum Associates.

Novikoff, A. B. (1945a). The concept of integrative levels and biology. *Science, 101,* 209–215.

Novikoff, A. B. (1945b). Continuity and discontinuity in evolution. *Science, 102,* 405–406.

Pacheco, A. M., Lucca, N., & Wapner, S. (1985). The assessment of interpersonal relations among Puerto Rican migrant adolescents. In R. Diaz- Guerrero (Ed.), *Cross-cultural and national studies in social psychology* (pp. 169–176). North Holland: Elsevier Science Publishers.

Piaget, J. (1967). *Six psychological studies.* New York: Random House.

Proshansky, H. M., Ittelson, W. H., & Rivlin, L. G. (Eds.). (1976). *Environmental psychology: People and their physical settings.* New York: Holt, Rinehart & Winston.

Rogoff, B. (1990). *Apprenticeship in thinking: Cognitive development in social context.* New York: Oxford University Press.

Schneirla, T. C. (1949). Levels in the psychological capacities of animals. In R. W. Sellars, V. J. McGill, & M. Farber (Eds.), *Philosophy for the future* (pp. 243–286). New York: Macmillan.

Schutz, A. (1971). *Collected papers* (M. Natanson, Ed.). The Hague, Netherlands: Nijhoff.

Strauss, A. A., & Werner, H. (1942). Disorders of conceptual thinking in the brain-injured child. *Journal of Nervous and Mental Disease, 96*(2), 153–172.

Tenglund, M., & Demick, J. (in preparation). *Physical, interpersonal, and sociocultural aspects of stress in the workplace.* Manuscript in preparation, Suffolk University, Boston, MA.

Turvey, M. T. (1977). Preliminaries to a theory of action with reference to vision. In R. Shaw & J. Bransford (Ed.), *Perceiving, acting and knowing* (pp. 211–265). Hillsdale, NJ: Lawrence Erlbaum Associates.

Vygotsky, L. S. (1978). *Mind in society: The development of higher psychological processes.* Cambridge, MA: Harvard University Press.

Wapner, S. (1985). Martha Muchow and organismic-developmental theory. *Human Development, 28,* 209–213.

Wapner, S. (1987). A holistic, developmental, systems-oriented environmental psychology: Some beginnings. In D. Stokols & I. Altman (Eds.), *Handbook of environmental psychology* (pp. 1433–1465). New York: Wiley.

Wapner, S. (1991, June). *A holistic, developmental, systems-oriented approach to some aspects of clinical psychology.* Paper presented at Italian Psychological Association meetings, San Marino, Italy.

Wapner, S., Ciottone, R. A., Hornstein, G. A., McNeil, O. V., & Pacheco, A. M. (1983). An examination of studies of critical transitions through the life cycle. In S. Wapner & B. Kaplan (Eds.), *Toward a holistic developmental psychology* (pp. 111–132). Hillsdale, NJ: Lawrence Erlbaum Associates.

Wapner, S., Cirillo, L., & Baker, A. H. (1969). Sensory-tonic theory: Toward a reformulation. *Archivia Di Psicologia Neurologia E. Psichiatria, 30,* 493–512.

Wapner, S., & Demick, J. (1990). Development of experience and action: Levels of integration in human functioning. In G. Greenberg & E. Tobach (Eds.), *Theories of the evolution of knowing: The T. C. Schneirla conference series* (pp. 47–68). Hillsdale, NJ: Lawrence Erlbaum Associates.

Wapner, S., & Demick, J. (1991a). Some relations between developmental and environmental psychology: An organismic-developmental systems perspective. In R. Downs, L. S. Liben, & D. Palermo (Eds.), *Visions of evelopment, the environment and aesthetics: The legacy of Joachim F. Wohlwill* (pp. 181–211). Hillsdale, NJ: Lawrence Erlbaum Associates.

Wapner, S., & Demick, J. (1991b). The organismic-developmental, systems approach to the study of critical person-in-environment transitions through the life span. In T. Yamamoto & S. Wapner (Eds.), *A developmental psychology of life transitions* (pp. 25–49). Tokyo: Kyodo Shuppan.

Wapner, S., & Demick, J. (Eds.). (1991c). *Field dependence-independence: Cognitive style across the life span.* Hillsdale, NJ: Lawrence Erlbaum Associates.

Wapner, S., Demick, J., & Damrad, R. (1988, April). *Transition to retirement: Eight years after.* Paper presented at the Eastern Psychological Association annual meeting, Buffalo, NY.

Wapner, S., Demick, J., & Redondo, J. P. (1990). Cherished possessions and adaptation of older people to nursing homes. *International Journal on Aging and Human Development, 31*(3), 299–315.

Wapner, S., Kaplan, B., & Cohen, S. B. (1973). An organismic–developmental perspective for understanding transactions of men in environments. *Environment and Behavior, 5,* 225–289.

Wapner, S., & Werner, H. (1957). *Perceptual development.* Worcester, MA: Clark University Press.

Weisbord, M. R. (1991). *Productive workplaces: Organizing and managing for dignity, meaning, and community.* San Francisco, CA: Jossey-Bass.

Werner, H. (1926). *Einfuhrungin die entwicklungs-psychologie* [Comparative psychology of mental development] (4th ed.). Leipzig, East Germany: Barth.

Werner, H. (1940). *Comparative psychology of mental development.* New York: International Universities Press.

Werner, H. (1957a). *Comparative psychology of mental development* (3rd ed.). New York: International Universities Press.

Werner, H. (1957b). The concept of development from a comparative and organismic point of view. In D. Harris (Ed.), *The concept of development* (pp. 125–148). Minneapolis, MN: University of Minnesota Press.

Werner, H., & Kaplan, B. (1956). The developmental approach to cognition: Its relevance to the psychological interpretation of anthropological and ethnolinguistic data. *American Anthropologist, 58,* 866–880.

Werner, H., & Kaplan, B. (1963). *Symbol formation.* New York: Wiley.

Werner, H., & Strauss, A. A. (1941). Pathology of figure-background relation in the child. *Journal of Abnormal and Social Psychology, 36,* 236–248.

Wofsey, E., Rierdan, J., & Wapner, S. (1979). Planning to move: Effects on representing the currently inhabited environment. *Environment and Behavior, 11,* 3–32.

Wundt, W. (1912). Principles of physiological psychology. In B. Rand (Ed.), *The classical psychologists* (pp. 685–696). New York: Houghton Mifflin.

Author Index

Numbers in *italics* denote complete bibliographical citations

A

Acebo, S. C., 186, *196*
Adler, N. J., 71, *88*
Alexander, C., 23, *36*
Allport, G. W., 110, *126*
Alper, J., 161, *173*
Apter, D., 233, *236*
Arbuthnot, J., 40, *52*
Argyris, C., 84, *88*, 179, 181, *196*
Armon, C., 23, 24, 25, 26, 31, *36*, 162, *174*, 205, 206, *216*
Arthur, M. B., 221, *236*
Arvey, R., 142, *152*
Augros, R., 160, *173*
Avolio, B., 142, *153*
Axelbank, R., 141, *153*

B

Baker, A. H., 224, *239*
Barrett, G., 142, *153*
Barth, F., 201, *216*
Bartunek, J. M., 68, 69, 73, 80, 87, *88, 89*
Basseches, M. A., 4, *18*, 84, *88*

Baxter, J., 142, *153*
Baxter-Magolda, M., 59, *65*
Beck, M., 179, 181, 189, *196*
Bee, H., 109, *126*
Belbin, R., 141, 142, *153*
Bennett, R., 142, *153*
Bennis, W., 70, *88*
Ben-Shakhar, G., 63, *65*
Bibace, R., 225, *237*
Billings, R. S., 22, *37*
Blocher, D. H., 129, *137*
Bloland, P. A., 131, *137*
Boddy, D., 186, *196*
Boyd, R., 212, *216*
Bradford, A., 192, *196*
Bradford, D., 72, *88*
Brief, A. P., 130, 131, 132, 136, *137*
Bronowski, J., 157, *173*
Brown, D. P., 124, *128*
Buhlman, R. A., 200, *217*
Burke, K. W., 224, *237*
Burton, A., 93, 97, *107*

C

Cafferty, T., 143, *153*
Campbell, J., 156, 157, *173*

241

Subject Index